Khin Yi

THE DOBAMA MOVEMENT IN BURMA (1930-1938)

Southeast Asia Program
120 Uris Hall
Cornell University, Ithaca, New York
1988

© 1988 Cornell Southeast Asia Program

ISBN 0-87727-118-6

To my parents

U Ba and Daw Nyo

to whom I owe everything

The Southeast Asia Program would like to acknowledge with thanks the assistance of the following people in helping prepare this manuscript for publication: Dr. Aye Kyaw, of Cornell University; Dr. Dorothy Guyot; Dr. Myo Myint of the University of Mandalay and Professor Than Tun currently of Northern Illinois University. We would also like to thank Dr. Robert Taylor of the School of Oriental and African Studies in London for bringing the original thesis to our attention.

TABLE OF CONTENTS

FOREWORD BY ROBERT TAYLOR	ix
CHRONOLOGY 1930-1939	xvi
INTRODUCTION	1
CHAPTER I: THE FORMATIVE YEARS	3
CHAPTER II: THE GATHERING STRENGTH	26
The 1935 Yenangyaung Conference	26
The 1936 Myingyan Conference	34
The Komin Kochin Party	38
Building the Dobama Organization	42
The 1938 Prome Conference	52
CHAPTER III: THE YEAR OF STRIFE	57
i. The Oilfield Strike: Early Stages	57
ii. The Split in the Dobama	84
iii. The Second Indo-Burmese Riot	94
iv. The Breakdown of the Oilfield Strike	98
CONCLUSION	133
BIBLIOGRAPHY OF REFERENCES	136

TABLES AND DOCUMENTS

Tables

1.	Leadership of the Dobama	45
2.	Racial Composition of the Oilfield Workers	95

Documents

1.	The English Translation of the Dobama Song	9
2.	The 12 Demands of the November Meetings	60
3.	The 21 Resolutions of the January 9, 1938 Meeting	62
4.	Additional Resolutions of the January 9 Meeting	64
5.	Resolution of the January 20, 1938 Meeting	66
6.	Resolutions Passed at the February 13, 1938 Meeting in Yenangyaung	71
7.	BOC Concessions of September 19, 1938	82
8.	Resolutions of the RUSU Meeting of December 14, 1938	109
9.	Resolutions Passed at the January 9, 1939 Meeting at the Shwedagon Pagoda	117
10.	Further Resolutions Passed at the January 10, 1939 Meeting	120
11.	Manifesto Issued by the Dobama, January 16, 1939	121
12.	Resolutions of the February 9, 1939 Meeting	127

ILLUSTRATIONS
Following page 56

Thakin Ba Thoung, Founder of the Dobama Asiayone
The Dobama Emblem
The Patrons
The Presidents: 1935-1938
The KMKC Members

APPENDICES*

APPENDIX ONE	Reform Series No. I
APPENDIX TWO	(a) The original Dobama Song as Sung at Thaton Hall (b) The National Anthem
APPENDIX THREE	Reform Series No. II
APPENDIX FOUR	The Constitution of the ABYL
APPENDIX FIVE	The undated manifesto of the ABYL
APPENDIX SIX	"The undated First Manifesto" Manifesto I issued by ABYL
APPENDIX SEVEN	"The Second Manifesto"
APPENDIX EIGHT	"The Third Manifesto
APPENDIX NINE	Manifesto Number IV
APPENDIX TEN	"Preface to the KMKC Constitution"
APPENDIX ELEVEN	"Draft Constitution"
APPENDIX TWELVE	"Constitution of the Most Dependable Army of Burma"

*These Appendices, which are written in Burmese script, form a separate volume: Southeast Asia Program Monographs No. 2A.

FOREWORD

THE "DOBAMA ASIAYONE" IN BURMA'S POLITICAL HISTORY

The Dobama Asiayone was the central organization in the fundamental transformation which occurred in the nationalist movement of Burma during the decade prior to the Second World War. Before then, Burmese nationalist groups, represented first by the Young Men's Buddhist Association (YMBA) and subsequently by the General Council of Burmese Associations (GCBA), had remained constricted between the contradictory concepts and terminology of, on the one hand, the Burmese Buddhist political tradition as represented by the defeated monarchical state and the Theravada Buddhist *sangha*, and on the other, the definitions of modernity and progressiveness as presented by the British colonial state with its emphasis upon rationality, productivity, and instrumental power. The leaders of the nationalist groups were pulled between these two ideals, one learned from Burma's 1,000 year old culture and the other from the institutions of British science and imperialism. When the YMBA and GCBA political leadership moved toward the ideals of the past through the use of indigenous symbolism and devotion to the ethical principles of Buddhism, they received the support of wide sections of Burmese rural society. When they moved toward the realities of the British presence through their roles as lawyers, journalists, and elected politicians, they lost touch with their political supporters while, ironically, gaining access to positions of influence and wealth in the capital.

The success of the early Dobama Asiayone which Daw Khin Yi graphically describes in this volume, stemmed from its attempt to overcome this contradiction rather than being torn between the two seemingly opposed ideas. Symbolic of the radical difference between it and its predecessor organizations, which were better known by their English initials than their Burmese name, the Dobama Asiayone was and is best known by its full Burmese title.[1] Use of this title was an attempt to

---

1. The Burmese name for the Young Men's Buddhist Association was Buddha Batha Kalyana Yuwa Athin (Association to Care for the Well Being of Buddhism) but it was commonly referred to in Burmese as the YMBA. Similarly, the General Council of Burmese Associations was normally referred to as the GCBA in Burmese rather than by its indigenous name, Myanma Athin Chok (Supervising Burma Association). The attempt by European writers to refer to the Dobama Asiayone by its initials failed but not before causing a good deal of confusion. In older writings the organization is usually referred to as the DAA. British police records followed this practice. The use of these initials reveals a confusion about the Burmese spelling of the name. *Do* stands alone signifying "We" but is often written and pronounced in the possessive form *Do* and then means "Our." *Bama* means either "Burman," "Bur-

find a way of fusing the power of what was believed to be Western technique with the essence of what it was to be Burmese. Out of this effort would arise a new man and a new set of political ideals, capable of coping with the British on their own terms while, at the same time, retaining the support of the broad mass of the people. The founders of the Dobama Asiayone intended that it would address the fundamental political problems of colonial Burma and would ignore the divisive political issues that the British created, such as the question of Burma's separation from India in 1932, in favor of the overriding political question of the period, the achievement of independence. In so doing, however, the leadership was forced to confront, in both theoretical and practical terms, the question of whether class or race provided the most appropriate category for analyzing Burma's economic and political situation. In this regard, the formation and development of the Dobama Asiayone was a part of the strengthening class and ethnic consciousness of late colonial Burma.

The idealistic intentions of the founders of the Dobama Asiayone and of their successors soon came up against the realities of the colonial politics which they were helping to recast. But despite its shortcomings, the Dobama Asiayone's attempt to reform the nature of political thinking in Burma was sufficient to reshape the prevalent assumptions for political action of a generation of nationalist students and union leaders. In the best tradition of Burma's historians, Daw Khin Yi reveals the mistakes and shortcomings of the individuals involved in the making of history without denigrating the importance or sincerity of their actions.

The history of institutions is normally less tidy than the history of ideas. There were no winners or losers in the internal history of the Dobama Asiayone in Daw Khin Yi's account. There were important consequences flowing from their actions. The split within the leadership which Daw Khin Yi examines was a result of the inability of old and new Dobama leaders to agree on how to overcome the contradictions of Burma's colonial political dilemma. An internationalism which pulled toward a broad nationalist orientation and emphasized the common class interests of Burma's Indian and Burmese workers and peasants struggled against a narrow nationalism which sought to define the dominant political problem in terms of race alone. The positions of the leaders were not absolutely fixed on these points, but the underlying dilemmas which they faced as political leaders forced them to think in these terms. The new intellectual contradiction which arose as a result of the Dobama leaders' attempt to surpass the early colonial political contradiction remained unresolved at the time of the Japanese occupation in 1942. The question was overtaken by events and did not recur in outward form again until independence was achieved ten years after Daw Khin Yi's history concludes.

---

mese," or "Burma," thus Do Bama can be either the more narrowly nationalistic "We Burmans," the broader "We Burmese," or the most encompassing "Our Burma." *Asiayone* stands as one unit meaning "association," "organization," or, more precisely, a "tightly bound group of men." Properly, therefore, any attempt to provide English initials for *Do Bama Asiayone* should have been DBA.

The critical place of the Dobama Asiayone, and the larger Thakin movement which it represented, did not become apparent to observers of Burma's politics until after independence. J. S. Furnivall's classic *Colonial Policy and Practice*, written a few years after the events described in this volume, apparently mentions the Dobama Asiayone only twice. Dobama is referred to as a "patriotic group" noted for its campaign to boycott foreign goods and foreign styles. Furnivall also finds the patriotism of the group significant when he records that among the few members of the House of Representatives opposed to political corruption were "adherents of the *thakin* (extremist) party, and it is interesting to note that it was the extremist party, most keenly opposed to foreign government, which was the most solicitous for pure administration."[2] But Furnivall at that time foresaw no particular future for the Dobama members in government after the war. When, however, many of them became the first rulers of independent Burma, he served as an adviser to them.

Those historians and political analysts who wrote after Burma achieved its independence were able to see more clearly the crucial place of the Dobama Asiayone in the shaping of Burma's nationalist politics. Professor John Cady, in his standard history of modern Burma, devotes a four page section to the "The Thakin Party or Dobama Asiayone." He noted that the founding of the organization was at the time "seemingly unimportant but potentially significant."[3] Frank Trager's political analysis written in the mid 1960s devotes more than twice as many pages to the Thakins as did Cady but his analysis is one-sided and ignores not only the founding of the movement which Daw Khin Yi describes, but underplays the personalized factionalism and intellectual disputes that divided the movement.[4] Curiously, Donald Eugene Smith's valuable study, *Religion and Politics in Burma*, almost ignores the Dobama Asiayone and when it is briefly discussed, many of the statements concerning it are misleading or false, as Daw Khin Yi's work demonstrates.[5] Other authors have merely ignored the significant

---

2. J. S. Furnivall, *Colonial Policy and Practice* (New York: New York University Press, 1956; first published by the Cambridge University Press, 1948). Neither *Dobama Asiayone* or *Thakin* appears in the index. The quotations come from pp. 166 and 171 respectively.

3. John F. Cady, *A History of Modern Burma* (Ithaca: Cornell University Press, 1958), pp. 375-78, quotation on p. 375; activities of the Thakins, both as an organization and as individuals after the period Daw Khin Yi describes are noted on pp. 417; 419-20; 448; 471-74; and 528.

4. Frank N. Trager, *Burma: From Kingdom to Independence* (London: Pall Mall; New York: Praeger, 1966), pp. 44, 53-63, 82, 95, 130-31, 150-51, and 167.

5. Donald Eugene Smith, *Religion and Politics in Burma* (Princeton: Princeton University Press, 1965), pp. 115-16 and 118-19. On p. 115, for example, Smith states that the *Dobama* was founded in 1935 and he accepts uncritically a claim by Aung San that, despite its origins, it was "the only non-racial, non-religious movement that ever existed in Burma." On the next page he confuses the continuing role of many

role of the Dobama Asiayone in creating much of the spirit and ideas of the late colonial nationalist movement and their impact on subsequent events.[6] The only major published study of Burma's politics devoted to the period which included the foundation and growth of the Dobama Asiayone, Albert D. Moscotti's *British Policy and the Nationalist Movement in Burma, 1917-1937*, mentions the Dobama Asiayone and Thakin only three times.[7] My own study of Burma's elite politics between 1937 and 1942 failed to relate the growth of the Dobama Asiayone and its own politics to the larger political world.[8]

To begin to understand the importance of the Dobama Asiayone in modern Burma's politics, one has to turn to Burmese scholarly writing in English. In Dr. Maung Maung's *Burma and General Ne Win*, although the main protagonist, Ne Win, plays only a marginal role in the founding and leadership of the Dobama Asiayone other than through his association with his uncle, Thakin Nyi, the author devotes nearly the whole second chapter to the growth and development of the Thakin movement and the role of students in it.[9] The most complete discussion

---

prewar Thakin in politics with an unfounded implication that this group remained united around previously held secular nationalist goals. By positing a Buddhist nationalism against a putative Thakin secular nationalism on pp. 118 and 119, Smith creates a degree of consistency for Thakin thought which never existed in the clarity which his argument requires.

6. Professor Josef Silverstein in the discussion of the "Sources of Burmese Political Culture" in *Burma: Military Rule and the Politics of Stagnation* (Ithaca: Cornell University Press, 1977) does not refer to the organization, but later identifies it in a footnote as a "movement . . . launched by young Burmese in the early 1930s as a way to recapture pride and to enlist Burmese in a truly nationalist movement." See p. 45, fn. 20. The movement is not listed in the index of David I. Steinberg's *Burma's Road Toward Development: Growth and Ideology Under Military Rule* (Boulder: Westview Press, 1981).

7. Albert D. Moscotti, *British Policy and the Nationalist Movement in Burma, 1917-1937* (Honolulu: University Press of Hawaii, 1974), pp. 56, 65-66, and 120.

8. Robert Henry Taylor, "The Relationship Between Burmese Social Classes and British-Indian Policy on the Behavior of the Burmese Political Elite, 1937-1942" (Ph.D. dissertation, Cornell University, 1974). See the account on pp. 181-205. This is based almost entirely on British police and political reports. The events Daw Khin Yi describes in her chapter 3, "The Year of Strife," are told from the perspective of the government in my chapter 5, "The Fall of the Ba Maw Ministry," pp. 289-369. Accounts in Burmese include Ba Tin, *1300 Pyi Ayeidawbon Hmattan* [Record of the 1300 Revolution] (Rangoon: Myawadi, n.d.) and Kyaw Win Maung, *Mandalei 1300 Pyi Ayeidawbon hme Nechet Towhlanyei Tho* [To the Anti-Imperialist Revolution, the Mandalay 1300 Revolution] (Rangoon: Banmaw Sapei, 1984) as well as the volume noted in fn. 11 below.

9. Maung Maung, *Burma and General Ne Win* (New York: Asia Publishing House, 1969), "Chapter 2, The Struggle Gathers Momentum," pp.

of the organization and its genesis and development before the publication of Daw Khin Yi's study is U Maung Maung's *From Sangha to Laity: Nationalist Movements in Burma 1920-1940.*[10] However, the Dobama Asiayone is not the focus of this study, though the organization does play a crucial part in U Maung Maung's implicit thesis about the rise of new secularist political forces as the population became disenchanted with the religious hypocrisy and political inconsistency of the older leaders of the GCBA generation.

It is when Burmese are writing in their own language that full attention has been given to the development of the Dobama Asiayone in both its intellectual and institutional forms. Popular magazines and newspapers carried many articles on the role of the Dobama Asiayone in the nationalist period, and politicians were reluctant to abandon the Thakin title, but no full study of the organization was published until 1976 when *Do Bama Asiayone Thamaing* [History of the Do Bama Asiayone] appeared.[11] This two-volume study, prepared by a committee working in the late 1960s and based on interviews with Thakin activists and on collections of Dobama Asiayone documents, is an example of the encouragement given by the government of Burma in the 1960s and 1970s to the study of nationalist history. Daw Khin Yi had the use of some of these materials, as well as the draft of this history, when she was preparing her Masters thesis which forms the basis of this present monograph. Stylistically her work is also similar to the authorized Burmese version, and it has the flavor of much contemporary Burmese historiography. Subsequently, in 1980 a biography was published of the founder of the organization entitled *Myanma Naingnganyei hnit Thakin Ba Thoung* [Burma's Politics and Thakin Ba Thoung], by *Myan Alin* [*Light of Burma*] journalist Tin Htun Aung.[12] These works reprint the original "National Building" tracts translated in Daw Khin Yi's Appendices I and III as well as the conference resolutions to which she refers in the main text. Later tracts by members of the majority faction after the split in the organization in 1938 are collected in Thein Pe Myint's *Bun Wada Hnit Do Bama.*[13]

The story of the initial eight years of the Dobama Asiayone which Daw Khin Yi recounts is, in broad outline, a familiar one in colonial

---

30-61; there is also a discussion of the later Dobama ideology on pp. 65-67 and mentions elsewhere.

10. Maung Maung, *From Sangha to Laity: Nationalist Movements of Burma 1920-1940*, Australian National University Monographs on South Asia No. 4 (New Delhi: Manohar, 1980).

11. Do Bama Asi Ayun Thamaing Pyuzuye Ahpwe, *Do Bama Asi Ayun Thamaing* (Akyinchok) (Do Bama Asiayone History Preparation Group, History of the Do Bama Asiayone [Abridged]) (Rangoon: Sapei Biman, 1976), two volumes.

12. Tin Htun Aung, *Myanma Ngannganyei hnit Thakin Ba Thoung* [Burma's Politics and Thakin Ba Thoung] (North Okkalapa: Sapei-u, 1980).

13. Thein Hpei Myint, ed., *Bun Wada hnit Do Bama* (Rangoon: Bawsado Sapei, 1967).

Southeast Asia.[14] A small number of men and women, well educated in comparison with the majority of the population, at home in both their own and a major European language, living in a major cosmopolitan commercial city, and familiar with political, economic, and social movements in other parts of the world, especially within the colonial empire of which they were a part, felt a strong sense of dissatisfaction with the behavior of the indigenous political leaders who had been cooperating with the colonial rulers. They sought a new departure in politics and morality, condemning the past as both defeatist and corrupt. Initially much of their inspiration came from the intellectual excitement that accompanies the reading of radical critiques of Western civilization and then attempting to apply these to their own situation.[15] The moral aspect of their effort drew in some members who otherwise believed that purely political action held little immediate promise of solving social issues. In the case of the Dobama Asiayone, many of the members who became active from this basis came from the All Burma Youth League and similar organizations, such as the earlier Youth Improvement Society.[16] In later years, many of these leaders, such as former Prime Minister U Nu and his close adviser, U Ohn, would reject outwardly political solutions for social problems and would launch religious appeals to improve the moral tone of society.

The intellectual energy of the Dobama Asiayone derived from the wide variety of political views espoused by its members, definable in terms of their origins from forms of "National Socialism" on the right to "International Communism" on the left. The social origins of the leaders provided them with no firm class perspective from which to view these doctrines, though over time the more established members of society came to distrust the more ardently socialist ideologists. But none of the leaders were able to grasp in a politically effective manner the profound consequences that colonial rule was having on the position of the workers and peasants. When worker and peasant movements arose, they did so usually without the leadership of the Thakin, and the peasant and labor union leaders were often distrustful of the urban and theoretical biases of the ideologically motivated intellectuals. As Daw Khin Yi shows, in the case of both the Saya San peasants revolt and the 1300 *Ayaydawbon* (Revolution) of 1938, the leaders of the Dobama Asiayone were often found wanting. On the other hand, the leaders recognized that without a clear understanding of the actual political situation and a progressive leadership, peasant revolts and urban strikes would always be defeated by the colonial government.

The split in the Dobama Asiayone which occurred at the end of the 1300 *Ayaydawbon* was in part motivated by disagreements as to how

---

14. It has its parallel in the Partai Nasional Indonesia (PNI) founded in 1928, the Vietnamese Revolutionary Youth League founded in the late 1920s, and the Kesatuan Melayu Muda (Young Malay Union) founded in 1938.

15. Thakin Ba Thaung was much influenced by the philosophy of Nietzsche and the nationalism of Mazzini and the Sinn Fein movement. Marxist and socialist thought more generally came in the later 1930s.

16. See the discussion in Maung Maung, *From Sangha to Laity*, pp. 74-79.

the urban radical nationalists could provide leadership for the workers and peasants without, at the same time, becoming enmeshed in the political machinations of political party leaders like Dr. Ba Maw and U Saw. A resolution of the meaning and consequences of the 1938 split was soon overtaken, however, by other issues including the position of Burmese nationalists on the question of collaboration with Japanese fascism. That story is beyond the history Daw Khin Yi has written, but it too was eventually overtaken by events during the subsequent anti-fascist resistance and post-war independence struggle against the British. But the 1938 split, and those that followed, have their roots in the development of the Dobama Asiayone and the legacy of these splits has shaped Burma's post-independence politics.

During the 1950s and early 1960s, it was commonly recognized that many of the individuals in top positions in the ruling Anti-Fascist People's Freedom League (AFPFL) and its major armed and unarmed opponents had been active Thakin in pre-war nationalist politics. General Aung San himself was a Thakin and had been a secretary general of the Dobama. Prime Minister Nu, Deputy Prime Minister Ba Swe, and other leading officials in the government, as well as underground Communist leaders such as Thakin Than Tun and Thakin Soe also play prominent roles in Daw Khin Yi's account. But it was not until the establishment of the Revolutionary Council government following the March 1962 military coup that some of the ideas of the Dobama Asiayone were implemented and its symbolic legacy was renewed by the state. The Revolutionary Council's Burma Socialist Programme Party was founded on July 4, 1963, thirty years to the day from when Thakin Ba Thoung, with about eight others, established the first Dobama Asiayone organizing committee.[17] Later the Revolutionary Council government erected statues to Thakin Po Hla Gyi along with those of Saya San to commemorate the workers' strikes and peasant revolts of the 1930s. The constitutional structure of the state since 1972 is near in form to that of the pre-war Dobama Asiayone manifesto issued soon after the 1938 split. Since 1980, surviving members of the Dobama Asiayone have been given state awards and political pensions for their dedication to the nationalist cause. The ambivalent attitudes of the government about class and race in its policies and in its statements regarding entrepreneurial and alien groups reflect the legacy of the 1930s and the origins of the Dobama Asiayone. It is therefore useful to have Daw Khin Yi's history of the organization up to 1938 available to a wider audience.

Robert H. Taylor

Department of Economic and Political Studies
School of Oriental and African Studies
March 24, 1987

---

17. Maung Maung, *From Sangha to Laity*, p. 120.

CHRONOLOGY
1930-1939

May 10, 1930	Telegu Dock Workers' Strike
May 26, 1930	First Indo-Burmese Riot
June 1930	Publication of *The Dobama Sadan*
July 15, 1930	First statement issued by the Dobama
July 19, 1930	Dobama Song sung at the Thaton Hall
July 20, 1930	Dobama Song sung at the Shwedagon pagoda
September 1930	Formation of the All Burma Youth League (ABYL)
December 22, 1930	Outbreak of the Peasants' Rebellion
January 2, 1931	First Sino-Burmese Riot
January 1931	Formation of the Yetat
January 21, 1933	Launching of the *Dobama News Weekly*
July 4, 5, 6, 1933	"Conference" of the Six
November 1933	By-election at Shwebo
September 1934	Formation of the Temporary Central Executive Committee
March 30, 1935	First Conference of the Dobama and the ABYL
June 27, 28, 39, 1936	Second Conference of the Dobama and the ABYL
July 19, 1936	Formation of the KMKG
January 28, 29, 1937	First Conference of the ABC
January 29, 1937	Draft Constitution of the Dobama approved
March 25, 1937	Launching of the *Dobama Bulletin*
April 1, 1937	Anti-Constitution Demonstration
September 4, 1937	Formation of the Bama Latyone Tat
January 8, 1938	Outbreak of Oilfield Strike
January 30, 1938	Resolution passed to give support to the strikers
February 3, 1938	Strike Relief Committee formed
February 5, 1938	Formation of Strike Enquiry Commission by Governor of Burma
February 13, 1938	Protest against Strike Enquiry Commission

March 22, 23, 24, 1938	Third Conference of the Dobama
March 23, 1938	Formation of the Oilfield Strike Enquiry Committee
April 1, 1938	Anti-Constitution Demonstration
May 1, 1938	First May Day held in Burma
July 3, 1938	The last ABC meeting held at Moulmein Zayat
July 26, 1938	Second Indo-Burmese Riot
November 14, 1938	Decision reached to stage the "long march"
November 23, 24, 1938	Conference held at Panswe by Ba Sein faction
November 30, 1938	Marchers leave Chauk
December 4, 1938	Section 144 proclaimed at Magwe and the decision made by the Central Executive Committee to lead the marchers
December 8, 1938	Tat Bos despatched to Magwe
December 11, 1938	Ba Hein and Ba Swe arrested
December 15, 1938	Protest demonstrations staged by students
December 20, 1938	Secretariat Incident
December 23, 1938	Death of Aung Gyaw
January 8, 1939	Arrival of the marchers at Shwedagon
January 9, 1939	Formation of All Burma Peasant's Organization and The All Burma Worker's Organization
January 23, 1939	Dawn raid at Shwedagon
January 31, 1939	Protest demonstrations at Allanmyo and death of Thakin Po Ba
February 8, 1939	Students and monks arrested at Mandalay
February 10, 1939	Massacre of the Seventeen at Mandalay
March 8, 1939	End of Student Strike
April 6-9, 1939	Conference held at Moulmein by the Thein Maung faction
July 1939	End of Oilfield strike

INTRODUCTION

There are few major events in modern Burmese history so important as the Thakin movement. It represented a generation of radically minded youths who, blinded by intense patriotism and a desire for complete independence, disregarded all else and joined hands to flaunt the authority of the British overlord, ultimately overthrowing it. For over two decades after the attainment of independence, key positions in the country were held by members of the movement or those connected with them.

The Thakin movement has been much discussed, yet inadequately treated. Thakin Ba Sein and Thakin Tun Ok, leaders of the Ba Sein faction of the Dobama, have each produced a short account, and the Dobama Asiayone Thamaing Pyuzuye Aphwe, represented by the Thein Maung faction, also published in 1976 a two-volume account of their movement. Well documented, this is an immeasurably useful source of information for historians. Nevertheless, no comprehensive account exists written by a non-Thakin who sympathizes with the Thakins as a whole, but has no factional bias. This study is an attempt to fill this void. As a complete study of the movement would extend beyond permissible limits, only an eight-year span is presented here, covering the years 1930-1938, which roughly constitute the period of unity among the Thakins before factional jealousies and strife were to rip them apart.

This study has three main parts: the first covers the initial phase, the second the growing momentum, and the third the movement at its zenith and the split that then occurred. The activities and events are described and analyzed in chronological order. The terms Burman and Burmese are both used to denote all the indigenous races of Burma with no reference to any particular ethnic group. The split occurred in 1938, the year which the Burmese chronicles describe as "The Year of Strife." That year marks the most important period in the history not only of the Thakin movement but also of modern Burma, because repercussions from the events of that year are still being felt today. For these reasons, a detailed study is made of this period. However, analysis of the split is not an easy task. Aware of the controversial nature of the subject, I have tried to introduce as many factual records as possible and a large number of quotations have been included in the text so that the records might speak for themselves.

In preparing this study, all available data have been studied and evaluated. Many prominent Thakins were interviewed and, whenever possible, the author attended some of the informal meetings where the old Thakins nostalgically recall their past. A questionnaire was also circulated among the Thakins in an effort to obtain autographed accounts of their participation in the movement, but this venture was a failure since the response to it was negligible.

The author hopes that eventually a complete history of the Dobama will be written, from its inception to its merging with the Dobama Sinyetha Party to form the Mahabama. This would not only prove to be an invaluable source of information and inspiration to those who study history but it would also enkindle the hearts of the youth of all ages with love for the country and a dauntless spirit to defend her just as the young Thakins did a couple of generations ago.

CHAPTER I

THE FORMATIVE YEARS

The Dobama Asiayone (the "We Burmans Association"), commonly known as the "Thakin Party" came into existence on May 30, 1930 [*Do Thamaing*, I, 1976, 137, 177; Ba Maung, 1975, 323] through the endeavors of a group of like-minded youths imbued with the idea of delivering the country from alien rule.[1] Although the members of the group sprang from diverse social and economic backgrounds, they were bound together by an ardent desire for national independence. A more tangible bond for them was their adoption of the appellation "Thakin" in place of the usual affix of U, Ko, or Maung.[2]

The founder of the Dobama, Thakin Ba Thoung, was not, however, the first person to suggest the Thakin affix. U Sandima, the Abbot of a monastery at Wetkathay, a small village in Taungdwingyi township had earlier instructed the villagers there to hang on their houses name-plates using Thakin titles, as a means of developing their consciousness of being their own masters and of the superiority of the Burmans as a race [interview, Thakin Kodaw Hmine]. Perhaps impressed by this practice during a visit to Wetkathay village, Thakin Ba Thoung on his return to Rangoon suggested to his close friends that they should also adopt the Thakin appellation. This they did, although reluctantly.

Thakin Ba Thoung's early life is rather obscure. He was a protégé of U Tun Shein, one of the three delegates of the Young Men's Buddhist Association (Pe, Pu, Shein) who went to London on July 7, 1919 to protest the Craddock Scheme. Ba Thoung's name first came to public notice in 1930 when he won the Prince of Wales Translation Prize, Rs. 1,000 Award of the Rangoon University College, for his translation of the *Outline of General History* by V. A. Renouf [Ba

---

1. On July 15, 1930, the *Sun Daily* (Thuriya Nezin), a leading Rangoon newspaper, carried the first Dobama announcement that all official declarations would be made by the association's secretary . Its address was given as 33 Yedashe Road, the residence of Thakin Ba Thoung, the founder of the group [*Sun Daily*, July 15, 1930].

2. Thakin means Lord or Master. Earliest mention of this word can be found in the Raza Kumar Inscription of AD 1112. What prompted the young patriots to adopt the word was not love for the word itself but aversion when an Englishman or, worse still, an Indian used it in place of Mister, such as Brown Thakin or Banerjee Thakin. Usage of this appellation also earned the young Thakins much ridicule and contempt from the older generation of politicians and the general people alike. It was considered too presumptuous on the part of the young and seemingly unimportant men to use such a noble term of address.

Thoung, 1940, 7]. At that time he was serving on the editorial board of a bilingual magazine, *Gantaloka, The World of Books* a monthly publication issued by the Burma Educational Book Club. At the same time he was a part-time translation tutor in the Department of Oriental Studies at the Rangoon University College and also on the payroll of the Burma Book Club as a part-time salesman [Ba Thoung, 1940, 7 and interview]. At the time of the Dobama's founding, Thakin Ba Thoung was tutor-cum-editor-cum-salesman.

Thakin Ba Thoung met with his friends and discussed the social and political conditions of the time. During this period his close friends were Ko Thein Maung and Ko Hla Baw [*Do Thamaing*, I, 1976, 127]. Ko Thein Maung was a Mathematics Honors student recently returned from London where he had been sent by the Burma Educational Book Club to study the management of book stores; and Ko Hla Baw was a laboratory assistant employed at the E. M. D'Souza Pharmacy in Rangoon.[3]

In 1928 these friends first attempted to attract public attention by staging a political play depicting the disastrous effects on the country of the existing political parties, but after a couple of months' rehearsals the play flopped [*Ko Min Sar Zu*, I, 1936, 1]. It was only two years later that the obscure group was brought to the forefront of the political arena by the Indo-Burmese riot which broke out in Rangoon on May 26, 1930.

On May 10 about 2,000 Telegu dock workers had gone on strike against the Scindia Steam Navigation Co., Ltd. Initially the company refused to comply with their demand for an increase in their daily wage from Rs 1.50 to Rs 2 and replaced the strikers by some 2,000 Burmans. On May 22 an agreement was reached between the company and the striking dock workers to raise their daily wage to Rs 1.75 [Soe, 1966, 92-93]. The company, however, did not inform the Burmese workers of the settlement. On the morning of the 26th when the Burmese workers came to the Lewis Street Jetty, the reinstated Indian workers flung insults and taunts at them. Infuriated, the Burmese workers responded violently, and the brawl developed into a racial riot between Burmans and Indians [Desai, 1959, 407].

The riot lasted four days [Soe, 1966, 94]. As a result of concerted efforts by the town elders, both Indians and Burmese, and the appeals made by the Sayadaws from Aletawya, Bagaya, Thadu, and Zawtanayama monasteries, a peaceful reconciliation was finally effected. According to the government reports, over 250 Indians and a few Burmans lost their lives. The total number of Indians who sustained injuries was estimated at 2,500 [Ba Khine, 1964, 157].

The Indo-Burmese riot served as a powerful medium to expose the deplorable social and economic conditions in Rangoon. To be insulted by the Telegu coolies, regarded as the lowest stratum of the resident aliens in Rangoon, was enough to arouse indignation in the most feeble

---

3. Later additions to this small group were Ko Tha Doe, YMB Saya Tin, Ko Ohn Khin (Mogyo), Ko Ohn Pe of Wakema, Ko Maung Maung Toe, Ko Yi, Ko Hla Pe (Pinbyu), and Ko Tin Sein [*Do Thamaing*, I, 1976, 34].

of the self-respecting citizens. The young Thakins immediately seized upon the favorable political climate created by the riot to make their political debut and the Dobama Asiayone came into existence.

Although the riot had economic causes, the young Thakins turned it into a political issue and used the opportunity to propagate their ideas and popularize their cause. Within a few days of the incident they issued a manifesto, the Dobama Sadan, also known as the *Reform Series No. 1* (Appendix I), and distributed it free of charge. There they openly declared that the manifesto had been issued to commemorate and honor those who had received wounds and those who had given up their lives for the national cause during the Indo-Burmese riot. On the title page of *Reform Series No. 1* [Nainggan Pyu Sar Zu I] [*Do Thamaing*, I, 1976, 127] was the six-line motto which soon became the Thakin slogan:

> Burma is Our Country
> Burmese is Our Literature
> Burmese in Our Language
> Love Our Country
> Cherish Our Literature
> Uphold Our Language

The main theme of the manifesto was "Burma for the Burmans." This theme was repeatedly stressed with the aim of arousing a spirit of unity and fraternity among Burmans, and implanting the attitude: "We (are) Burmans" (Dobama Wada). To raise public awareness of matters concerning economic welfare, the manifesto pointed out that "wealth is the foundation of all power" and urged Burmans to engage in petty business which hitherto had been in the hands of the Indians and Chinese. To stimulate a spirit of militance, the old Burmese adage "Non-aggression quells aggression" was altered to "Non-aggression breeds more aggression and only aggression quells aggression." Finally the dictum "Let him who desires peace prepare for war" was adopted as their slogan.

Several aspects of this manifesto should be noted. It was issued almost immediately after the incident on May 30, 1930 [*Do Thamaing*, I, 1976, 127]. It is worth remarking that, although the Thakins made use of the opportunity to propagate their ideas and ideals they employed no word or phrase to incite any fresh recurrence of rioting. Rather the manifesto urged the people "not to hate the Indians but to love one another more." They viewed the incident as a manifestation of capitalist manoeuvers rather than racial strife. This view can also be taken as an early indication of their international outlook.

In pointing out the reasons for the Burmese people's inherent weakness, a parallel was drawn with the ancient Greeks. Regional loyalties and attachments to one's own place of birth and upbringing had caused rivalry among the Greek city states and had brought about gradual deterioration and ultimate ruin. The manifesto appealed to the Burmans to restrain themselves from harboring such narrow sentiments and to uproot and destroy any thought or action which would cause disunity among the people. The people were further urged "to consider and cherish the whole length and breadth of the country as their own hearth and home."

The manifesto's exhortation to set up petty business is indicative of the awareness of the Thakins that the country's immediate need was economic stability. The futility of political awakening without economic stability was repeatedly stressed. Their maxim "wealth is strength" clearly indicates that the young Thakins were not merely idealistic in their outlook, but that they had their feet firmly rooted in reality.

The portion of the manifesto devoted to the "half castes" is also worthy of mention. These half castes were not condemned for having alien blood, but were accepted on an equal standing with fullblooded Burmans. (The Thakin prediction that a day would come when people of mixed blood would proclaim that they too are Burmese has come true. At present Burmese citizenship is much sought after and in court people of mixed parentage are producing proof of their Burmese ancestry.) Lastly, the manifesto gave expression to the radical nature of the Thakin youths. Their insistence that a fool should be honored differed from the teaching of the Buddhist scriptures that "to shun a fool is a blessing." This was a foretaste of later radical maxims such as "run out and meet the onslaught of danger" or "live dangerously."

One of the far-reaching effects of the manifesto was to give impetus to the Burmanization movement which challenged the dominance of alien languages. At the time all place names and street names were written in English; telegrams had to be sent in English or in Hindi; knowledge of Hindi was necessary to ride a bus in the city; and the official language of the court was English. Schools were divided into European, Anglo-Vernacular, National, and Vernacular. Products of the vernacular schools were employed at the lowest rung of the occupational ladder. The common couplet used by the privileged few who could attend the expensive schools to taunt their counterparts from the monastic schools aptly expressed the situation:

    Students of English Schools are superior
    Students of monastic schools are mere beggars

Song recitals were a new tactic the young Thakins adopted to attract public attention. The first rendition of the Dobama Song took place on July 19, 1930 at the Social and Reading Club of the Thaton Men's Hostel at Rangoon University College. The event was planned and organized by Thakin Ba Thoung and Thakin Thein Maung assisted by Ko Nu (an Arts student, who later became Thakin Nu) and Thakin Tun Sein, a demonstrator in Mathematics [*Do Thamaing*, I, 1976, 134]. A fairly large crowd attended the recital, including two young students, Ba Sein and Lay Maung [*Do Thamaing*, I, 1976, 134-35] who were later to figure in the history of the Dobama organization.

The song presented at the Thaton Hall was the outcome of a concerted group effort. The idea was supplied by Thakin Ba Thoung; the words were written by YMB Saya Tin, and then polished by Thakin Hla Baw and Thakin Thein Maung. The tune was the work of YMB Saya Tin alone [Shwe Thway, 1965, ii]. Although one of the first to join the group and adopt the Thakin appellation, Saya Tin is best known as YMB Saya Tin, the YMB affix having been acquired from a private school and a musical troupe he had founded in Mandalay prior to his venture in Rangoon [Shwe Thway, 1965, 42].

The song, which embodied the political ideas of the Thakins, quickly gained popular acceptance and at the second conference of the Dobama, held at Myingyan in 1936, it was declared to be the national song [Shwe Thway, 1965, 116]. During the Japanese occupation it became the official national anthem. After independence, the Dobama Song again became the national anthem with a slight alteration made to suit the times [Shwe Thway, 1965, 135]. (The original song, together with the various changes it has undergone, is given in Appendix II). In the mid 1970s the government considered adopting a new national anthem but decided to retain the Dobama Song.

The song's acclaim derived from its stirring appeal. While pointing out the deplorable and humiliating conditions of being a subject race, it urged the Burmese to strive for national freedom. In recalling past glories, it traced the original establishment of the First Burmese Dynasty at Tagaung by Abiraja. In an attempt to trace the legendary ancestry of the Burmese kings from Lord Buddha Himself, the song reminded Burmans of the claim that they belonged to the race of Sakyas (Thakiwun).[4] In recounting the victories over the neighboring states of India (sic) and Siam, the song recalled past greatness, so that the youth might recapture the splendor of their forefathers. It also appealed to the Buddhist mind, with its reminder of the law of change and the impermanence of material things, implying that the state of subjugation was also transient. The song also raised the people's hopes with the promise that a day would dawn when the country would lose its fetters and become independent.

The song provided an effective means of propagating the Dobama creed. Whereas their manifesto had reached only a fraction of the literate population the song now engulfed everyone as it was passed on from person to person. Its primary aim was an appeal for Burmanization and to give Burmans an awareness of themselves as a race apart. The song manifested the Thakin way of life and thought and served as a program to forge a social revolution with a vision of a new order yet to come. Its popularity lay not only with the choice of words and the tempo of the tune, but also with the song's philosophical content.

The song recital at the Thaton Hall was such a tremendous success that the performance was repeated the next evening at the U San Tun Tazaung at the Shwedagon pagoda when a larger crowd including women, children, and monks attended [*Sun Daily*, January 22, 1930]. One of the most striking features of the occasion was the way the Thakins attempted to instill a spirit of punctuality. A quarter of an hour before the performance began, the musical troupe entertained the audience with a series of classical songs, and at precisely 5 p.m. when the shrill ring of the alarm clock had hardly stilled, Thakin Ba

---

4. As a matter of fact, this legend which claims that the man who came to rule at Tagaung was a descendent of the Sakyan race does not claim that all Burmans are Sakyas. Modern scholars consider this story as a mere fabrication to glorify the Burmese king during the early Konbaung period (late nineteenth century). The story gained popularity when it appeared in a Third Standard Burmese Reader [*Daung Hpatsar Thit*, III, 1924, 116].

Thoung, acting as the master of ceremonies, announced the beginning of the song recital. He then requested the audience to remain standing with closed eyes for three minutes as a mark of respect for those who had fallen during the Indo-Burmese riot. At the audience's request, he first explained the song, phrase by phrase, the aims and objects of the Dobama [*Sun Daily*, July 22, 1930] and the reason for the adoption of the Thakin appellation. He also made use of the occasion to elucidate ways to promote the Burmans' own literature and language. Later, with only the orchestra seated, and the entire audience standing and listening, YMB Saya Tin took to the stage and sang the prelude. The audience joined in the chorus making the thunderous sound of "Dobama" resound throughout the pagoda precincts [*Sun Daily*, July 22, 1930]. The audience enthusiastically requested an encore. At the close of the recital, song sheets were sold for an anna (5 pyas) each to raise funds to meet expenses [*Do Thamaing*, I, 1976, 135].

After its successful debut, the song was sung on all occasions when a sizeable crowd gathered. Football matches, pagoda festivals, and fairs soon became concert halls [Shwe Thway, 1965, 70]. On September 21, 1930 to commemorate the first anniversary of the death of U Wisara--a leading political monk--one thousand candles were lit at the Shwedagon pagoda and the song was again sung [*Sun Daily*, September 26, 1930]. In their efforts to popularize their song, the Thakins employed all available media. Contradicting their own principle of using only Burmese, the Thakins had an English translation made and inserted in the 1931 issue of the Rangoon University College Annual Magazine (see Document 1). Through such endeavors, the song became popular overnight.

For the Thakins, their song recitals served as an effective tool to propagate their cause. Therefore, not only did they sing but they also taught the audience to sing along with them. Every song recital was accompanied by a session of explanation. The song was interpreted phrase by phrase and certain terms adopted or coined by the Thakins were explained in detail [*Do Thamaing*, I, 1976, 136]. Thus the song recitals also provided a platform for the Thakins' political speeches.

During this initial phase the requests for song recitals pouring in from all over the country indicated the song's effectiveness as a propaganda medium. The first invitations came from the Delta towns of Dedaye, Kyaiklat, Pantanaw, and Pyapon [*Do Thamaing*, I, 1976, 136]. The National School Teachers' Association and the Sayeikya Yowa Association of Pantanaw gave the first invitation. Ko Ohn Khin, Ko Kyaw, and YMB Saya Tin performed in Pantanaw at 11 a.m. on August 29, 1930 at the National High School. At 7 p.m. the same evening over 3,000 people attended a repeat performance at the office of the District Council, local government body established in 1921. The owner of the Myo Lone Kyetthaye Press, U Ohn Maung distributed the song leaflets. Ko Thant (who later became the Secretary General of the United Nations) explained why the Thakins had come to sing. As representatives of the Dobama, Ko Ohn Khin (later proprietor of the Bama Khit Newspaper) explained the song. The entire audience joined in the chorus. The visitors gave another performance the next day at the Cooperative Bank [*Sun Daily*, September 5, 1930].

At about the same time Thakin Ba Thoung went to Kyaiklat with a musical troupe led by Po Ni. Dedaye and Zalun also played hosts to

DOCUMENT 1

THE ENGLISH TRANSLATION OF THE DOBAMA SONG

"We Burman" Song

Long, long live "our Burman's" fame;
In history shines "our Burman's" name.
Our race well known the world over.
Should we now prove inferior?
Tut! tut! not we, not we,
For Burman, Burman are we!
Are we not Burman? We are, we are,
Then unite and act, "Father's sons" we are,
Not for us, but for those of hereafter.
Be brave, be brave, like a true Burman,
Burma, Burma for us Burmans.
Act and behave like Masters,
For Burmans are a race of Masters,
Under the heaven and on earth,
High-minded and of Zamayi's blood.

<u>Chorus to be repeated twice</u>

For so long as the world will last,
Burma is ours, Burma is ours.
This is our country, this our land,
This our country till the end.
This is our country, this our land,
This our country till the end.

Let all our countrymen
Consider this as our land,
Our duty then
Is to love Burman.
Mark ye, Burman, Burman are we;
And all must work for nation's cause.
Our glorious time will come
As sure as the rising sun.
We Burman, we Burman
Consider the whole of Burma
As our true home sure.
Consider it as ours, Man!
This is like a true Burman.

<u>Chorus to be repeated twice</u>

For so long as the world will last,
Burma is ours, Burma is ours.
This is our country, this our land,
This our country till the end.
This is our country, this our land,
This our country till the end.

S.C.P.

[The University College Magazine, Vol. XXII, No. 1, 1931, (Monsoon Number) 42.]

the singers of the Dobama Song. As was their wont, the song recitals were accompanied by an explanatory session. The contacts made in these towns proved to be valuable in the Dobama's later organizational campaigns.[5]

By this time, the Thakins had formed themselves into a loose organization under a collective leadership.[6] While some of the group were engaged in song reciting tours, others attempted to reach the public through the printed word.

The fruit of their endeavor was the publication of a thirty-six page booklet containing eight articles which had formerly appeared as editorials in the *Gandaloka Magazine* [Ba Tin, 1964, 15]. It was issued under the title of *Reform Series No. II* (Appendix III).[7] A notice in the newspapers announced that the booklet would be sent to those who enclosed a one anna stamp in a self-addressed envelope [*Sun Daily*, July 28, 1930] and further cautioned that all letters be written in Burmese, thereby making the Thakin aim for Burmanization felt from the very outset.

Publication of the *Reform Series No. II* was made possible by a contribution of one hundred rupees from U Khin Maung, rice merchant, Thamanyadi Rice Mill of Thayettaw village. Fifteen hundred copies were printed for distribution. A notification published in the July 28 issue of *Sun Daily* stated that the pamphlets were then available, but actual distribution began only in the middle of August [*Sun Daily*, August 15, 1930].

The cover of the booklet bore the silhouette of a young Burman with a traditional Burmese chignon. He is clad only in a pasoe khadaunggyaik, a longyi gathered in front and passed between his legs to tuck in back. Holding a flaming torch over his right shoulder, he is seen striding resolutely towards a set destination. With the rays of the rising sun as backdrop for the silhouette, on the right is portrayed a ruined city with toppling towers and spires while on the left rises a modern industrial city resplendent with chimneys and derricks and airplanes overhead, all of which signify Burma's march towards modernization and industrialization.

The picture, however, was not an original Thakin creation, but was a clever adaptation from the cover of a history of the Russian Revolution which Thakin Ba Thoung had bought with the money he received from the Prince of Wales Translation Prize. The original picture, a

---

5. Another song composed by YMB Saya Tin also became famous. It is the valiant marching song of the Letyone Tat. With a few words altered, it has become one of the forces' favorites, the Ye Ye Dauk.

6. In this group were Thakins Ba Thoung, Hla Baw, Thein Maung, Ohn Pe, Tha Doe, Ohn Khin, Tin Shein, Maung Maung Toe, Ko Yi, Ko Hla Pe (Pinbyu), and YMB Saya Tin [*Do Thamaing*, I, 1976, 136].

7. The articles were, "On Translation"; "Our Land and Literature"; "When Monastic Schools become Academies for Scientific Learning"; "The Marble Statue"; "The Year 2028"; "The Wonders of Science"; "Science and Farming"; and "The Way to Success."

worker shouldering a huge hammer, had a row of buildings as background[8] [Ba Tin, 1964, 13].

Of the eight articles in *Reform Series No. II* the first two dealt with translations. The first, "On Translation," claimed that only through translation could vistas on global affairs be widened and it stressed the need for translation to fulfill the requirements of the future independent state. The article further stated that existing Burmese literature was no longer sufficient to meet the demands of present-day life. Lokaniti was excellent as a didactic poem, while recitation of Payeikkyi was soothing to the mind. But they could not teach the art of manufacturing automobiles, trains, or airplanes. Neither could they provide for the people's daily needs or protect the country from the onslaught of enemies.

In the second article, "Our Land and Literature," a comparison was made between Burma and Japan. The article contended that the two countries had been simultaneously exposed to the impact of the West. Yet Japan had achieved great advances in science and technology due to its people's proficiency in translation, while Burma remained in the backwaters for having ignored this urgent need.

The third article, "When Monastic Schools become Academies for Scientific Learning," claimed that the high rate of literacy in Burma derived from the good services of the Buddhist monks and that the decline in the monastic education system had hampered the nation's progress. The article further advocated compulsory primary education and free education up to the university level.

The fourth article, "The Marble Statue," recounted an observation made by a certain German visitor to the Orient who likened (the people of) the east to a huge, serene, and immobile marble statue. Citing the legend of a monk, Khin Gyi Phyaw,[9] who, when ridiculed as being too old to learn the scriptures, flaunted the pestle tied with twigs saying the pestle had sprouted leaves, for which he came to be known as "Learned Mr. Pestle," the article urged its readers to try their utmost to animate the statues. In encouraging the readers to foster the spirit of enterprise, it added that "to be alive for an hour of fame is better than a hundred years of obscurity." The article concluded that the

---

8. Thakin Ba Sein, who later became the leader of the faction which bears his name, gave a different interpretation of the symbol. According to him, when the Aryans conquered Europe they entered Rome brandishing torches. The soldiers of Alaungmintaya, the founder of the last dynasty, held torches while vanquishing their foes. Further, the torch symbolizes the intention of the Dobama to incinerate the British imperialist ogres [Ba Sein, 1943, 53-54]. Another interpretation of the symbol is that it is an adaptation of the *Iskra*, the *Spark*, a revolutionary newspaper launched by Lenin in December 1900 [*Myanma Lu Nge Kyway Kyaw Than*, 1938, Vol. I, No. 5, 2].

9. *Sic*. The accepted hero of the legend is, however, Shin Ditharpamauk.

statue had at last bestirred itself, when U Kyaw Yin[10] took a flight in an inflated balloon and Maung San Wa and his friends set out on a global tour.

The fifth article, "The Year 2028," expressed aspirations for independence. The article by its title indicated the Burmese willingness to spend one hundred years if need be in the struggle for independence, citing Sun Yat Sen's forty years' devotion to freeing his country from foreign interference.

The sixth article, "The Wonders of Science," recounted the attempts made by foreigners to introduce scientific knowledge into Burma. According to this article, the introduction of the steam engine was suggested by Solomon De Cotte (?) during the reign of Anaukpetlun.[11] The unfortunate man was condemned as a lunatic and put into prison in 1604. Again in 1811, Bodawpaya imprisoned a Col. Stevens (?) for a similar suggestion. Other scientific discoveries made throughout the world were enumerated and readers were urged to do their utmost in their search for scientific knowledge.

The seventh article, "Science and Farming," discussed the techniques employed in scientific farming and the benefits of using chemical fertilizers. The article pointed out that in Burma, the peasantry constituted 80 percent of the entire population and the methods of farming were still rudimentary. It therefore suggested that a chemical fertilizer by the trade name of "Amophos" be used.

The eighth article, "The Way to Success," emphasized the importance of interpreting *kan*. In attempting to dispel its accepted meaning as fate, the article stressed that the word was a derivation from Pali, Sanskrit, and Hindi, and that in these languages, *kan* meant work. Therefore, success in any enterprise lay not in fate but in work.

The *Reform Series No. II* was milder in tone than the *Reform Series No. I*. This is understandable when one considers the circumstances of its publication. The first pamphlet expressed the indignation felt by the Thakins over the insults to the nation during the Indo-Burmese riot, while the second was only a compilation of articles which had formerly appeared in the *Gantaloka* magazine, a purely literary publication. But the stress on translation, exhortations to youth to venture and to dare, and the insistence on the quest for scientific knowledge carried a strong message despite the mild tone.

The Thakin program included mobilization of the young people, and the All Burma Youth League (ABYL) was founded in September 1930. Led by University students and school masters from the Myoma National school, a large gathering of youths, about five thousand, met at U Nageinda Mandat on the Shwedagon pagoda. As an expression of anti-British sentiment, imported British cigarettes were burned in a

---

10. He was a drawing master from Tavoy who built a large balloon, about sixty feet in diameter, filled it with smoke, and rode in a basket chair attached to it.

11. It is impossible to believe this story since Anaukpetlun reigned from 1605-28. Similarly there was no Col. Stevens in the service of King Badon (popularly known as Bodawpaya) who died in 1819.

bonfire. The organizers distributed pamphlets urging youths to boycott imported British goods and to patronize homespun clothes and cheroots [*Do Thamaing*, I, 1976, 139].

At the close of the meeting the All Burma Youth League was formed. The avowed aims of the League were to

1. boycott British goods;
2. patronize home-made goods and promote home industry; and
3. strive for the unity and progress of the youth. [*Do Thamaing*, I, 1976, 139-40]

A working committee was formed with the following office holders:

President	Myoma Saya Tint
Secretary	Ko Nu
Treasurer	Ko San Thein
Information Officer	Saya Hein (Myoma)
Committee Members	Thakin Ba Thoung
	Ko Ba Tun
	Ko Lu Tun
	Ko Ohn
	Thakin Lay Maung
	Thakin Ba Sein

The meeting resolved that all members would go about the city during weekends to urge the people to boycott cigarettes and encourage the use of home-made goods. Soon, through their efforts, food stalls, hair-dressing saloons, and small shops were set up in Rangoon and in the districts [*Do Thamaing*, I, 1976, 139-40].

Six months after the Indo-Burmese riot of May 1930 another riot broke out in Rangoon. This time it was Chinese who were involved. On January 2, 1931 [*Sun Daily*, January 5, 1931] some Burmese laborers who went to a circus staged at the corner of Godwin and Strand Roads got into an argument with the owner of a wayside Chinese restaurant over the payment for "Khaukswe" (noodles), and a clash followed. When the infuriated shop owner vented his anger by throwing a spear at a passing monk the situation got out of control. Sporadic clashes went on for about ten days before the situation returned to normal [Ba Khine, 1964, 159-60].

This provided the Thakins with another opportunity for further mobilizing the young people. Seizing the opportunity, Thakin Hla Baw called a mass gathering at the maidan in Botahtaung, Rangoon, which was attended by over two hundred people. Thakin Hla Baw urged his audience to unite against all enemies. Assembled under the fluttering Peacock Flag, shouting their vow to defend the country from all her enemies, and amidst cries "Dobama! Dobama! Dobama!" the Dobama Ye Tat (Our Burmans Army of Braves), a paramilitary organization and forerunner of the Bama Letyone Shat Ni Tat (Burman's Most Dependable Army of Red Shirts), was born [Ba Khine, 1964, 160].

But as the movement of Thakins and youths was gaining momentum, a greater force, which eclipsed all other movements, swept through the Burmese political scene. This was the agrarian revolt led by Saya San which broke out on December 22, 1930. Although Saya San's uprising ended in fiasco, its impact on the people was nevertheless overwhelming. As a result, the popularity of the Dobama temporarily waned and did not rise again until the by-election at Shwebo in 1933.

As individuals, the Thakins may have given support to Saya San's cause, but there is no indication that they did so as a body [Ba Sein, 1943, 37]. Had they decided to back Saya San, they might well have been able to draw strength from the peasantry as well as from their urban supporters centering on the educated middle class. To emphasize this lost opportunity to forge a stronger and more formidable force, it would not be incongruous to mention Dr. Ba Maw's defense of Saya San at his trial. Although he lost the case, Ba Maw's attempt to champion the cause greatly enhanced his popularity. And upon this wave of popularity Dr. Ba Maw rose to political fame.[12]

The year 1931 was the most uneventful in the history of the Dobama. Only two efforts by the association were recorded during that year. First, in the summer of 1931, a debate was held under the aegis of the Rangoon University Students Union on "Whether or not Burma should sever its ties with India." Speaking for separation were U Ba Pe, U Soe Nyunt, and U Tun Win while Dr. Ba Maw, U Kyaw Myint, and Ramree Maung Maung opposed them [Do Thamaing, I, 1976, 151]. At the debate, Thakin Ba Thoung stood up and told the audience:

> to vote for anti-separation means to remain a British slave, while to vote for separation would mean to remain a British bondsman

He further stated that to ask whether Burma wished to remain linked with India or not was like asking her whether she wished to remain under the left heel or the right heel of the British raj. He boldly stated that the Dobama Asiayone which he represented favored neither separation nor anti-separation; the Dobama's sole desire was nothing short of complete independence.

To emphasize his point, he cited a familiar Burmese tale about a thief named Ngatetpya. When Ngatetpya was tried before King Thado Minpaya, he was given a choice as to the manner of his death and was asked whether he preferred his throat to be slit or to be crucified alive. Ngatetpya boldly replied that he favored neither and if he were to state his heart-felt desire, he desired the king's own queen. For this bold rejoinder, Ngatetpya was not only reprieved, but was richly rewarded [Do Thamaing, I, 1976, 151]. Thakin Ba Thoung's words truly reflected the hopes of the masses who were interested neither in separation nor in anti-separation. The Thakin slogan "separation means slave and anti-separation means bondsman" became a popular catchword.

---

12. It should be noted, however, that Thakin Mya also defended Saya San, and Saya San donated Rs. 169 to Dobama Asiayone, a sum he had received as royalty from the *Sun Daily* for publication of his book *Letkhanuzu Kyan* (Diagnosis of Diseases). With this money Dobama founded the Saya San library.

The Dobama also made its presence felt at the departure ceremony for delegates to the Burma Round Table Conference in London scheduled for November 27, 1931. On October 15, 1931, the delegates left for England [*The Sun Magazine*, October 25, 1931, 4]. On the jetty at Rangoon the delegates received a grand send-off befitting the occasion. But just as they were about to embark, some Thakins and youths presented each of them with an envelope in which was a cartoon poster by U Ba Gale. The cartoon showed a man at the helm of a boat with a rod in his hand, to the end of which was tied a bone, while dogs tethered to a chain swam to catch the bone. The boat represented Burma, the man at its helm the British Prime Minister Mr. J. Ramsay MacDonald, the bone the worthless new Constitution, and the dogs the very delegates who were about to set out on their futile mission [*Do Thamaing*, I, 1976, 149-50]. This action by the Thakins brought much public censure. In particular, the portrayal of the delegates as dogs was considered too discourteous. Thus *The New Light of Burma* (Myanma Alinn) one of the leading newspapers, ran an editorial asking parents to keep their sons from associating with such unmannerly elements.

Undaunted by such threats, many youths continued to align themselves with the young Thakins, and it soon became necessary to reorganize the All Burma Youth League (ABYL). Many people who had been instrumental in forming the organization were either too busy with personal problems or were disinterested, while for some, their enthusiasm for youth affairs had waned with maturity. Saya Tint, the former president, and Saya Hein, who was formerly in charge of the information bureau, were now occupied with teaching. Ko Nu, the secretary, had returned to his native town of Pantanaw to teach. U San Thein, an Executive Committee member, had taken up regular occupation as an income tax officer [*Do Thamaing*, I, 1976, 156]. Therefore, when Thakin Lay Maung set out to reorganize the ABYL towards the end of 1932, new members had to be recruited to fill these vacancies.

Thakin Lay Maung rented a house at 172 Suburban Road, Ahlone, and, assuming the post of general secretary, set up a new Executive Committee with the following members:

Thakin Ba Sein, Ko Thi Han, Ko Ba Kyaw, Ko Kyaw Sein, Ko Ba Thwin, Ko Hla Maung and Ko Hla Pe. [*Do Thamaing*, I, 1976, 156]

Very soon the newly reorganized ABYL Headquarters became the rallying ground for former adherents and some students from the Rangoon University College and Myoma, Cushing, St. John's, and Methodist High Schools. About this time, they were also joined by Thakin Than Tun, then a student at the State Teachers' Training College [*Do Thamaing*, I, 1976, 156].

The motto adopted by the ABYL was "failure means death and burial, yet the throne itself is the reward for success and survival." The ABYL was very different from the then-existing youth organizations such as the Youth Temperance League and the Youth Improvement Society, which aimed at the social and moral uplift of youth and confined their activities to imparting general knowledge, setting up libraries, and founding orphanages and borstals. The ABYL, on the other hand, strove to create a generation of politically awakened patriotic youth (Appendix IV). In order to implement this aim, the ABYL contacted the Anti-Imperialist League in London and carried on a regular correspondence with it. The reorganized ABYL moved to 81 Suburban Road [*Do Thamaing*, I, 1976, 169], and in 1933 its newly elected Executive Committee consisted of:

President	--	Ko Tint
Vice-President	--	Ko Khant (brother of U Thant, UN)
Treasurer	--	Ko Thi Han
Secretary	--	Thakin Lay Maung
Committee Members	--	Thakin Ba Sein (Judson College)
	--	Ko Hla Pe (51st Street)
	--	Ko Tun Tin (U.C.R.)
	--	Ko Ba Thwin (Sanchaung)

It declared its chief aim to be to strive for independence and its program, laid down in a statement issued soon after the merging of the ABYL and the Dobama, included the following:

1. To dominate matters concerning the administration and the economy of the country;
2. To suppress foreign investments by denying foreigners the right to own land and property;
3. To raise the living standards (of the people) in order that all may obtain at least their basic needs;
4. To introduce a universal education system;
5. To guarantee equal opportunities to all Burmans;
6. To guarantee freedom of expression and press;
7. To nationalize important public concerns;
8. To annihilate factional tendencies and forge a patriotic spirit;
9. To promote self discipline, physical culture, and defense (of the country) by (a) forming Yetat, (b) conducting group activities, which would promote fraternity and moral courage;
10. To recognize only the Burmese Language and Literature in Burma (Appendix V).

The advent of the ABYL and the Dobama on the political scene challenged the long accepted notion that young people should not burden themselves with political and national issues, and instead promoted the new concept that, as future citizens of the country, youth should play an important part in the struggle for the country's freedom.

Many were sympathetic towards youth activities.[13] When a Japanese businessman, Mr. Jirozaemon Ito, visited Burma on a global tour, he was introduced to the leaders of the ABYL by U Ottama, an Arakanese monk who had resided in Japan for many years. Branch youth organizations in Mandalay, Myingyan, and Yenangyaung gave Ito a rousing welcome. This paved the way for later cordial relations

---

13. Prominent supporters included U Ottama, U Kaytu, Shin Ariya, U Kyaw Tint, U Pe Maung Tin, U Soe Thein, U Thein Zan, and U Su [*Do Thamaing*, I, 1976, 157].

between the Thakin youth and the Japanese Consulate in Rangoon [*Do Thamaing*, II, 1976, 478].

To form a network of branch organizations, Thakin Lay Maung set out on a tour of the towns along the railroad between Rangoon and Prome. Stopping at Paungde, at the home of Ko Thi Han, he contacted fellow students from Nattalin, Zigon, and Gyobingauk. At Prome Thakin Nyi assisted him in organizing the young people. In this manner youth activities came to be linked with the Dobama [*Do Thamaing*, I, 1976, 156].

The manifestos issued by the ABYL were concerned mainly with encouraging the use of homespun articles, and the shunning of foreign cigarettes. The undated first manifesto (Appendix VI) urged and stressed that the wearing of homespun pinni and pinbyu would not only revive the long neglected art of weaving, but would also provide a livelihood for many people. The manifesto pointed out that because of the response given to the ABYL appeals in 1930, and the abstinence from cigarettes, cheroot-rolling enterprises had mushroomed throughout the country. The manifesto stated that smoking cheroots and wearing rough homespun clothing would bring economic prosperity and stability to the country, and it concluded "unity and thrift are the two greatest blessings."

The second manifesto (Appendix VII), also undated, urged the youth to live by the motto "failure means death and burial, yet the throne itself is the reward for success and survival." It also beckoned them to join the League whose aim was to usher in an independent and responsible government in Burma.

The third manifesto (Appendix VIII), also undated, extolled the past glories of the country, and compared them with the deplorable state of the present where in some cases a laborer earned a paltry sum of three annas for a working day of ten hours. The living conditions of such laborers were so poor that the proverbial situation of "no place to turn to and no means to meet the expenses," had become a stark reality for them.

In tracing the causes of such a state of affairs, the manifesto claimed that lack of skill and poverty were inter-dependent. Poverty must be removed by giving all-out encouragement to the workers so as to ensure better workmanship. Therefore it urged the people to:

1. smoke cheroots instead of cigarettes;
2. wear homespun instead of imported textiles;
3. use Burmese umbrellas instead of foreign ones;
4. wear slippers instead of foreign shoes;
5. furnish homes with Burmese wares;
6. patronize Burmese food instead of foreign cuisine; and
7. substitute domestic goods for foreign goods wherever and whenever possible.

The ultimate aim was the realization of the long-cherished dream of the youth, i.e., an opportunity to create a new Burma, which would take her place in the family of nations. Therefore, the ABYL made a direct appeal to the students, at the same time enumerating the benefits and advantages of joining the League as follows:

1. Fraternity among the Burmese youth would form a nucleus of national unity;
2. Not to smoke cigarettes would mean not only thrift, but also clear headedness;
3. To wear homespun clothes and use home-made goods would mean an outward manifestation of the patriotic spirit;
4. Constant use of things made in the country would help create national consciousness (Appendix IX).

Having to a certain extent regained their foothold in the political arena through their youth activities, the Thakins took up the task of publishing a party organ. The *Dobama News Weekly* (*Dobama Thadinzin Hmattan*) was launched on January 21, 1933.[14] Its stated aims were to familiarize the general public with the ideals and aspirations contained in the Thakins' six-line motto and to solicit new ideas [*Do Thamaing*, I, 1976, 155]. The journal was to serve partly as a sounding board and partly as an open forum. The first issue declared that it was published neither for financial gain nor for the glory of the organization. The first eight issues appeared weekly, but the later ones were somewhat irregular. The twelfth and final number of the first volume appeared on April 22, 1933, while the one and only number of the second volume was published on July 22, 1933.

One regular feature of the journal was entitled "Our Heroes," and biographies of U Wisara, U Addisawuntha, and Ashin U Gawtha appeared in the first, second, and fifth issues respectively. To imbue very young people with new and radical ideas, a column was reserved for children to express their radical concepts. The radical nature of the journal is well expressed in a declaration made in the "Six Political Statements of the *Dobama News Weekly*," published on February 25, 1933:

1. Only Burmese must be spoken and written;
2. All offices and public buildings must display only the peacock standard;
3. Lest martyrs such as U Wisara be forgotten, bronze statues in their likeness must be erected;
4. The term "government" (Asoya Min) should be done away with and the term "Public Servant" (Pyi Asegan) used instead;
5. Likewise, the titles of Commissioner (Mingyi), Deputy Commissioner (Ayebaing), Subdivisional Officer (Ne baing), and Inspector of Police (Yazawut Wun) should be done away with and replaced by the terms Divisional Public Servant (Taingpyi Asegan), District Public Servant (Khayaing Pyi Asegan), Subdivisional Public Servant (Ne Asegan), and Public Servant for Crime (Yazawut Pyi Asegan) instead;[15]

---

14. The journal's circulation at its height was estimated at 1,000 and its cost was 2 annas (10 pyas) per copy.

15. The term Pyi Asegan was publicized during the Shwebo by-election in November 1933 by the Thakins [*Do Thamaing*, I, 1976, 157, 158, and 159].

6. Those who kowtow (Shikkho) to the above-mentioned Public Servants and address them as "My Lord" (Ashin Hpaya) and those who still have the slave mentality (Kyunzeik) should be hanged. [*Ba Sein*, 1943, 41-42.]

Another expression of the Thakins' radical outlook is found in their interpretation of time-honored maxims. The very first issue of the journal invited the readers to come with a clean slate (*tabula rasa*), lest old ideas mingle with the new and confuse their minds. Time-honored maxims were not to be taken as Gospel truths, for they were not always correct. As an example, the maxim

> If you wish to understand the workings of another man's mind
> Place yourself in his position and you cannot be wrong

was altered to: "Never place yourself in another's shoes." One man may be a thief while the other man may be good. Therefore to apply the maxim regardless of time and place would be wrong. Another maxim they changed to emphasize their point was "if one obeys the command of one's parents even the iron sheets and massive rocks can be smelted down to a boiling mass." In other words, all obstacles would disappear if one honored one's parents. They declared that the above maxim was not always correct, and mentioned the case of Prince Siddhattha.[16] However, they advocated that one should obey explicitly the commands of parents who are wise and whose knowledge extends beyond that of their children. The commands of parents whose wisdom was on the same level as that of their children should be obeyed after carefully weighing the pros and cons. Finally, the words of parents whose intelligence was less than that of their offspring should be flatly rejected.

In an article entitled "The Unemployed," a quick and sure method of eradicating unemployment was given as follows:

1. All high-ranking government officials including the governor and his ministers be reduced in monthly salary to Rs. 500;
2. All foreign-owned property be confiscated and shared equally among all nationals.

The journal also served as a means to enroll candidate Thakins. In each issue a column published the names of newly recruited Thakins, but such enrollments were few and far between [*Ba Tin*, 1964, 17-18]. The Thakins who used this facility, rank among the old veterans

---

16. Prince Siddhattha, is the princely name of Lord Gaudhama Buddha. He was confined to a life of ease and pleasure and was forbidden by his royal father to venture out of the palace walls. Disregarding the royal orders, he went to the city. There he came across the Four Signs which so changed his outlook on life that he renounced all his worldly possessions including his wife and infant son. This renunciation and ascetic life led him to the Enlightenment. The argument here was that had he abided by his father's command, he would not have attained Buddha-hood.

because their names were listed long before district organizations were established.

The publication of the journal came to a stop with the first number of the second volume.[17] A contributing factor to its failure was the lack of funds, for no separate moneys had been reserved for the journal, and donations from interested members had been its mainstay. It did not have the support of a general readership nor was there a district organization to act as a base. A political organ, dependent on advertisements from the bourgeoisie and petty business enterprises, it is small wonder that the journal was shortlived.

At this juncture, Thakin Ba Thoung wanted to have a kind of conference of all Thakins to draw up a program of more consolidated activities. The conference was scheduled to be held at the then Headquarters of the Dobama at 33 Yedashe Road, Bahan, on July 4, 5, and 6, 1933. Of the many Thakins with whom he made contact only a couple appeared at the scheduled time. Three more arrived later, so that the conference came to be called "The Conference of the Six." The stalwarts who attended were Thakin Ba Thoung, Thakin Thein Han (Bogale), Thakin Thein Maung, Thakin Hla Baw, Thakin Tun Shwe, and Thakin Ba Tin. Thakins Ba Sein and Ohn Khin attended as observers [Ba Tin, 1964, 23-24].

Thakin Ba Tin, a participant in this "conference" later recalled that, as a veteran of the GCBA and accustomed to conferences attended by overwhelming masses, for him this first conference of the Dobama presented a pitiable sight. He said:

> Having declared in bold words that the primary, secondary, and tertiary aim was independence and to achieve that aim, the adherents were willing to face exile, the hangman's noose, and even death, and to find only six who came to attend the conference, I could not express the feeling of disillusion I felt at that time. [Ba Tin, 1964, 25.]

Thakin Ba Tin further recalled that Thakin Ba Thoung seemed to divine the suppressed feelings of disillusionment and disappointment among the participants, and to dispel them he told the gathering after dinner that day:

> I cannot fully express my joy to see you today. Out of the thousands who enlisted as Thakins I am glad to find at least five who have heard the clarion call. In fact it is heartening to find that besides myself, I have five other gallants. Compared to Hitler, I am far more fortunate because when Hitler first set up his party he was alone and his funds were hardly worth mentioning. He had about thirteen annas (approximately eighty pyas). [Ba Tin, 1964, 25.]

---

17. There is, however, a contradictory statement that only one number (i.e. Vol. I, No. 1) of the *Dobama News Weekly* was ever published [*Do Thamaing*, I, 1976, 156].

The only resolution passed at the "conference" was to draw up a program for an extensive organization throughout the country.

The young Thakins soon found a new medium to propagate their ideals and aspirations. The untimely death of U Thuta, a member of the House of Representatives, created the need for a by-election in Shwebo in November 1933. The group decided that Thakin Ba Thoung should contend for the seat in order to propagate Dobama ideals. He left for Shwebo, accompanied by Thakins Thein Maung and Ba Sein. En route, they were joined by Thakin Thein Maung's brother, Thakin Tun Shwe, who had taken a month's leave as a school teacher at Toungoo for the sole purpose of assisting the Thakins in their new venture [*Do Thamaing*, I, 1976, 157].

At Shwebo, the young Thakins established their headquarters at the residence of Thakin Ba Khant, where they hung a signboard bearing the legend Komin Kochin, to denote their intention to install their own government.[18] Their public speeches were a rousing success in this ideal location. Shwebo was the home of Alaungmintaya, the founder of the Konbaung, the last of the Burmese dynasties. The tomb of Alaungmintaya lay in the center of the city in a state of disrepair and devoid of the honor due to a monarch. The Aungmye, the victory soil outside the city which the Konbaung kings had trod before setting out on major expeditions, had been turned into a burial ground and the palace site had become a jail. All these were eloquent testimonies to Burma's sorry plight. The Thakins were able to set people's minds against colonial rule without much difficulty.

As was their wont, each public speech was preceded by a song recital with elaborate explanations. Since the Thakins' purpose was to spread their creed rather than actually to obtain the seat, they took no stand on the major issue of the day, advocating neither separation nor anti-separation. Seditious words inflamed the minds of the audience with a desire to revive the glorious past: "Freedom must be fought for"; "what is lost through violence must be retrieved by violence"; "It is a historical fact that India (Manipur) and Siam were once under the sway of our forefathers whose only weapon was a bamboo staff"; "Although enslaved now, as sure as the sun rises in the east, a day will dawn when we will be masters again" [*Do Thamaing*, I, 1976, 157].

Although the majority of the audience were enthralled by such fiery speeches, those favoring the authorities dubbed the young Thakins as Maik Yuu Ye--reckless crazy fools. To this taunt, the Thakins replied at their meetings with their own interpretation of the epithet: they were crazy to crave for the independence of the country; they were daring to face all dangers to achieve their aims. In all, the Thakins made forty such public speeches before they were served with an ultimatum to leave the town within forty-eight hours. They defied the orders and were arrested under Section 144 of the Indian Penal Code [*Do Thamaing*, I, 1976, 157].

---

18. *Ko* means "our own," and *min* "king" or "government," *Kochin* means "we together" or "ourselves." So probably Komin Kochin means "our own government and our own people." The Komin Kochin Aphwe was founded on August 8, 1936 (Appendix X).

If the authorities had expected the arrests to intimidate the young Thakins, they were mistaken. The arrests and the reports of the arrests carried in the local papers served to promote the popularity of the Thakins and gave them fresh impetus. At the news of the arrests in Shwebo, Thakin Lay Maung and Thakin Han immediately set out to assist their comrades. They were joined at Toungoo by Thakin Hla Maung, who was to earn the name of "Khwegaungbyaungbyankat," the sticker of the dog stamp upside-down. On a letter to a colleague in Rangoon, he had written under the stamp which bore the likeness of the British king, "I have stuck the dog stamp upside down." For this mischief he was promptly placed under arrest. He soon earned the name of "the returnee of the seven prisons."

On arrival at Shwebo, these three gallants not only conducted fresh public meetings but also managed to found a library and a volunteer force. Thakin Lay Maung founded the Yadana Theinhka Reading Club, and Thakin Hla Maung founded the Yangyi Aung Ye Tatseik, a volunteer organization affiliated to the Dobama Yetat [*Do Thamaing*, I, 1976, 158].

The arrests of the Thakins at Shwebo also helped to bridge the gap between the two age groups in politics. Till then the old political veterans had looked upon the undertakings of the Thakins with condescending indulgence and had not identified with them. However, when the Thakins arrested at Shwebo were sentenced to four months' rigorous imprisonment and were separately sent to the jails at Mandalay, Myingyan, Rangoon, and Thayetmyo, they staged a hunger strike in prison.

When this news reached the public, the first to take up their cause was the Rate and Tax Payers' Association. A protest meeting was held at Bagaya Uyin Kyaung Taik at Kemmendine, Rangoon and was attended by students, Thakins, and veteran members of the GCBA (General Council of Burmese Associations) [*Do Thamaing*, I, 1976, 158]. Funds collected by the Rangoon Myodaw Pyu Pyin Ye Association enabled Thakin Lay Maung and Thakin Han to proceed to Shwebo. U Thet Su, U Hla Tun Phyu, Daw Ant, U Min O, U Po Mhin, and U Soe Tin, who were members of the association, personally approached Dr. Ba Han, a prominent barrister to plead the cause of the Thakins. Through his efforts Mr. Justice J. R. Das passed orders for their release [*Baho Akhun Htan*, 1965, 20-21]. An overwhelming mass of people, comprising Wunthanus, Thakins, and youths gave the Thakins a rousing welcome as they stepped out of their respective jails.

Soon after their release, Thakin Ba Sein and Thakin Lay Maung, together with Shin Ariya, a brother of U Ottama who had recently returned from deportation, launched a propaganda tour. They chose the hot month of April which was vacation time for students. Their itinerary included a rail journey from Rangoon to Prome and a river trip along the Irrawaddy to Mandalay, the ultimate destination being Shwebo where they intended to "tread on the victory soil" for the second time. Their tour carried them to Allanmyo, Chauk, Letpadan, Mandalay, Meiktila, Myingyan, Prome, Sitkwin, Tharawaddy, Thayetmyo, Yenangyaung, and Zigon. To people gathered at these various stops, Thakin Ba Sein explained the Dobama Song and Thakin Lay Maung spoke of the duties and the tasks of the young people, while Shin

Ariya highlighted his experiences in expounding on the role played by the young monks in the fight for freedom [*Do Thamaing*, I, 1976, 159].

There were no untoward incidents at the various stopping places. However, within an hour of their arrival at Shwebo, Section 144 of the Code of Criminal Procedure was proclaimed. Despite this, the Thakins continued with their scheduled program, announced by the town crier. The next day they were arrested, tried, and sentenced to three months' hard labor. In protest against the harsh measures meted out to the Thakins and in sympathy with their cause, the bazaar sellers of the Shwebo Municipal Bazaar closed their premises [*Do Thamaing*, I, 1976, 164].

Protest demonstrations were staged at Yenangyaung, Myingyan, and Toungoo. Thakin Kha was delegated to Shwebo to replace those arrested, and he toured the countryside delivering speeches at the neighboring villages of Seikkhun and Chiba. The Thakins were later sent to Mandalay jail and on their release after the completion of their jail term the citizens of Mandalay welcomed them with great honor [*Do Thamaing*, I, 1976, 165]. While their comrades were under detention, Thakin Thein Maung and Thakin Han toured Myaungmya and Wakema. Thakin Nyi and Thakin Tun Ok carried on the work begun by the Thakin leaders and formed branch organizations for youth activities at Prome [*Do Thamaing*, I, 1976, 166].

There was one other setback. This time, it was due to the founder leaving the organization. The rift occurred over the issue of fund raising. Thakin Thein Maung was convinced that the Thakins should first gain the confidence of the people by their example of self-lessness and that, once public confidence had been gained, their financial problems would be automatically solved. Thakin Ba Thoung, on the other hand, believed that the primary concern of the party should be self-sufficiency, and suggested various ways of gathering funds before launching a political campaign. Failing to convince Thakin Ba Thoung, Thakin Thein Maung in exasperation told him to go in search of funds and to rejoin them later. Thus differences of opinion led the founder to abandon the organization which he had brought into existence [*Do Thamaing*, I, 1976, 166]. Later Thakin Ba Thoung set up a new organization known as the Hsinyetha Min Hsinyetha Chin Party and when the short-lived party became extinct, he faded from the political scene.

His departure, however, did not much affect the organization as a whole. The one change was the transfer of the headquarters from his residence to that of Thakin Han at Linlun Kwetthit, though the headquarters of the ABYL continued to be at 172 Suburban Road, Alon [*Do Thamaing*, I, 1976, 166]. For some time in September 1934, both the Dobama and the ABYL had their headquarters at 81 Suburban Road, Alon [*Do Thamaing*, I, 1976, 169].

In September 1934, a temporary Executive Committee of the Dobama was formed.

President	--	Thakin Thein Maung
Vice President	--	Thakin Lay Maung
General Secretary	--	Thakin Ba Sein
Joint Secretary	--	Thakin Tun Ok

            Treasurer   -- Thakin Han
            Propaganda Officers   -- Thakin Nyi and
                                            Thakin Tun Shwe
                              [*Do Thamaing*, I, 1976, 169]

Thakin Thein Maung and Thakin Han had the responsibility of working at the headquarters in Toungoo and, with the help of Thakin Tun Shwe and Thakin Hla Maung, organized the people of central Burma. Thakin Ba Sein and Thakin Tun Ok were sent to Yenangyaung to make arrangements for holding the First Conference there [*Do Thamaing*, I, 1976, 169].

The formative years of the Dobama--the five-year period preceding their first Conference held at Yenangyaung in 1935--were chaotic. Brought into the world during the turmoil of the Indo-Burmese riot of May 1930, the group lacked all semblance of a political party in the accepted sense of the word. No proper organization was formed until the First Conference, although the Thakins gained a fair amount of support, especially from the politically awakened youth among the educated classes and from the downtrodden masses, by their song recitals and pamphleteering in the early phase and later by their public speeches during the election campaign at the Shwebo by-election.

Leadership was tacitly vested in the hands of the entire group, but their inability to provide organized leadership during these five long years indicated their inherent weakness and lack of foresight. This weakness was particularly manifest at the time of the peasants' uprising in 1930-1931. If the Thakins had not allowed themselves to be eclipsed by the greater force of these events that convulsed the whole country but had rather used this force as a springboard to raise themselves so they could ride the rising crest of popular support, the course of their history and that of the country itself would have been different.

Not only did they lack organized leadership and foresight, but they also lacked a clear-cut pattern of organization. While their sister organization, the ABYL, whose aim was more social than political, was equipped with its own Constitution, branch organizations, and a well established secretariat, the Dobama, the political counterpart, lacked all these facilities. It was only on the eve of calling a conference that a provisional Executive Committee was hastily formed.

With such haphazard leadership, it is small wonder that no systematic membership existed. Apart from those who enrolled as members through the columns of the *Dobama News Weekly* no membership campaign was launched. The leaders of the Dobama seem to have been content with the vast crowds that attended their public speeches and to have overlooked this important facet of political life. They apparently did not realize that membership is the very life-blood of the party itself.

The lack of a written Constitution or an open declaration makes a retrospective assessment of their ideology during this period difficult. It has been proclaimed that their song was the embodiment of their sentiments and aspirations. But while use of the song as a means for rallying support is understandable, to convey their ideology through the medium of the song is neither plausible nor practical. Most

Burmese words are ambiguous and differences in interpretation could promote misunderstanding and cause seeds of discord to be sown among the movement's adherents. For the purposes of propagation and standardization of their ideology they ought to have produced a written Constitution by the time their First Conference was held. Their failure to do so clearly indicated a lack of thoroughness in their capacity as promoters of a political creed.

With such shortcomings, it is remarkable that the party gained popular support, especially from the downtrodden masses. As these people constituted the majority of the population, the Dobama's support during the early years of its existence outstripped that of its rival organizations. The party attracted public sympathy as the underdog subjected to oppressive measures from the British authorities. The anti-British sentiments of the inarticulate mass of people found eloquent expression in the fiery and seditious speeches delivered by the Thakins at their public meetings. Thunderous applause and ovations at such meetings and the singing of the chorus at the song recitals were the only means by which the discontented masses could give vent to their suppressed feelings. Thus, the Thakin public meetings were highly successful.

However, the party's other propaganda medium, the *Dobama News Weekly* did not progress satisfactorily. Pamphlets or periodicals used for the purpose of propagating an ideal or a cause should be sold at almost a give-away price. The *Dobama News Weekly* at 2 annas (10 pyas) a copy was too expensive when the per capita income of an average Burman in the early 1930s was probably less than Ks 70.00 [*EDB*, 1956, 6]. To be able to sell it at a much lower price, the party needed financial support. When the popular epithet used for the Thakins was "a budding Thakin has to undergo six months' rigorous imprisonment," it was not easy to find well-to-do people willing to support their cause. Therefore, their propaganda activity through the publications medium failed miserably.

Lack of organized leadership, absence of a clear-cut policy, except for what may be called a blind patriotism, coupled with the lack of monetary backing were responsible for the haphazard situation which prevailed during the initial phase of the Dobama's history.

CHAPTER II

THE GATHERING STRENGTH

The three years following the First Conference of 1935 were the most fruitful years in the history of the Dobama Asiayone. These three years roughly corresponded with a period of unity which existed until the Dobama fell into discord leading to an eventual split.

Thakin Aung San, as general secretary of the Dobama for 1939, stated in the preamble to the proceedings of its Fourth Annual Conference that "the annual conferences are milestones by which the progress of their party is gauged" [*Do Nyi Largan*, 1939, 3]. The growth, split, and decline of the Dobama are clearly discernible in the events leading from one conference to the next. An attempt will be made here to study the growth of the party through these conferences. Of the five, the first three covered a period of unity and gathering strength. The first of these was held at Yenangyaung on March 30, 1935 [*CM* 7/1935].

The 1935 Yenangyaung Conference

The need to set up a regular party and systematic organization became apparent to the Thakins from the sympathetic public response during and after the election campaign at Shwebo. It was to satisfy this need that a countrywide convention was called during the summer of 1935. The young Thakins looked forward to the occasion and worked diligently to realize their aim. As mentioned above, in September 1934 they formed a temporary central Executive Committee. The first tangible actions taken by this newly formed Executive Committee were to move their headquarters and to allot specific duties to each of the individual members. With the exception of the president and the treasurer, who remained in Rangoon and took charge of the administrative duties, all other members were sent out to the districts to organize and make the necessary preparations for the conference.

During the first week of March 1935, a Reception Committee was formed at Yenangyaung with the following members:

President	-- U Aung Pe
Vice Presidents	-- U Ba Thit
	U Yan Shwe
Secretary	-- U Nyi Pu (Pleader)
Joint Secretaries	-- Thakin Tun Ok
	Thakin Ba Tin
Treasurer	-- U Ba Htein (Baho Mandaing press)
Fund Collectors	-- U Soe Thein (Municipal)
	U Ngwe Thaung

[*Do Thamaing*, I, 1976, 169]

The program for the conferences was worked out as follows:

1. Recitation of the Pancasila--the five precepts
2. Welcoming speech and chanting of Ratu
3. Dobama Song
4. Election of a Patron
5. Election of a Master of Ceremonies
6. Presidential speech
7. Reading and accepting of the Annual Report of the Dobama and the ABYL [All Burma Youth League] [*Aung Myin*, April 2, 1935].

Preliminary proposals were:

1. to pray for the repose of the souls of those who had given their lives during the Saya San uprising; to recognize their patriotism although their expression of it is open to criticism;
2. to pray for the release of those placed under detention (both lay and clerical) in anticipation of the New Constitution soon to be conferred upon the country;
3. to refrain from participation in the forthcoming Silver Jubilee Celebrations in order to express the general feelings of the people who, though reduced to a subject race, still mourn for their monarch and whose hearts grieve at such a lamentable condition;
4. (a) to free the country (from alien rule) and to set up a constitutional form of government which would ensure equal opportunities for everyone;
   (b) to have the central Executive Committee draw up a program systematically to organize students, youths, workers, and peasants;
   (c) to join forces with any political faction or organization holding similar aims and objectives;
5. (a) to urge all Burmans to patronize national enterprises by using home-made goods;
   (b) to encourage the Burmans to practice spinning with a view to replacing foreign imported textiles with homespun;
6. to elect an All Burma Executive Committee for the coming year, and the elected Executive Committee to form the central Executive Committee with the following offices:

>President,
>Vice President,
>Treasurer,
>Secretary,
>Joint Secretary

and the committee who will be responsible for the organization of Workers, Peasants, Youth, and Yetat Voluntary Corps;

7. to urge the companies concerned to comply with the rightful demands made on behalf of the oilfield workers by the Yenangyaung Labor Congress;
8. to recognize the triumph of the Anti-separationists at the elections [*Aung Myin*, April 2, 1935].

Together with the program and the proposals issued by the Dobama, the president of the General Council of Burmese Associations (GCBA) of Yenangyaung issued an invitation addressed to all the people of Burma, including monks. It reads:

> Everyone is aware that this association [the GCBA] has acted in accordance with the resolutions made at the conferences held at Shwebo, Meiktila, Pegu, Minbu, Toungoo, and Sagaing (where it was called off), without deviating from the declared policy and has served with selflessness for the welfare of the country. Due to the tactics employed by the Government, the country is now rent into numerous factions, and the national enterprise is thereby undermined. If we allowed this state of disunity to be prolonged, it is inevitable that we shall all suffer in the end. In order that a program be drawn up and the effective remedy be given, it is urged that all interested persons attend the Conference of the Dobama and the ABYL who have promised to serve the country in all humbleness. The attendance of at least three representatives from each village and town is solicited. [*Aung Myin*, March 22, 1935.]

The conference was scheduled to commence on March 26, 1935, and shortly before, a notice dated March 25, 1935 was sent by U Po Han, the subdivisional magistrate at Yenangyaung, to U Ba Htein, treasurer of the Reception Committee, a representative of the Thakins. The notice read:

> You in conjunction with the other members of the Dobama, All Burma Youths, and Thakins Associations have made poisonous and inflammatory speeches in the past. There is fear of repetitions of such highly objectionable speeches at the forthcoming Conference Meeting to be held at Yenangyaung on the 30th March 1935, and if not prevented there is immediate danger of disturbing the public peace. You are now called upon to show cause in person or by pleader why an order under Section 144 of the Code of Criminal Procedure should not be passed against you by the 28th day of March 1935. [*CM*, 7, March 25, 1935.]

On March 28, 1935 the magistrate issued another notice stating:

> WHEREAS it has been made to appear to me that you, in conjunction with other members of the Dobama, All Burma Youths League, and Thakin Associations held public meetings and inflammatory speeches, which, if repeated may lead to a disturbance of the public peace.

> I do hereby, prohibit you U Ba Htein, from holding or attending any Political Meeting or Conference held in connection with the aforesaid Dobama, All Burma Youths League or Thakin Associations within the jurisdiction of the Yenangyaung Subdivision for a period of two months from the day of the original notice, viz. 25-3-35. [*CM*, 7, March 28, 1935.]

However, in defiance of Section 144 of the Code of Criminal Procedure, 1898, promulgated for the occasion, the youth leaders from Myingyan took the lead in staging a mass meeting on March 28, 1935. At that meeting, Thakin Bo proposed a protest against the prohibition, which was seconded by Thakin Ba Nyein and unanimously endorsed [*Do Thamaing*, I, 1976, 173]. The following message was sent to the governor and the Home Ministry:

> The notice issued by the District Magistrate Yenangyaung forbidding the entry of forty Thakin leaders (into Yenangyaung area) and enforcement of P.C. [Indian Penal Code] Section 144 is not merely a prohibition against the holding of the Conference scheduled to be held on 30 March 1935, it is an obstruction preventing the Thakins in the discharge of their legitimate actions.
>
> Therefore, we, the All Burma Youth of Myingyan district, vehemently protest the above-mentioned action. Should this enforcement entail any breach of public peace, the Government shall bear the sole responsibility for the consequences. [*Do Thamaing*, I, 1976, 173.]

The following tract was also distributed to the general public:

> Just as we are about to conduct the Conference a notice has been served demanding why the Section 144 of the Criminal Procedure should not be passed against us. . . . Negotiations made by Thakin Han had failed. According to the Subdivisional Magistrate Section 144 is being enforced because
>
> (1) Speeches made by the Thakins are inflammatory and seditious;
> (2) The Conference of the Dobama Asiayone coincides with the Industrial Show and it is feared that clashes might occur;
> (3) Yenangyaung, being the oilfield area, interrelationships between the workers and oil companies exist. Besides unemployment problems are rampant. If the Conference champions their cause it is feared that a state of unrest might occur;
> (4) When a few residents of Yenangyaung were consulted, they were of the opinion that the conference would disturb the peace.

On March 24, 1935, notices regarding the promulgation of Section 144 were distributed individually to the Thakin leaders. Mounted police were sent to the villages within Yenangyaung jurisdiction and village criers made announcements to the villagers [*Do Thamaing*, I, 1976, 172].

The Reception Committee of the conference had sent Thakins Ba Sein and Thein Maung to Maymyo to put their case before the authorities. The home minister was fairly impressed by the explanations given by the Thakins in which it was stated that:

(1) Although the speeches delivered by the Thakins were accused of being inflammatory and seditious, no Thakin had been convicted under Section 144. Therefore it is to be construed that the speeches delivered were within limits of freedom of speech. Should they overstep the bounds of the above-mentioned rights, action should be taken against them accordingly. In the past this freedom has been denied to the citizens. There had been an incident where some Thakins in Shwebo were charged with a non-existing ruling and were banished from the area. Later, the Magistrate of Shwebo had to rescind the order and withdraw the groundless charge. On the second occasion, when a similar incident was reported at Shwebo, the District Magistrate was once again found to be in the wrong. No incident of violence has been recorded at any of the public meetings conducted by the Thakins. It is evident that the Thakins love their country and are interested only in the rights of the citizens. Therefore, the first accusation is unfounded.

(2) The exhibition (Industrial Show) is held for the purpose of promoting national industry which is in line with the Thakin aspirations. Therefore, the second allegation that the conference would clash with the exhibition is also unfounded.

(3) The Thakins have been active in the oilfield area for the past four or five years assisting the Workers and the Labor Congress. There has been no occurrence of lawlessness. Besides, it should be stated that the demands of the workers to be placed before the conference are honest and legitimate ones.

(4) The fourth allegation does not call for any refutation as it is merely an assumption made by a few individuals.

Under the pressure of such a loud protest, the home minister agreed to have the District Magistrate Magwe, rescind the orders issued by the subdivisional magistrate and permission was granted for the convening of the conference with a stipulation that the following items from the agenda be excluded:

(1) Notwithstanding the regularity or the irregularity of their actions, due recognition be given to those

persons both lay and cleric who had given up their lives during the Tharrawaddy uprising. To offer prayers for the repose of their souls in accordance with the traditions of the Buddhists.

(2) To pray that those persons (both lay and cleric) placed under detention for services to the country and religion may enjoy good health and their grievances be speedily remedied. As the New Constitution is about to be conferred, the conference is of opinion that they should be released without any delay.

(3) The Burmese nationals are denied the privilege of being ruled by their own king. As a subject race, they mourn for the Burmese monarchs. To express this lamentable condition, the conference deems it proper (for the nationals) to refrain from participation in the Silver Jubilee celebrations (to be held) to mark the twenty-fifth anniversary of the coronation of King George V.

The Thakins conceded to the demand to omit the above items from their agenda, and the subdivisional magistrate of Yenangyaung immediately rescinded the order [*Do Thamaing*, I, 1976, 174-75].

Although the authorities were successful in removing what seemed to them objectionable items from the agenda they had inadvertently helped to popularize the Thakins as champions of the oppressed. By their refusal to allow the Thakins to conduct the conference peacefully and without restraint, what might have passed unnoticed by the general public became, in the dexterous hands of the Thakins, a powerful weapon to expose the infringement by the authorities of freedom of expression.

The conference was declared open at the Sekkalampa Tazaung at Lebaw Kyaung Taik on March 30, 1935 at 2 p.m. After the chairman U Soe Thein's inaugural speech, the meeting was adjourned till noon the next day [*Do Thamaing*, I, 1976, 175].

The leaders met *in camera* that night and again in the morning, where the decision was made to call off the conference. An explanatory declaration printed details of the items forbidden to be discussed at the conference and added:

As the agenda for the conference was drawn after careful deliberations at the grassroot and divisional level . . . and had been put up to the conference for formal approval . . . all youthful members should not be mindful of the restrictions but carry out the tasks as assigned in the agenda. [*Do Thamaing*, I, 1976, 176-77.]

The most noteworthy incident that took place during the conference was the enrollment of Mr. Maung Hmine. Mr. Maung Hmine is one of the pseudonyms of U Lun, a well-known literary figure who was later to be a winner of the Stalin Peace award. To oppose any Burmese use of the "Mr." affix, he took the name of Maung Hmine, the hero of a popular novel *Chinbaung Ywetthe Maung Hmine* [The Roselle leaves seller, Maung Hmine] by Wunsaye U Kyi. In the novel Maung Hmine was a philanderer who earned the contempt of the general public for his escapades. By calling himself Mr. Maung Hmine, a combination of a hated affix and an obnoxious name, U Lun attempted to discourage the use of the "Mr." affix by the Burmans [Maung Thuta, "Sayagyi Thakin Kodaw Hmine," 1971, 595-98]. On becoming a Thakin, he called himself Thakin Kodaw Hmine, an equivalent to Master Lord Hmine.

Despite governmental interference, the Thakins were able to elect the following Executive Committee for the year 1936:

President	-- Thakin Ba Sein
Vice President	-- Thakin Lay Maung
Secretary	-- Thakin Thein Maung
Joint Secretary	-- Thakin Tun Ok
Treasurer	-- Thakin Tun Khin
Information	-- Thakin Nyi
Members	-- Thakin Han
	Thakin Tun Shwe
	Thakin Ba Ba

[*Do Thamaing*, I, 1976, 176]

Thus after five years in the political arena the Thakins were for the first time able to form a proper party with a central executive. Judging from their agenda and the proposed resolutions they had not come very far from the well-trodden path of the traditionalists. They professed to be radicals, but at heart they were still conservatives. They still considered recitation of Pancasila an important part of the occasion, and it appeared reasonable to them to intone the welcoming speech in ratu verse and to invoke the supernatural powers for the speedy release of the political detainees. Besides, they seem to have hoped that the 1935 Constitution would usher in a more liberal form of government, for they proposed to "pray" for the release of the political detainees "now that the New Constitution is (soon) to be conferred upon the country."

The third item in the agenda, banned by the authorities, was glaring evidence of a traditional outlook. In it the Thakins openly mourned for the long-departed Burmese monarchs. One might argue that their action was governed by their desire to enlist the support of conservative elements, yet it cannot be denied that it exposed a chink in the armor of their radicalism.

The fourth item proposed a united front against imperialism. One cannot help but wonder what prompted them to adopt such an attitude. They were convening their First Conference. They were on the threshold of a new life. Did they not consider themselves strong enough to stand alone? Or was the proposal a mere formality?

The fifth item, the proposal for the revival of spinning and promotion of home-made goods, is clearly the contribution of the ABYL. Although the conference was admittedly a joint affair, the inclusion of a reformist program was incongruous in a conference discussing political problems. The last item in the agenda surpassed all others in its absurdity. The Dobama had taken a neutral stand towards the separationists and Anti-separationists, yet they now publicly rejoiced at the triumph of the Anti-separationists.

Nevertheless, their interest in the working class and their intention to mobilize workers, peasants, youths, and students were laudable. The sixth item proposed support for the demands made by the Yenangyaung Labor Congress on behalf of the oilfield workers. They were to reap a rich dividend from this enterprise. In later years they reached the zenith of their popularity through their association with the labor conflict at Yenangyaung.

Without any formal resolution passed at the conference, there was no clear-cut program to give guidance to the Executive Committee during its tenure of office other than the conference agenda. Out of the eight items mentioned in the agenda, the assignments which directly concerned the central Executive Committee were drawing up a program and systematically organizing the students, youth, workers, and peasants. However, at the close of their tenure of office there had been little progress to report. Except for two visits abroad [*Do Thamaing*, I, 1976, 181-85] and some improvements in organization at home, nothing spectacular was achieved.

Soon after the First Conference, the president, Thakin Ba Sein, made a brief tour of the principal towns in India. He traveled there at the invitation of U Ottama, a veteran political monk who was at the time serving as the president of the Hindu Maha Sabha in India. Ba Sein left Rangoon early in June accompanied by Sayadaw U Ketu. His first stop was at Calcutta, where he met Babu Rajendra Prasad, Pundit Mohan Malavia, and other Congress leaders. At Patna and Gaya, at the invitation of Indian youths, he delivered several lectures explaining the current political situation in Burma and emphasizing the awakening of the young people. He also stressed the need for an Asian Youth Organization. His lectures were carried in the local newspapers and interested youths from Bombay and Bengal invited him to speak to them. Because of the seditious nature of Thakin Ba Sein's speeches, he and U Ottama were served in Northern India on July 29, 1935 with a notice under Section 144 forbidding them from making public speeches. Therefore they returned to Burma, arriving at Rangoon on August 13, 1935. They were given a rousing welcome at the jetty and a reception in their honor was held at the Jubilee Hall on September 2, 1935. The reception, attended by adherents from different political parties and people from all walks of life, was formally opened with the singing of the Dobama Song by YMB Saya Tin and a chorus of the Thakins. Thakin Kodaw Hmine served as the chairman, and prominent among the speakers were Barrister U Paw Tun, Mr. Ganga Singh, Amyotha U Myint, University Ko Aung Thein, Thakin Saw Gyi, and Thakin Tun Saing.

The vice-president, Thakin Lay Maung, left Rangoon on July 6, 1935 at the invitation of an Indian journalist, Sri Hari Rao. After paying homage to U Ottama in Calcutta, he made a tour of South India accompanied by Sri Hari Rao, stopping at Kakinada, Muzatpattam, Vishakhapatham, Sita Nagaram, Bazawada, and Madras. At Madras he attended a meeting held by students and municipal workers on November 7, 1935 to celebrate the Russian Revolution. In Bombay he not only attended the conference of the Radical Youth, but delivered a short speech on behalf of the youth of Burma. Thakin Lay Maung's visit to India lasted about six months.

These Indian tours enabled the Thakin leaders to study at first hand the activities of the Indian political parties, to gain a wider perspective in aligning their own problems with those of international politics, and to reassess their former achievements with socialist ideology. These tours also helped to bring about a better understanding and a closer tie between Burma and India in their fight against British imperialism [*Do Thamaing*, I, 1976, 184].

The 1936 Myingyan Conference

While the two Thakin leaders were away in India, their comrades in Burma launched a countrywide campaign to form district organizations. The extent of their achievement can be gauged by the number of delegates registered at the Second Conference held at Myingyan on June 27 through 29, 1936. While the Yenangyaung conference had been attended by forty delegates, the Myingyan conference was attended by over two hundred from seventeen districts: Henzada, Kyaukse, Magwe, Mandalay, Meiktila, Minbu, Monywa, Moulmein, Myaungnya, Prome, Pyapon, Rangoon, Sagaing, Shwebo, Tharawaddy, Thayetmyo, and Toungoo [*Do Thamaing*, I, 1976, 197].

The conference opened with the singing of the Dobama Song. The chairman was Thakin Kodaw Hmine while Thakin Ba Sein acted as the master of ceremonies. Conspicuously absent was U Soe Thein, who had acted as chairman at Yenangyaung. In a declaration explaining why he had withdrawn his patronage, he stated that, as a boycotter of the New Constitution, he could not participate in the Second Conference which was held to permit its members to stand in the general elections [*Do Thamaing*, I, 1976, 197].

In spite of the initial setback resulting from this unexpected announcement, the conference proceeded successfully according to schedule. Then on June 29, the last day of the conference, Thakin Ba Sein, Thakin Nyi, Thakin Aung Than, Thakin Than, and Thakin Tun Myint were arrested under Sections 120(B), 124(A), and 153(A) of the Indian Penal Code for seditious speeches given a few months earlier at Moulmein [Ba Sein, 1943, 59; *Do Thamaing*, I, 1976, 197].

If this government action was meant to warn the youths from joining the Thakins, its effect was the reverse. On the day that the Thakin leaders were arrested, the youth of Myingyan, students and Dobama Yetat, staged a protest demonstration. Marching through the streets and beating the Maha Sidaw Gyi--the royal drum--they denounced the government's action. At the mass meeting held at the Kohsaung Tazaung that night where practically the whole town turned up, over a hundred youths stood up on the stage amidst thunderous applause and announced publicly they were joining the Thakins [*Do Thamaing*, I, 1976, 198]. The most outstanding of the new members thus enrolled was Prince Hteik Tin Kodaw Gyi, a grandson of the Crown Prince Kanaung [Ba Sein, 1943, 60]. As the arrests were made on the last day of the conference, the remaining Thakins were able to bring the conference to a successful close.

The seven resolutions that were passed at the conference were:

1. Firmly believing that the New Constitution will perpetuate slavery and impoverish the populace, the people of Burma have strongly objected to the promulgation of the same. Despite repeated protests, the New Constitution is about to be forcibly conferred upon us. Therefore, the conference is of opinion that it should allow its members to contest the elections and resort to an effective means to wreck the Constitution. In order to activate this resolution, the conference accords full authority to the Executive Committee of the central organization.

2. To propose a vote of respect to those patriots both lay and cleric, who gave their lives for the country's cause.

3. To form special bureaus to assist the peasants and workers in gaining their legitimate rights and also to make home-made goods easily accessible to them.

4. The conference is of opinion that the action of the government in forbidding the students of certain schools in Burma to participate in political activities deprives the youth of Burma from gaining the basic political knowledge and prevents them from acquiring political consciousness in their youth and thus prolongs the tenure of slavery. Therefore, the conference strongly protests against such restrictions.

5. Burial rites are still denied to the late King Thibaw and his Queen. Their bodies still remain in Ratnagiri. The conference deems it proper that their remains, together with the remains of the late Queen Mother at Rangoon, be returned to Mandalay Palace to be interred alongside those of their forebears.

6. The conference is of opinion that the proscription orders placed upon the political organizations at Motaung village in Sagaing District are uncalled for.

7. In order to define clearly the tasks of the Yetat, the conference sanctions full authority to the Executive Committee to draw up the Constitution. [*Do Thamaing*, I, 1976, 198-99.]

One outstanding event at the conference was the recognition of the Dobama Song as the national song. It had been acclaimed as the Party's song since its inception, now it was elevated to national status.

The central Executive Committee members elected for the year were:

President	-- Thakin Lay Maung
Vice President	-- Thakin Nyi
Secretary	-- Thakin Tun Ok
Joint Secretary	-- Thakin Tin Maung
Treasurer	-- Thakin Tun Khin
Information	-- Thakin Thein Maung
	Thakin Mya
	Thakin Ba Ba
	Thakin Ba Sein
	Thakin Hla Baw

[*Do Thamaing*, I, 1976, 199]

The All Burma Committee was formed with sixty-three members from thirteen districts: Henzada, Insein, Mandalay, Myingyan, Pakokku, Pyapon, Rangoon, Sagaing, Tharrawaddy, Toungoo, and Yenangyaung. The first woman Thakin (Thakinma) to be elected to the All Burma Committee was Thakinma Ma Thein Tin of Prome [*Do Thamaing*, I, 1976, 197].

The 1936 Myingyan conference was a second milestone in the march of the Dobama towards consolidation of their strength. It revealed a leftist bent within the organization although no formal declaration was made to that effect. The first resolution was indicative of this tendency. At the First Conference, the Thakins seem to have fostered some hope that the New Constitution would usher in a more liberal form of government. But at the Second Conference their attitude towards the Constitution had changed totally. The futility of their protests had become apparent and therefore, they decided to participate in the general elections only in order to wreck the Constitution from within.

In the classic Marxist view, bourgeois-democratic parliaments as instruments of the ruling capitalist class do not qualify as agencies for effecting genuine political change. Lenin held this view during the 1905 Russian Revolution, and scorned legislative action. But later, he contended that in circumstances which made direct revolutionary action impracticable, participation in bourgeois parliaments could be a most useful auxiliary weapon. In an essay "Should We Participate in Bourgeois Parliaments" Lenin declared that as long as elements of the masses had faith in the parliament, parliamentary participation to destroy that faith was an obligation. The modus operandi of Communist parliamentary behavior may be summarized as:

1. Ally with . . . other friendly legislative groups;
2. "Expose" government policy at every opportunity;
3. Assert, first, the interests of the working class and, second, those of allied classes such as the peasantry;
4. Propose legislation for its propaganda value;
5. Observe strict party discipline;
6. Combine work in the parliament with political action outside--including illegal actions where necessary.
[Overstreet & Windmiller, 1959, 466-68.]

The decision of the Dobama to participate in the general elections held under the New Constitution had a similar intention of disrupting the proceedings of the legislature and wrecking the Constitution from within.

Another indication of the leftist tendency in the Dobama is to be found in the presidential speech delivered by Thakin Lay Maung. He condemned the existing form of government, pointing out its shortcomings and weaknesses. He accused the New Constitution of being a weapon aimed at perpetuating colonial rule. Most important, he suggested the setting up of "lawka neikban," an allusion to socialism.

However, the Thakins were not able to renounce their basic nationalistic conceptions. Although they no longer mourned for the death of the Burmese monarch, as they did at the First Conference, a resolution passed at the Second Conference indicated their concern for the mortal remains of the royal family. Resolution No. 5 was in error when it stated that the remains of King Thibaw and Queen Supayalat were in Ratnagiri with burial rites unperformed and that the remains of Dowager Queen Hsinbyumashin were in Rangoon. After King Thibaw died at Ratnagiri on December 16, 1916, Queen Supayalat returned to Burma, died at Rangoon on November 25, 1925, and was buried there at her own wish. Dowager Queen Hsinbyumashin died in Rangoon on February 26, 1900 and her remains were interred in the Mandalay Palace enclosure.

By resolving that the students should take a leading role in politics, the Dobama paved the way for the entry of students which momentarily strengthened the organization. But this inflow, together with the leftist tendency, was later to cause a rift within the organization, splitting it into two factions.

At the Second Conference, an attempt was also made to consolidate the volunteer organization of the Yetat and to draw up a Constitution to define their tasks. By contrast, no Constitution was drawn for the parent organization, although more than half a decade had passed since it was first organized.

Judging by the resolutions passed at the Second Conference and the leaders' inability to provide a clear-cut program, it is apparent that the Thakins were still fumbling in the dark. Some elements among them visualized a socialist state. But nothing definite was decided. Even the term "socialism" was avoided. Instead the term "lawka neikban," more utopian than socialist, was used. Probably the Thakins were afraid to abandon their nationalistic stand so abruptly in favor of an internationalist one, which would signify a total change from their earlier views. Their song, their slogans, and their speeches had always reeked of nationalist sentiments. "For one's own religion, one's own nation" had always been their battle cry. Their reluctance can therefore be well appreciated. This also partly explains their tardiness in formulating and publishing their Constitution. It needed time and audacity to reconcile the two conflicting interests within the party.

The time span between the Second Conference which ended on June 29, 1936 and the Third Conference which began on March 28, 1938, was a long twenty-one months. Despite vehement opposition and the unwillingness of the general public, the much despised Constitution of 1935, had come into effect on April 1, 1937. The Thakins spent the greater part of 1936 and the early months of 1937 in preliminary preparations for their "war" against the Constitution. The guiding principle for their activities during this period was the first resolution passed at the Myingyan conference which declared that they would contend for seats in the House of Representatives in order to wreck the Constitution from within [*Do Thamaing*, I, 1976, 201].

The Komin Kochin Party

At the meeting of the central Executive Committee held at their headquarters now at 229 Phayre Street, on July 19, 1936 at 2 p.m., the Komin Kochin Party (abbreviated as KMKC)[1] was formed to serve as a spearhead in the Dobama's assault against the Constitution. The preface to the KMKC Constitution (Appendix X) issued on August 8, 1936 gives the reason for establishing the organization:

> The Komin Kochin party is formed with a view to make known to the world our true feelings. We, the people of Burma detest being held in slavery. Our one desire is to set the country free from all restraints. What we hanker after is true freedom in the same spirit as the earliest inhabitants of the world had hankered after the sun and the moon.

The aims of the KMKC according to their Constitutions were: (a) to protest against the New Constitution soon to be conferred upon the nation; (b) to prove by actions the worthlessness and futility of the New Constitution; and (c) to make use of the platform provided by the general elections for propagation of the Dobama ideals.

In implementing these aims, the KMKC was to seek the advice of the central Executive Committee of the Dobama in all matters and to abide by the modus operandi chosen by it. Members of the KMKC were forbidden from accepting official positions in the House of Representatives and were to refrain from supporting those who did so. Membership of the KMKC was extended to all members of the Executive Committee of the Dobama, and to the candidates contesting for seats in the House of Representatives on the KMKC ticket. Those standing as candidates were to give a written pledge to uphold the Dobama ideals and to abide by the regulations laid down by the Dobama. Therefore, a member of the KMKC automatically became a Thakin and held dual membership. However official status was granted to the KMKC member only when the candidate was elected to the House of Representatives. Furthermore, the candidate elect was required to contribute not less than fifty rupees towards the funds for the upkeep of the KMKC party. The office bearers for the KMKC were nominated by the central Executive Committee. For disciplinary reasons, the central Executive Committee reserved the right to expel any member without the benefit of explanation, should he be found guilty of either obstructing or acting contrary to the ideals and the interests of the Dobama. The central Executive Committee also reserved the right to abolish the KMKC party. The party's Executive Committee members elected on the day of its inception were:

---

1. On the meaning of Komin Kochin, see above, p. 21.

President	-- Thakin Han
Vice President	-- Thakin Mya
Treasurer	-- Thakin Tun Khin
Secretary	-- Thakin Kan Tint
Information	-- Thakin Thein Maung
Member	-- Thakin Ba Sein

The first task of this newly formed organization was to launch a national campaign against the New Constitution. For this the leaders of the Dobama made an extensive tour of the country soon after the formation of the KMKC. Thakin Hteik Tin Kodaw Gyi and Thakin Han, together with members of the Executive Committee of the Myingyan District, arranged campaign stops throughout Upper Burma. Thakin Kodaw Hmine, Thakin Tun Ok, Thakin Lay Maung, and Thakin Thein Maung, together with Thakin Tin Maung, Thakin Kan Tint, and Thakin Kyaw Yin toured Lower Burma. In all, during the four month's campaign they covered twenty districts and one hundred townships, and held more than one hundred public meetings.

During this campaign, Thakin Kan Tint, Secretary of the KMKC, became ill and died on September 22, 1936. This slackened the groups' activities for a while. On resuming their campaign, the organizers were divided into four groups assigned to specific areas headed by Thakin Tun Ok, Thakin Kyaw Yin, Thakin Hteik Tin Kodaw Gyi, and Thakin Tun Shwe. Thakin Kodaw Hmine and Thakin Lay Maung made a general tour of the whole country. However, their activities were greatly hampered by the lack of coordination between the organizers and those at the headquarters.

During this campaign, the Dobama issued the *KMKC Manifesto I* (*Komin Kochin Sardan Amhat I*, 1936) and ten thousand copies each of the *KMKC Declaration I* (Kominn Kochinn Sarsu I, Do Dikar) and handbills advertising the KMKC emblem (which was identical with that of the Dobama). The *KMKC Manifesto I* disclosed their aims and objects and stressed the worthlessness of the New Constitution. The elections were likened to cattle markets where the astute buyer inspects the animal before buying. While an unwise choice of cattle would prove to be only a bad bargain, indiscreet voting could ruin the whole country. The *KMKC Declaration I* opened with a brief account of the aims of the Dobama and the program of the KMKC and then appealed to the general public to vote for KMKC candidates. The *KMKC Manifesto II* was withdrawn soon after its publication as its contents were considered to be in conflict with the Dobama ideals.

Although it had previously been decided that all publications concerning the KMKC and the general elections were to be made by the central Executive Committee alone, individual members disregarded this important injunction. Not only was the authorization of the publication made without the prior sanction of the central headquarters but so also were such important decisions as the nomination of candidates. Despite such disorganization and lack of coordination, twenty-eight candidates contesting the elections drew 80,000 votes (*Myanma Lu Nge Kyway Kyaw Than*, 1938, I, v., 3) in the general election of November 13, 1936.

The three KMKC members elected were Thakin Mya, B.Sc., B.L. for Tharrawaddy (South); Thakin Hla Tin for Henzada (East); and Thakin Ant Gyi for Pakokku (South). Thakin Mya, about 40 years old at that time, had been one of the boycotters of the 1920 student strike. Thakin Ant Gyi, also about 40, was one of the leaders of the Hlaing-Pu-Gyaw GCBA on the district level and was serving as the treasurer of the Dobama and president of the KMKC school at Pakokku. Thakin Hla Tin was about 35 years old. He had been educated in Ceylon and at the time of the election, was serving as the president of the KMKC at Henzada.

Although few in number, the KMKC members of the House of Representatives were noticeable. At the first session of the House of Representatives, held on February 10, 1937, they expressed their contempt for alien rule by remaining seated when the entire House stood up to greet the governor as he entered the Assembly. They also refrained from joining the other members when they stood to pledge their allegiance to the crown. (However, the proceedings of the Burma Legislature declares that the motion, moved by the home minister, to convey congratulations to His Majesty King George VI on the occasion of his accession to the throne and to pledge devotion to his royal person, was carried unanimously.) The KMKC members withheld their votes in the election of the Speaker and the Deputy Speaker, maintaining that they considered both incapable of standing up for the interests of the country against those of governmental authorities. Their most startling action during the first session was their dramatic walk-out in protest against the stipulation that all members of the House of Representatives proficient in the English language must conduct debates in it.

The occasion which gave rise to the language question was the introduction of the Burma Tenancy Bill, 1937. When the bill was circulated to the members of the legislature to elicit their opinion, U Ba Thi, member of parliament for Mandalay district (South), spoke in Burmese. Under the Government of Burma Act, 1935, Section 30, all proceedings in the council were to be conducted in English, except when a person was not sufficiently acquainted with the language. Thakin Mya, in supporting U Ba Thi, spoke in Burmese. As a science and law graduate, Thakin Mya was urged by the Speaker to speak in English. Thakin Mya refused to comply, contending that his proficiency in English was comparable to that of Burmese spoken by a Coringhee [*BLP*/FHR, 1937, I, i-iii]. The three members of the KMKC then trooped out of the assembly, followed by a good many other members of the opposition [*Myanma Lu Nge Kyway Kyaw Than*, I, v, March 15, 1938, 35].

A mass meeting to denounce the action of the speaker was then held at the Town Hall with Thakin Ba Gwan in the chair, and Thakin Tun Ok as master of ceremonies. The meeting was attended by a large crowd which included many monks. The KMKC issued a pamphlet entitled: "No Burmese to be spoken in Burma is an insult to the whole Nation." The first paragraph asked; "If speaking Burmese is not permitted in Burma, in what country shall it be spoken?" The pamphlet pointed out:

> Speaking of Burmese was permitted under the Dyarchy system. . . . Under the New Constitution, this privilege is being denied. . . . The Constitution conferred upon Burma is the same as the one given to India . . . yet, in India, the Speaker not only permits the use of indigenous lan-

> guages even by those who are fluently conversant with English, but the display of the national flag and chanting of the national song is allowed. . . . Furthermore (in Burma) the Speaker of the Upper House permits Burmese to be spoken . . . the prohibition against speaking Burmese in the legislature is an insult directed not only at the handful (present at the chamber) but it is an insult to the whole nation.

It further urged all Burmans, within and outside the House of Representatives to strive for the privilege of speaking Burmese in the legislature. Despite such protests, the authorities did not relent. Nevertheless, the Dobama did make effective use of this issue to propagate their ideals and publicize their Burmanization movement.

Their other activities in the House of Representatives were less spectacular but they made use of every opportunity to harass the government. One such opportunity was a confrontation during the question period, when it was normal procedure to challenge and embarrass the government. The KMKC members demanded information about Hmankyaung Sayadaw U Ariyawuntha of Okpo who had been exiled in connection with the Saya San uprising, and about U Nageinda imprisoned in a jail in Bengal. They also inquired about the Thakins detained in prison.

Another device for challenging the government was the adjournment motion which could be used to postpone the scheduled business of the House in order to open discussion on urgent public matters. Such motions were common but were rarely admitted by the Speaker, who decided whether the question was of sufficient importance to justify a special debate. When Thakin Tun Ok was arrested on February 23, 1937 under Sections 124(a) and 153(a) of the Indian Penal Code, an adjournment motion was moved by Thakin Ant Gyi, and was seconded by Thakin Hla Tin. Over the question of "Speaking Burmese in the House of Representatives" Thakin Ant Gyi again proposed an adjournment motion. On both occasions, the motions were rejected. An adjournment motion jointly moved by Thakin Hla Tin and U Sein Win (Pegu) to discuss the flood question was, however, accepted [Do Thamaing, I, 1976, 269].

The KMKC party entered more electoral contests. Thakin Thein Maung ran third in the Khayan-Thongwa (Hanthawaddy) by-election and Thakin Ba Than ran second in Bassein (West). However, these defeats should not be considered complete failures, because the primary aim of the KMKC in contesting elections had always been to make use of the electoral platform to propagate their ideals. At the fourteenth meeting of the central Executive Committee on May 16, 1937, the KMKC decided to expand their scope of activities by contesting municipal and district council elections throughout the country [Do Thamaing, I, 1976, 269]. The meeting was attended by Thakins Lay Maung, Hla Baw, Mya, Ba U, Thein Maung, Ba Gwan, and an observer Thakin Bo. Resolution No. 5 expressed their intention to contest seats in the municipal and district councils on the KMKC ticket. At the 15th meeting of the central Executive Committee held on July 13, 1937, it was decided to appoint five additional officers to the KMKC. The officers, chosen from among the central Executive Committee of the Dobama, were Thakins Tun Ok, Ba Sein, Ba U, Nyi, and Ba Gwan.

A special manifesto announced the KMKC aims in contesting local elections to be propagation of Dobama ideals and consolidation of the strength of party sympathizers. They proposed replacing representatives of the propertied minority with KMKC members and abolishing celebrations which glorified colonial rule and perpetuated the slavery of the people, such as Empire Day, Coronation Day, welcoming receptions, and others. On the constructive side, their program included endeavors to gain official recognition for the tricolor flag and the Dobama Song, recognition of Burmese as the official language of the courts, and construction of monuments and statues of such national martyrs as U Wisara [*Do Thamaing*, I, 1976, 267-68]. For the public welfare, the following program was appended: (1) Free universal education; (2) Establishment of Libraries and Museums; (3) Teaching of Technology, Commerce, and Economics; (4) Free medical facilities; (5) Housing accommodation for the homeless and destitute; (6) Provision of comfortable traveling facilities and public health amenities; and (7) General public welfare of the cities and towns [*Do Pyandan*, III, 1938].

With regard to the problem of taxation, the KMKC proposed doing away with laws and regulations which were considered detrimental to the interests of the taxpayers, preventing wasteful and indiscriminate expenditure of funds, and putting a stop to the malpractice and corruption indulged in by the members of the municipal and district councils. To benefit the taxpayers, such capitalist enterprises as trams, telecommunications, electricity supply, and pawn shops were to be taken over by the municipal and district councils, and the profits derived from these enterprises were to be used exclusively for the taxpayers and to reduce the tax rates. And finally, services considered by Dobama headquarters to be beneficial to the taxpayers were to be performed as and when necessary [*Do Pyandan*, III, 1938].

Due to the paucity of data, it is not known how many KMKC members were elected to the municipal and district councils. However, the report of the Rangoon District Conference held at the U Hain Gyi-Daw Hnin Zayat in the precincts of the Shwedagon pagoda on May 18, 1939 stated that "as Thakin Captain Ba Hpu, a KMKC member who was elected to the municipality is expelled from the Dobama, no KMKC member now remains in the municipal council [*Baho Akhun Htan*, 1965, 52].

Building the Dobama Organization

While the KMKC members were harassing the authorities in the Legislative Council, the remaining leaders of the Dobama concentrated their attention on building up their organization. Their efforts resulted in the establishment of branch organizations in Akyab, Amherst, Bassein, Bogale, Chauk, Danubyu, Hanthawaddy, Henzada, Insein, Mandalay, Maubin, Monywa, Moulmein, Myanaung, Pantanaw, Pakokku, Pegu, Prome, Pyapon, Pyinmana, Rangoon, Sagaing, Sandoway, Shwebo, Tharrawaddy, Thayetmyo, Toungoo, Wakema, Yamethin, Yandoon, and Yenangyaung.

The formation of a network of organizations necessitated setting down rules for the behavior and conduct of members and a system of communications linking the central organization with individual members. Before formulation of the Dobama Constitution the political concepts were rather vague, in part due to the reading habits of the founding fathers. They were voracious readers. They read biographies, political theories, and memoirs of such personages as Bose, Casement, Gandhi, Garibaldi, Lenin, McSweeny, Marx, Mazzini, Nehru, Nietzsche, Rizal, Rousseau, Shaw, Stalin, Sun Yat-sen, de Valera, and Voltaire. They also studied the French Revolution, the Irish revolt, the Russian Revolution, the Gandhian movement, Fascism, Democracy, and Communism. Illustrious figures of Burmese history such as Alaungmintaya, Bandoola, and Bayinnaung were also studied [Ba Sein, 1943, 43]. Thus nationalism, internationalism, chauvinism, jingoism, all found their way into the political expressions and aspirations of the young Thakins. The Second Dobama Conference at Myingyan in March 1936, had entrusted the task of drawing up a draft Constitution to the central Executive Committee, and at the Moulmein Zayat, in the precincts of the Shwedagon pagoda in Rangoon, on January 29 and 30, 1937, the draft Constitution was presented to the All Burma Committee for approval. Forty-two of the eighty-four members of the All Burma Committee, attended the conference. On the first day of the meeting, they unanimously endorsed the draft Constitution, which was published on February 2, 1937 (Appendix XI).

As a campaign piece to the Constitution, the Dobama ideology (Dobama Wada) was enumerated in fifteen items [*Do Thamaing*, I, 1976, 252-55]. The first two items defined the words "Dobama" and "Thakin." Dobama was defined as the indigenous races of Burma and those who promoted the welfare of Burma according to the Dobama ideology. Thakins were those who strove to attain equal human rights and raise the standard of living. The aim of the Dobama was to champion these causes, and thus all members of the Dobama were Thakins.

In the third item, the Dobama championed the downtrodden masses of the world. In the fourth and fifth items, the Dobama expressed the conviction that as long as capitalism prevailed, class distinctions based upon wealth would exist. The affluence of the propertied class corresponded proportionately to the penury of the poor.

The sixth item advocated the dethronement of capitalism and the setting up of a new form of government where equal rights and equal opportunities would be ensured. The seventh item enumerated the steps to be taken in setting up "heaven on earth":

> To set up such a government, under the leadership of the proletariat class, private ownership of the privileged class must be turned into state ownership . . . class distinctions (based upon wealth and ownership) must be removed, and equal distribution of wealth must be effected. . . . Since capitalism stems from imperial and colonial interests, such a system must be replaced by one which guarantees human rights for all.

The eighth and ninth items expressed the Dobama intention to annihilate capitalism in Burma and set up a Komin Kochin form of government.

> The social and economic ills which beset the downtrodden masses derive from imperialism. Therefore, imperialism must be rooted out both economically and politically. In so doing the vision of the ultimate aim must never be lost to sight. The ultimate aim is the independence of the country, and the establishment of a Komin Kochin form of government.

Komin Kochin was defined as neither monarchic nor despotic, but as the supremacy of the proletariat. The tenth and eleventh items stated that the annihilation of imperialism, the attainment of freedom, and the setting up of the Komin Kochin form of government could only be achieved through concentrated efforts and unity among the people. The steps to be taken were given in the twelfth article: to contend for seats in the House of Representatives; to form mass organizations; to employ strike tactics; to stage protest demonstrations; and to undertake other systematic agitation and propaganda strategies.

The thirteenth and fourteenth items declared that to realize the above aims, political power was essential and must be acquired at all costs. There were to be two distinct periods in its acquisition, a preparatory period and a period of actual contention for power. The last item declared that all actions must be guided by the principles laid down in the Constitution of the Dobama Asiayone.

The Constitution itself contained fourteen articles. It stated the aims of the Dobama to be complete independence for Burma and a socialistic "heaven on earth" in which all Burmans would enjoy equal opportunities. To realize the above aim all legitimate means were to be used.

The text of the Constitution dealt with the organizational structure. Honorary membership would be extended to any person whose services to the country were considered by the central Executive Committee to be worthy of the honor. Ordinary membership would be open to all Burmans and members of indigenous races who had attained the age of eighteen and professed to abide by the aims and aspirations of the Dobama. Non-nationals were allowed to be members with the formal sanction of the central Executive Committee. The sponsorship of two members was necessary for admission into the organization, except in areas with no branches where the sanction of the central Executive Committee would be sufficient. All applicants were to adopt the Thakin affix and pay an annual fee of four annas (25 pyas).

The Constitution further defined the organizations to be affiliated and the tasks and responsibilities of the central Executive Committee and the All Burma Committee. The affiliated organizations to the central body were (a) the Komin Kochin; (b) the Letyon Tat; (c) the All Burma Workers' Association; and (d) the All Burma Peasants' Association. The structure of the Dobama was based upon "democratic centralism." Policy-making authority was vested in the central executive body and decisions made by the central body were binding on subordinate organizations. Although authority was exercised from the top downwards, since the central body was elected from the grass-roots level by a successive series of conferences, authority was built from the bottom upwards. Differences of opinion were permitted before a decision was reached, but the expression of opinion was the prerogative only of individuals and not of organized groups, as a mechanism for preventing contests for supremacy within the party.

The principle of "democratic centralism" resulted in a hierarchical organization based on indirect elections. At the bottom was the local branch, a group of members in a village or urban neighborhood, which elected representatives to the township conference. The township conference elected representatives to the district conference, and the district conference elected delegates to the All Burma executive conference which, in turn, elected the central committee and the president.

Thus, general authority of the Dobama was vested in a very small elite at the apex of the organizational pyramid. The Constitution required that the All Burma Executive Committee conference be convened every Tabaung, the last month of the year in the Burmese calendar. In the interval between the conferences, full power was vested in the fifteen-member central committee. This body chose from within itself the vice president, the general secretary, and the treasurer. The Constitution stipulated that the central committee should meet at least once a month. Therefore day-to-day decision making fell to the general secretary and three other members. This tiny core of leaders virtually monopolized the day-to-day exercise of authority (see Table I).

TABLE I

LEADERSHIP OF THE DOBAMA

Elected at Conference	1st Yenangyaung, 1935	2nd Myingyan, 1936	3rd Prome, 1938
President	Ba Sein	Lay Maung	Thein Maung
Vice President	Lay Maung	Thein Maung	Hla Baw
General Secretary	Thein Maung	Tun Ok	Lay Maung
Treasurer	Tun Khin	Tun Khin	Ba Gwan

In addition to its Constitutional prerogatives, the Dobama leadership had certain other important instruments of authority. Chief among these was the inner-party communicative system. Alongside the openly circulated pamphlets, the Dobama maintained a regular system of private communications. These included circulars and memoranda issued from time to time. In addition to the communications flowing down, there was a regular system of reports flowing up. The Dobama Constitution provided that each unit must submit regular reports to the next higher unit. In principle, communication was strictly vertical, each unit receiving information about party activities and policy only through communications flowing down from the center. In practice, however, each unit obtained considerable information through informal contacts. It was true that the system of internal communications as an instrument of authority was not perfect, but it was an indispensable aid to the leadership in its endeavor to create an efficient, centralized agency of political action.

Augmenting this communications system, a periodical was circulated as a further means for basic ideological indoctrination and as an instrument of communication. A quarterly bulletin known as the *Dobama Bulletin* (*Dobama Pyandan*) was launched early in 1937. The annual subscription rate for the bulletin, including postal charges, was one rupee. However, only three numbers were issued. The first appeared on March 25, 1937, the second on July 22, and the last number on September 27, 1937. The aim of the bulletin was to keep members and party sympathizers informed about party and KMKC activities. However, since the publication was so short-lived, its utility as a propaganda medium is difficult to gauge. No reason was given for the publication's demise but lack of funds may have been the chief cause just as it had been for its precursor, the *Dobama News Weekly* (*Dobama Thadinzin Hmattan*).

Very little is known concerning Dobama finances. No annual balance sheet was published except for the budget estimate for the year 1939-1940 which appeared in the report of the Fourth Annual Conference held at Moulmein in April 1939.

The party Constitution required that each member pay an annual membership fee of four annas. Besides this income, the Dobama was subsidized by monthly contributions from members and wellwishers. There was also an indirect subsidy, in the form of profits from the sales of books and pamphlets. However, the exact amount involved is not known. The report presented by the secretary of the All Burma Executive Committee at the first meeting held at Rangoon on January 29-30, 1937, stated that, although funds were not adequate for the upkeep of full-time staff members at the party secretariat, party finances had greatly improved.

The first attempt at keeping party finances in order was made at the fifteenth monthly meeting of the central Executive Committee held at the headquarters at 211 Lewis Street, Rangoon, on June 13, 1937. A resolution was then passed to keep a strict account of expenses incurred and to collect funds systematically. The funds were to be collected under five headings: welfare funds; party funds; annual fees; funds for the upkeep of the permanent staff; and funds for the publication of the bulletin.

The resolution further explained that the welfare fund was to be used exclusively by members of the central executive to defray legal and other expenses when governmental action was taken against them, and for the expenses they incurred when traveling to and from the districts where such governmental action was taken against district members. The annual fees were to be reserved for operating expenses, such as purchase of stationery for the Secretariat. The expenses for the upkeep of the permanent staff were to be met out of the monthly contributions and subsidies given by wellwishers and party sympathizers. Under no circumstances were the permanent staff to use other funds. The publication fund was to be used exclusively for publishing purposes and for issuing the quarterly bulletin. With the exception of the publications fund, all funds were to be sent to the treasurer, through the secretary. The publications fund was to be sent directly to Thakin Aung Than by name, who was responsible for the publication of the bulletin (pyandan). It is not known to what extent these rigid rules were observed. Despite such elaborate arrangements, since no balance sheet is available, it is not possible to gauge the income and expenditure of the Dobama.

The program of the Dobama included mobilization of peasants, workers, and youth. Their attempt to mobilize the peasants began in 1937. The Tharrawaddy branch of the Dobama arranged for Thakin Lay Maung to deliver speeches at peasant gatherings. Commencing with April 3, 1937, for a fortnight, discussions on political and peasant affairs were held and peasant organizations were formed at Gyobingauk, Letpadun, Minhla, Gyogon (West), and Kaingpyingyi (East), Tapun, Tharrawaddy, and Thonze [*Do Thamaing*, I, 1976, 230]. Although it had a favorable beginning, the venture was not pursued in earnest. In a country where the peasantry formed an overwhelming majority establishment of a handful of peasant organizations was indeed negligible. No further attempt was made in this field till the peasants from Waw and Thaton marched into Rangoon in support of the oilfield strike and encamped themselves at the Shwedagon pagoda in January 1939 [*Do Thamaing*, I, 1976, 327-30].

The attempt to organize the workers was even less adequate. During this period the Dobama leadership was preoccupied with KMKC activities [*Do Thamaing*, I, 1976, 222-24]. Only when the oilfield marchers arrived at the Shwedagon, was the All Burma Workers Association formed on January 9, 1939, a few hours after the formation of All Burma Peasants' Association [*Do Thamaing*, I, 1976, 375 & 379-80].

In 1930 at the time of the formation of the Yetat there was a rival organization, known as the Ye Sein Tat, the green-shirt army, formed by U Maung Gyi, the member for education in the Legislative Council [*Do Thamaing*, I, 1976, 133, 218]. Although the organizational pattern of the two groups was somewhat similar, their political outlook differed greatly. However, the leaders of the Ye Sein Tat from Chauk, Myingyan, and Toungoo brought their units into the Yetat, when they attended the First Annual Conference of the Dobama held in Yenangyaung in 1935. At the conference, the Yetat was re-named as Dobama Yetat and the task for organizing it was entrusted to Thakin Ba Ba of Chauk [*Do Thamaing*, I, 1976, 218-19]. Branch organizations of the Dobama Yetat were formed at Pakokku, Shwebo, Myingyan, and Yanangyaung. Prominent Yetat leaders during this period were Thakin Ba Ba (Chauk), Thakin Bo (Myingyan), Thakin Hla Maung (Toungoo), Thakin Tun Shwe (Toungoo), Thakin Tin U (Rangoon), and Thakin Ba Tha (Rangoon) [*Do Thamaing*, I, 1976, 219].

At the Dobama's Second Annual Conference held at Myingyan in June 1936, Thakin Hla Pe (Pinbyu) was given the task of reorganizing the Dobama Yetat. This reorganization was not the "brain child" of any one person. By a consensus of its leaders, Thakin Hla Baw, Thakin Tun Shwe, Thakin Hla Maung, Thakin Ba Tha (Rangoon), Thakin Tun Oo (Moulmein), Thakin Bo (Myingyan), Thakin Tin Oo (Rangoon), and Thakin Ba Ba, the Dobama Yetat came to be known as the Bama Letyone Tat [*Do Thamaing*, I, 1976, 219]. At the Second Conference of the All Burma Executive Committee, held at Rangoon on September 4, 1937, the task of drawing up a Constitution for the Bama Letyone Tat was given to Thakin Hla Pe, Thakin Tin Oo, and Thakin Tun Shwe. It was also unanimously decided that the draft Constitution be put up to the Dobama central Executive Committee for approval [*Do Thamaing*, I, 1976, 220].

The pamphlet [Hla Pe Pinbyu, 1937] issued on the occasion of the inauguration of the Bama Letyone Tat enumerated three methods by which a subject nation could achieve freedom. The first method was to trust in the generosity of the "foreign overlord" who at the ripe moment would deign to bestow freedom upon the country. The second method was that of non-violence and non-cooperation adopted by the Mahatma Gandhi and the Indian Congress in 1931. The third method was to enlist aid from countries hostile to the ruling race and with their help resort to armed resistance. The pamphlet added that whatever method was adopted it was essential that the youth whose task all over the world was to uproot the old and establish a new order should possess physical fitness, discipline, and agility. The pamphlet claimed that the Bama Letyone Tat was founded to meet these needs. It further added that the Constitution of the Bama Letyone Tat was formulated by choosing the essence of several constitutions of youth organizations and was patterned to suit the temperament of the Burmese youth.

The *Constitution of the Most Dependable Army of Burma* (Appendix XII) contained one hundred and fifty items under the following headings:

(1) Name, place, aim, qualification, and uniform.
(2) Relationship between the Dobama and the Bama Letyone Tat.
(3) Relationship between the Bama Letyone Tat and other organizations.
(4) Defense.
(5) Communication between the units and the general headquarters.
(6) Appointment.
(7) Discipline.
(8) Arbitration.
(9) Officer Corps.
(10) Method for amendments.

The formation of the Bama Letyone Tat was welcomed by the more adventurous young people. In a country where the bearing of arms was strictly prohibited and recruitment into the regular army was denied to Burmans and Shans, this paramilitary organization served as an outlet for their militant spirit. Although the Bama Letyone Tat was primarily designed for young men, in some areas like Aphyauk in Henzada District and Nyaung-U in Myingyan District young women calling themselves "Mai Letyone" joined in the activities [*Do Thamaing*, I, 1976, 220].

Data are lacking on enlistment figures for the Bama Letyone Tat but it can be assumed that a fairly large portion of the youthful members of the Dobama joined it.

By its own admission, the organization was subsidized by wellwishers and party sympathizers [*Do Thamaing*, I, 1976, 220]. But just as in the case of parent organization, very little is known concerning the finances of the Bama Letyone Tat.

Because of their youthful zest, radical ideas, and their demand for nothing less than complete independence, the Thakins were looked upon as a breed apart by the older politicians. Yet the Dobama's members cooperated with other political organizations in rallies, demonstrations, and campaigns.

Their attempt to participate in the fifteenth National Day [one of the main results of the 1920 students' boycott movement] celebrations held in Rangoon on November 19, 1935 was a failure. Although Thakin Aung Than, as the Dobama representative was permitted to deliver a speech, the Thakins' proposal to open the ceremony with the Dobama Song and to salute the Dobama tricolor flag was turned down by the National Day Celebration Committee whose members were predominantly members of the 21 Party (GCBA). Nevertheless, their attempts in the districts were successful [*Do Thamaing*, I, 1976, 190-91].

However, on the occasion of the sixteenth anniversary of National Day, November 7, 1936, the Dobama flag was displayed and the Dobama Song sung. The presidential speech was delivered at Victoria Park (Fytche Square), Rangoon, by Thakin Lay Maung, the president of the Dobama. Thakin Lay Maung likened Burma to a prison where there was no freedom of speech and expression. Citing the examples of Alaungmintaya, Hitler, and Mussolini, who had risen from the common fold, he urged the people to overthrow the foreign capitalist yoke and set up a proletarian state as in Russia. He defined the ills of the New Constitution and boldly stated that "reforms are like patched clothes, and what the country wants and needs is not patched up clothes but brand-new ones." In other words, he declared that what Burma wanted was complete independence (*Myanma Lu Nge Kyway Kyaw Than*, 1938, I, xii).

An organization associated with the Dobama was the Rate and Taxpayers' Association. It will be recalled that this association had befriended the young Thakins when they were arrested during the Shwebo by-election campaign. This friendship was further strengthened when some Thakin members were included on the association's executive body in 1934 [*Baho Akhun Htan*, 1965, 20]. On November 25, 1936, the Lanmadaw Council, an organization similar to the Taxpayers' Association invited it and the Dobama to attend a meeting to discuss ways and means of protesting against the extravagance of the Rangoon Municipal Corporation's proposed reception of the visiting Governor-General of India scheduled for January 8, 1937. The meeting formed a sub-committee including Dobama president Thakin Lay Maung to prevent the extravagant use of public funds [*Baho Akhun Htan*, 1965, 27]. The sub-committee conducted a vigorous campaign against the reception through public meetings, personal approaches, and newspaper columns. This pressure produces a compromise in which the municipal corporation announced that the Italian marble flooring for the municipal building and the proposed use of Rs 10,000 to entertain the visiting Governor-General would be dropped from their program, and that only Rs 1,000 would be used instead of Rs 3,000 to defray the expenses of the mayor's dinner to honor the governor. The members of the Lanmadaw Council were satisfied with the compromise and withdrew from the scene [*Baho Akhun Htan*, 1965, 28] but the Dobama and the

Rate and Taxpayers' Association intensified their efforts. The Indian Rate and Taxpayers' Association hurriedly formed on December 9, 1936, gave full support to the condemnation of the municipal corporation [Baho Akhun Htan, 1965, 29].

A meeting held on the premises of The East Rangoon Rate and Taxpayers' Association on December 13, 1936 unanimously decided to hold a protest demonstration at the Sule pagoda at 6 p.m. on December 14, the day of the mayor's dinner [Baho Akhun Htan, 1965, 30]. At 5:30 p.m. on that day while the demonstrators milled around the Pagoda and Victoria Park, a 200 strong pony-cart "brigade" took their position on the eastern side of the park in front of the municipal building. Then the demonstrators gave a grand feed to a pack of stray dogs brought for the purpose. The onlookers called out the names of municipal corporation members as choice pieces of bone were thrown to the dogs [Baho Akhun Htan, 1965, 31].

In the gathering dusk, the loud slogans of "Don't feed on our tax" and "May you spit blood if you do" reverberated through the precincts of the pagoda and the park. At 6:30 p.m. Thakin Ba Yin announced the start of the ceremony. With Thakin Ba U in the chair, U Ba Khine, Thakin Ba Yin, Thakin Lay Maung, Mr. Ganga Singh, U Aye Maung, Thakin Aye, U Ba San, and Mr. M. I. Khan gave speeches. Because amplifiers were used for the occasion, the speeches were clearly audible to those inside the town hall waiting for the governor, Sir Archibald Cochrane, who had not arrived on schedule. Soon, the lord mayor, Mr. Mirza Md. Rafi, sent for Thakin Ba Yin and requested him to withdraw the demonstrators from the scene, promising that the cost of the dinner would not be borne out of the corporation funds. The promise was read out in Burmese and Hindustani, and at 7:45 p.m. after the president gave a speech, the protest demonstration was declared disbanded. However, the fact that the mayor did not redeem his promise is evident from the ledger of the annual budget where a sum of Rs. 1,360 was shown against the expenses incurred for the reception dinner held in honor of the governor [Baho Akhun Htan, 1965, 33].

The Dobama also joined hands with other political organizations in the anti-Constitution demonstrations held on April 1, 1937. By the eighth resolution passed at the First Conference of the All Burma Committee held at the Moulmein Zayat on the Shwedagon pagoda on January 30, 1937, the members decided to express their contempt for the Constitution to be conferred upon the country by ceasing work that day, flying the flag at half mast, and holding public meetings [Do Thamaing, I, 1976, 206].

Commencing in the second week of March, members of the central Executive Committee toured the country to organize protest demonstrations. Through their efforts similar demonstrations were held at Bassein, Bogale, Chauk, Henzada, Hsimeezwe, Htandabin, Letpadan, Moulmein, Myingyan, Pakokku, Prome, Syriam, Shwedaung, Tharrawaddy, Toungoo, Wakema, Yenangyaung, and Zigone.

In Rangoon, at about 7:00 a.m. on the morning of April 1, 1937, officials suspended traffic along the Montgomery and Sule Pagoda Roads leading to the municipal corporation building where the swearing-in of the governor was to be held. On either side of the roads, armed troops of the King's Own Yorkshire Light Infantry, and the Rangoon Volunteer forces lined up in front of the cordon of Rangoon Police. Behind the cordon stood the spectators. The governor, accompanied by Lady Cochrane and their entourage, arrived at the town hall at about 8 a.m. [*Sun Daily*, April 3, 1937]. At about the same time, at the southernmost end of the Sule Pagoda Road near where the Sir Harcourt Butler monument stood, the Thakins were assembled, displaying the tricolor flag at half-mast. They distributed red arm bands and handbills to willing demonstrators. Many held aloft placards bearing the slogans "Wreck the Constitution"; "We condemn the swearing in"; "Publish newspapers with freedom"; "Speak without restraint"; "Factories are for the workers"; "Freedom of education"; "Reject the capitalist imperialists"; and "Exorcise the vampires accepting the New Constitution" [*Sun Daily*, April 3, 1937].

At 9 a.m., a young man, Maung Htein Win, announced from a car the purpose of their gathering and the manner in which the Constitution was to be wrecked. Then, Thakin Thein Maung announced the order of the day and invited people of all backgrounds to join in the activities. The program was also announced in Hindustani by Thakin San Tun Aung. Then led by the Deputy Speaker of the Lower Chamber, U Hla Pe, and U Kyaw Myint, an advocate, the procession of about one thousand Burmans and Indians walking four abreast and holding the tricolor flag at half-mast [*Sun Daily*, April 3, 1937] marched along the Strand towards Edward Street and from thence to Maung Khine Street. Although the main body of the procession marched in an orderly manner and dispersed at the end of the demonstration, a group of youths led by Ko Nu and Ko Hla Pe broke away, and taking along a photographer, marched to the High Court building. There, at the entrance to the building, they set fire to the Union Jack and the copies of the Constitution which they had brought for the purpose [*Sun Daily*, April 3, 1937].

Although the Dobama was essentially a political organization, it did not hesitate to serve the humanitarian cause when such action was called for. When an unexpected rainfall inundated most of the paddy fields in Arakan and Lower Burma during the monsoon of 1937, the Dobama invited individuals plus all political and social organizations in Rangoon to join in aiding the victims. The meeting held at their headquarters, on August 11, 1937, formed a temporary organization for the flood relief. The organization undertook to collect funds and to make appeals to the government authorities, and municipal and district councils to take immediate steps towards relief measures. The organization also distributed pamphlets appealing to the general public to give all-out assistance to the flood victims. Appeals were also made to the members of parliament, the teaching staff of the university, and the foreign diplomats. The Student Union and other student bodies responded to the appeals and contributed generously to the relief funds. Pandit Jawaharlal Nehru in his capacity as the president of the Indian Congress sent a wire to the Congress Party in Burma urging them to aid the Dobama in the mission of mercy [*Do Thamaing*, I, 1976, 232].

The Flood Relief Organization sent enquiry missions to the afflicted areas and their findings were announced at a meeting held at the city hall in Rangoon on September 5, 1937, attended by many political and social organizations in Rangoon. Through such efforts a certain measure of relief was given to the flood victims [*Do Thamaing*, I, 1976, 233].

Although they had no ulterior motives in launching this flood relief campaign, the venture benefitted the Thakins. The contacts made during the campaign helped to forge a strong link between the Dobama and the people living across the Arakan Yoma. During the campaign, Thakin Lay Maung, the Dobama president, and Thakin Kyaw Yin helped the flood victims and spread the Thakin ideals during their tour of Arakan. The places visited by the Thakin leaders were Akyab, Gwa, Kyaintali, Manaung, Minbya, Myebon, Myohaung, Ramree, and Sandoway. However, then they reached the Maze island in Sandoway district, Section 144 was proclaimed and this prevented them from holding public meetings [*Do Thamaing*, I, 1976, 232-33]. The lasting outcome of this Arakan tour was the formation of branch organizations at Akyab, Manaung, and Sandoway. The establishment of these district organizations was significant because it was the first time that branch organizations were established outside Burma proper. The enthusiastic response shown by one of the leaders from Arakan is worthy of mention. Thakin Aung Pe, the resident of the Sandoway District Dobama, crossed the Arakan Yoma on foot in order to attend the Third Annual conference held at Prome.

The 1938 Prome Conference

The Third Conference held at Prome was the most important milestone in the history of the Dobama. Although its significance was not apparent then, this was the last time that the Thakins met as a united body. Preparations for the conference were made a month ahead of the scheduled date. The 27th meeting of the central Executive Committee held at the Rangoon headquarters on February 20, 1938, passed the following resolutions:

1. (a) The Third Conference of the Dobama to be held at Prome on March 22, 23, and 24, 1938. The Prome district Dobama to form a Reception Committee which will be responsible for the conference.

    (b) The All Burma Executive Committee meeting at Prome on March 21, one day before the conference, will nominate the president and the Executive Committee for the coming year, and also to make amendments and approve the Constitution.

2. (a) Not less than two delegates from each branch organization to attend the conference.

    (b) The delegates to the conference to be nominated by the respective branch organizations.

    (c) The list of the delegates together with the delegate fee of Rs. 3 each to be remitted to the secretary, Reception Committee, stationed at No. 15 Yodayadan Prome before March 15, 1938.

3. The proposals and the annual reports to be submitted to the secretary, central working committee, temporarily stationed at No. 15, Yodayadan, Prome.

4. The Dobama headquarters to be stationed at No. 15 Yodayadan, Prome from March 7 and for the duration of the conference. [*Do Thamaing*, I, 1976, 149.]

At noon, on the scheduled date, March 22, 1938, the Third Conference of the Dobama was held at a pavilion built in an open space called Bali Kwin at Prome. The tricolor flag was flown at full mast behind the stage. The conference was declared opened by Thakin Kodaw Hmine. Then the audience stood at attention as YMB Saya Tin, accompanied by the band conducted by U Lu Gale, sang the Dobama Song.

The speech welcoming the delegates was read by Thakin Pu, president of the Reception Committee. He closed with the following words:

May the merits gained by the good deeds performed by the Reception Committee be instrumental in establishing socialist republics the world over, and gaining independence for Burma. [*Do Nyi Largan*, 1939]

The most outstanding feature of the conference was the first sign of a split which became apparent in the election of the president. Under Article IX, Section 3, of the Dobama Constitution, the president for the ensuing year was to be elected before the conference. In accordance with this regulation, Thakin Tun Ok had been elected president for the year 1938. However, he was arrested under P.C. 124(A) and was sentenced to one year's rigorous imprisonment on January 16, 1938 for having delivered an allegedly seditious speech at the National Day rally on November 27, 1937 [*Myanma Lu Nge Kyway Kyaw Than*, I, v, March 15, 1938, 12]. Therefore, it became necessary to elect a new president. Thakin Thein Maung and Thakin Nyi ran for the position, and Thakin Thein Maung was elected [Maung Maung, 1969, 59] by a very narrow margin. In his inaugural speech President Thakin Thein Maung told the audience that the motives in calling the conference were to discuss ways and means for attaining independence and to save the country from all miseries. He further added that:

All privileges rest with political power and we must strive hard till that power rests with the peasantry who constitute the great majority of the population. National affairs concern everyone, and this awareness must be created in their minds. Only when capitalism and imperialism disappear, will there be peace. The Dobama will never resort to violence as it is striving for world peace. . . . We are striving to eradicate poverty, famine, and unemployment. Whatever obstacle or opposition we have to face, the Dobama is of opinion that nothing can destroy us.

The four resolutions passed at the Prome conference were:

1. to set up an Oilfield Strike Enquiry committee--the task to be entrusted to Shin Ariya, Thakin Mya, and Thakin Tin Maung
2. to include the hammer and sickle in the center of the tricolour flag
3. to name April 1 as Anti-Constitution Day and to observe it every year
4. the KMKC members of the House of Representatives to refrain from accepting salary and to continue the fight within the House of Representatives to wreck it.

The conference divided the administrative body into nine bureaus: Workers, Peasants, Students and Youth, Letyone, Foreign Affairs, Finance, Propaganda, Organization, and KMKC [*Do Thamaing*, I, 1976, 251-52].

The Executive Committee members were appointed to a one year term by the newly elected president:

President	-- Thakin Thein Maung
Vice President	-- Thakin Hla Baw
Secretary	-- Thakin Lay Maung
Treasurer	-- Thakin Ba Gwan
Auditor	-- Thakin Mya
Workers	-- Thakin Thein Aung
Peasants	-- Thakin Khin Aung
Students and Youth	-- Thakin Khin Maung
Foreign Affairs	-- Thakin Aung Than
Letyone	-- Thakin Hla Pe
Finance	-- Thakin Kha
Propaganda	-- Thakin Ba Sein
	Thakin Kyaw Yin
Organization	-- Thakin Nyi, Thakin Thin and Thakin Aye
KMKC	-- Thakin Tin Maung

[*Do Thamaing*, I, 1976, 252.]

At the first meeting of the central Executive Committee the following executive body was elected by a unanimous vote:

President	-- Thakin Thein Maung
Vice President	-- Thakin Hla Baw
Treasurer	-- Thakin Ba Gwan
Auditor	-- Thakin Mya

	Secretaries	*Joint Secretaries*
Workers	--	Thakin Kha and
	Thakin Lay Maung	
Peasants	--	Thakin Than
KMKC		
	Thakin Tin Maung	Thakin Khin Aung
Foreign Affairs		

Propaganda	Thakin Kyaw Yin
	Thakin Ba Sein
Organization	Thakin Nyi
Student	Thakin Thin
	Thakin Aung Than
Finance	Thakin Aye
Letyone	Thakin Hla Baw

The annual conferences of the Dobama measure its progress. The Third Conference held in 1936 at Prome was conducted under strained circumstances because of the rival candidacies for the presidential chair. Four resolutions were passed at the conference, of which the second--to place the crossed hammer and sickle in the center of the tricolor flag--was most significant. The tricolor flag of yellow, green, and red had long been the standard of the Dobama. The Thakins had declared it to be the national flag at a meeting on September 19, 1935.[2]

Thakin Ba Han of Myingyan made the proposal at the Prome conference to include the crossed hammer and sickle and it was unanimously endorsed by the conference. The proposal gave an elaborate description and interpretation of the flag. It was to measure 5'x3' with deep yellow, dark green, and bright red stripes of equal lengths in ascending order. In the center, a white circle, occupying two thirds of the flag, was to have a red hammer and sickle crossed at an angle of 45°. The deep yellow symbolized the golden robe and represented the people, whose religious belief was Buddhism. The dark green was the color of paddy fields and green forests, on which the economy of the country rested, and the bright red represented the valiant spirit of the sons of the land, who were to be the saviors and protectors of the country. The white circle in the center symbolized purity of mind, the hammer represented the workers, and the sickle, the peasants. The inclusion of the hammer and sickle in the tricolor was significant. It was an outward manifestation of the international outlook which had penetrated the organization. This, and other differences among the leaders were to split the Dobama into two irreconcilable factions three months after the close of the conference.

The Third Conference at Prome was held in the eighth year of the Dobama's existence. It is worthwhile summarizing how far the Thakins had come from their humble beginnings.

They had moved not only figuratively but also physically. Their early headquarters was the home of the founder Thakin Ba Thoung, at 33 Yedashe Street, Bahan. When the founder and his colleagues parted company, the headquarters was moved to Linlun Kwetthit; and then to 81 and 172 Suburban Street, Ahlone; then to 277 Phayre Street; to 317

---

2. Attended by Shin Ariya, Thakin Lun, Thakin Kodaw Hmine, Thakin Han, Thakin Thein Maung, Thakin Ba Sein, Thakin Tun Ok, Thakin Tin Maung (1), Thakin Tin Maung (2), Thakin Bo, Ko Aung San (President, All Burma Students' Union), U Ngwe Zin, Thakin Kan Tint, and Thakin Aung Than [*Myanma Lu Nge Kyway Kyaw Than*, I, iii, 1938, 8].

Montgomery Street; and 201 Lewis Street. Force of circumstances and probably penury caused them to move so often. The Thakins had always been poor, and it was only in July 1937 that funds were systematically collected and accounts put in order. Before that their finances were managed haphazardly. When the association came into existence, there were no funds worthy of mention. Their early enterprises were partly financed by Thakin Ba Thoung from the thousand rupees he received as his translation prize. Attempts to raise funds through the sale of song scripts and pamphlets produced negligible sums. In 1936, a membership drive was conducted in earnest. However, since the membership fee was four annas per annum, the sum thus collected was still negligible. The main source of income was donations given by wellwishers and sympathizers. At the time of the Prome conference, the Dobama still depended on these sources. However, publication of the *Dobama Asiayone Pyandan*, a quarterly bulletin, partially helped to steady the balance.

By 1938 two important auxiliary organizations, the KMKC and the Letyone Tat, had been formed and placed under the direct control of the Dobama.

The most significant progress made by the Thakins over these years was in the field of ideology. Their political notions began with the Dobama Song script and advanced to a written Constitution, and from a purely nationalist outlook to an international one. The development received symbolic expression in the insertion of the hammer and sickle in the center of the tricolor flag. This progress had detrimental effects on the organization for it caused a rift between the older members who held to a nationalist outlook and the leftist-orientated younger generation.

Thakin Ba Thoung

Founder of the Dobama Asiayone

The Dobama Emblem (Courtesy: Dobama Historical Committee)

THE PATRONS

Shin Ariya
(Courtesy: Daw Ein Soe)

U Soe Thein
(Courtesy:Dobama Historical
Committee)

Thakin Kodaw Hmine
(From Ba Tin 1964)

Hteik Tin Kodaw Gyi
(From Ba Tin 1964)

Ledi Pandita U Maung Gyi
(From Dagon Magazine, Vol.CXCVII,
No. 224)

THE PRESIDENTS
1935-1938

Thakin Ba Sein

Thakin Lay Maung

Thakin Thein Maung

Thakin Tun Ok

Hteik Tin Kodaw Gyi
(From Ba Tin, 1964)

THE KMKC MEMBERS

Thakin Mya

Thakin Ant Gyi

(From Ba Tin, 1964)

Thakin Hla Tin
(Courtesy: Thakin Khin Nyunt)

CHAPTER III

THE YEAR OF STRIFE

Burmese Sakkaraj 1300 (1938) is a momentous year in the modern history of Burma. Because of the tempestuous nature of events which took place during that year, the period is known as "The Thirteen Hundredth Year Strife." These events are so closely linked with the activities of the Dobama that to study them closely is to trace the history of the Dobama itself. The strife began with the oilfield workers' strike, followed by the general strike of students and other workers. The chain of events culminated in the overthrow of the Ba Maw cabinet. The year also witnessed the second Indo-Burmese riot which broke out in Rangoon on July 26, 1938 and spread to most districts, lasting until September 8 [FRRIC 1939, 33-41]. The most pronounced feature of "The Year of Strife," however, was the factional struggle which arose within the Dobama itself.

i. *The Oilfield Strike: Early Stages*

The oilfield strike broke out at Chauk on January 8, 1938 [Khin Zaw, 1965, 10]. To a casual observer, it would seem ironic that an expansion of leave privileges should erupt into so serious a labor struggle. Early in October 1937, the Burmah Oil Company (BOC) authorities announced that they would grant ten days' holiday to the employees, in addition to the original ten days of holiday a year workers had enjoyed, all of which were religious holidays.[1] However, the Company withdrew several holidays from the proposed list: New Year's Day, the last day of the Thingyan holidays, and the first waning day of the moon in Waso, as well as the local pagoda festival holidays from the original list were withdrawn, thus bringing the total number of days off to seventeen [Ba Tin, 1964, 52-53].

On October 18, 1937, Thakin Ba Tin, secretary of the Dobama at Chauk met Thakin Khin Aung, Thakin Hlaing, and Thakin Ba Maung at Yenangyaung. After a short discussion they agreed to use religious factors to create a political issue out of the announcement [Ba Tin, 1964, 53]. The Executive Committee of the Yenangyaung workers' union readily accepted this proposal and resolved: to convert the committee for the organization of the workers into a working committee; and to stage mass meetings at Yenangyaung on October 30, 1937 and at

---

1. These were three days at Thingyan, the Fullmoon Day of Kason, the Fullmoon Day of Waso, the Fullmoon Day of Thadingyut, the Fullmoon Day of Tazaungdaing, the Fullmoon Day of Tabaung; and a day each for the Pin Pagoda festival and the Aye Zedi festival for the workers of Yenangyaung and Chauk respectively.

Chauk on October 31, 1937 [Ba Tin, 1964, 54]. Three speakers, chosen by the company to speak on the themes of oppression and on Buddhist belief, were Thakin Ba Tin, Thakin Kha, and U Thein Maung [Ba Tin, 1964, 55].

Accordingly, on October 30, 1937, over 5,000 workers attended a mass rally at Yenangyaung Balebba monastic grounds which was chaired by Thakin Aung Pe, with Thakin Hlaing as the master of ceremonies. At the close of the meeting, an Executive Committee for the working committee of the Yenangyaung Dobama Oilfield Workers' Association was formed with the following officers:

President	-- Thakin Ba Maung
Vice President	-- Thakin Myaing
Secretary	-- Thakin Hlaing
Joint Secretary	-- Thakin Soe Nyunt
Treasurer	-- U Taloke
Members	-- Thakins Ba Shin, Ba U, San Hlaing, and Mya Gyi

[Ba Tin, 1964, 55]

Thakin Kha reminded the workers of the oppressive measures taken by the different oil companies in the areas and of the methods employed by the 'Workers' Welfare Organization of the BOC in the selection of workers. U Thein Maung then delivered a speech which emphasized religion and its bearing on national aspirations. The meeting concluded with everyone shouting the slogans:

"Revenge for all sacrileges to religion";
"Master race we are, we Burmans";
"Triumph to the revolution."

At the conclusion of the mass meeting, a pamphlet urging the audience to defend their religion was distributed [Ba Tin, 1964, 55].

The resolutions passed at the meeting demanded

(a) the withdrawal of the holiday announcement as it amounted to religious persecution,
(b) a month's earned leave to be given in addition to the ten days' religious holidays,
(c) the abolition of the workers' welfare organization, which was a three-pronged organization represented by the government, the Company, and the workers under the supervision of Mr. Webster.

To implement the above demands, the participants empowered the Dobama Oilfield Workers' Association to act on their behalf. A similar mass meeting was held at 7 p.m. on the following evening in an open field near the Chauk market. That meeting elected office bearers for the Chauk Dobama Oilfield Workers' Association, and passed resolutions identical with those passed at Yenangyaung [Ba Tin, 1964, 58-59].

As a counter-measure, the BOC issued a pamphlet urging the workers not to be swayed by the idle rantings of the unemployed Thakins, but to accept graciously the leave proffered by the Company and endorsed by the government [Ba Tin, 1964, 60].

On November 14, 1937, a mass meeting was held in Yenangyaung and another was held in Chauk on the 20th. The meetings demanded the withdrawal of the announcement [*Do Thamaing*, I, 1976, 237] and issued "Twelve Demands" (see Document 2, p. 60). The Company granted only the first three of these [Ba Tin, 1964, 61], promising to improve the living conditions of its workers.

While such demands were being made, Thakin Lay Maung, accompanied by Thakin Aung Than (Bo Setkya), arrived at Chauk on Christmas Day of 1937. There they were welcomed by a display of a tricolor flag with a hammer and sickle in the center (sic) [Ba Tin, 1964, 62]. When Thakin Lay Maung returned to Rangoon, Thakin Kha took control.

In accordance with the directives received from the central organization of the Dobama, Thakin Kha on January 2, 1938, issued a notice to the workers' association at Chauk and Yenangyaung calling for three representatives to be sent to Yenangyaung on January 6, 1938 in order to launch an organized strike under the united leadership of the workers [Ba Tin, 1964, 64]. At that time it was not apparent that this invitation was to become the immediate cause of the labor upheaval. In order to attend the meeting Thakin Khin, a garage hand from the transport section of the Chauk BOC, absented himself from his duties and overstayed his leave by one day. On January 8, the day he reported back to resume his duties, Thakin Khin was served with a notice suspending him for a fortnight [Ba Tin, 1964, 64]. He appealed for reconsideration of the suspension order and succeeded in having it reduced by half [Ba Tin, 1964, 67]. Meanwhile, the superintendent of stores, Thakin Pe Than, approached the transport manager demanding that no action be taken against Thakin Khin and that the suspension order be withdrawn. The transport manager referred the case to the BOC chief agent who was uncertain whether Thakin Pe Than represented the workers or not. The BOC agent gave no definite answer, telling Thakin Pe Than to return the next day. Disgusted and riled by the agent's attitude Thakin Pe Than went around the workshops and garages inciting the workers to make a firm stand and demand their rights [*Do Thamaing*, I, 1976, 238]. Thus before the individuals involved reconsidered their stand, the workers had risen in protest against the suspension order served on Thakin Khin. Holding aloft a red banner made of the longyi stripped from his own body, Thakin Pe Than stood (in his underpants according to some reports[2]) in front of the workers whom he had incited to a state of frenzy lustily shouting:

"Re-instate Thakin Khin"
"Firebrand, Burn! Burn!"
"Strike! Strike! [Ba Tin, 1964, 68-69.]

Demonstrating workers spilled out of various workshops in the BOC compound. Led by a transport clerk, Thakin Hta, drivers who were shouting similar slogans converged with workshop and machine-shop workers led by Thakin Khin. At Singuchaung, they were joined by the crew from the dredger [Ba Tin, 1964, 69]. When they approached his

---

2. When interviewed, Thakin Pe Than declared he was fully dressed at the time of the incident. The extra longyi he brought with him served as the red banner.

DOCUMENT 2

THE 12 DEMANDS OF THE NOVEMBER MEETINGS

I. To improve the living conditions of the BOC workers.

II. To install electric light in the residence of the workers.

III. To provide an adequate water supply for the workers.

IV. To give free education to the children of the workers and build adequate schools for them.

V. To provide hospital facilities and pre-natal care to the wives of the workers.

VI. To grant annual leave with full pay to the workers.

VII. To provide drinking water at all work departments and to provide dining halls.

VIII. To provide recreation centers.

IX. To extend leave privileges with full pay on medical grounds.

X. To fill the vacancies created by people taking leave, and to grant acting pay to those who replaced them.

XI. In cases of death or of resignation, the vacancy thus created be filled with a person in-service rather than by an outsider. (Not to employ an outsider in case of the resignation or death of one of the workers.)

XII. Not to take oppressive measures against the members of the Workers' Association.

[*Dobama Thamaing*, I, 1976, 238.]

office, the BOC Manager met with Thakin Pe Than, Thakin Khin, Thakin Hta, Thakin Po Hla, and Thakin Ba Tin, five representatives chosen from among the crowd [Ba Tin, 1964, 70]. After apologizing for the suspension of Thakin Khin, the manager promised to withdraw the order. He urged the workers to forget the whole incident and report for duty on Monday morning. He retrieved the order from Thakin Khin and handed it to Mr. Bishop, the transport manager [Ba Tin, 1964, 70-71]. As the demonstrators marched away towards the Dobama headquarters, Mr. Bishop rode in front of them, and stopping his car, he declared the order issued to Thakin Khin had been withdrawn and urged the demonstrators to report for duty on Monday. Then he tore the order into pieces in full public view [Ba Tin, 1964, 72-73].

If by this final act of capitulation the transport manager had expected to achieve a peaceful settlement he was either ignorant of the dimensions of the labor discontent or he had underestimated the sway the Thakins exercised over the working masses. It was not long before he was to discover the futility of his attempt.

When the procession reached the headquarters of the Oilfield Workers' Association, Thakin Pe Than, Thakin Khin, and Thakin Ba Tin publicly pledged to lead the strike in the spirit of true Thakins, expressed in their slogan:

> First to be imprisoned,
> Then to be exiled,
> And finally to be executed at the gallows.

The same night witnessed formation of the Organization for the Protection (Welfare) of the Strikers.[3] Thakin Lay Maung and U Ba Hlaing arrived from Rangoon on the day of the strike. They proposed holding a mass meeting the next day, January 9, 1938 [*Do Thamaing*, I, 1976, 239]. At 7 p.m. over 5,000 workers attended the meeting at an open ground on the western side of the Chauk municipal market. The gathering passed twenty-one resolutions (see Document 3), after which the meeting adjourned peacefully at midnight and the demands were sent to the authorities.

At crack of dawn the next day, January 10, 1938, with hope surging in their breasts, the Executive Committee assembled in front of

---

3. It had the following officers:

President	-- Thakin Thet
Vice President	-- Thakin Thin
Secretary	-- Thakin Ba Tin
Joint Secretary	-- Thakin Pe Than
Treasurer	-- Thakin Khin
Members	-- Thakin Hta
	Thakin Tun Khin
	Thakin Toke Gyi
	Thakin Maung Gyi
	Thakin Po Hla Gyi
	Thakin Lwin

[*Do Thamaing*, I, 1976, 239.]

DOCUMENT 3

THE 21 RESOLUTIONS OF THE JANUARY 9, 1938 MEETING

(1) to condemn the action of the BOC for not informing the workers of its right to dismiss workers for absenting themselves from duty without permission;

(2) to raise the status of the daily wage earners to that of salary earners;

(3) to grant 53 days' leave privileges a year with full pay;

(4) to place the above three resolutions before the authorities and demand a reply within three days;

(5) to continue the strike if no satisfactory response is obtained;

(6) to place the schools run by the BOC under the management of the Committee formed by representatives of the workers;

(7) to include two medical officers chosen by the workers on the Medical Board;

(8) to demolish the existing living quarters of the workers and build spacious and hygienic quarters, with adequate facilities for light and water;

(9) to place "Rice Godown" [Company Stores] under the joint supervision of the representatives of the workers and Company representatives;

(10) to abolish immediately the Labor Bureau and to form a Labor Welfare Organization;

(11) to translate into Burmese the rules and regulations concerning the General Provident Fund and the bank regulations;

(12) to condemn the action of the Company in withholding the right of public assembly either at the living quarters or at the Buddhist chapel;

(13) to protest the Company and Labor Bureau meting out disciplinary action against the workers;

(14) to condemn the action of the "spies" employed by the Labor Bureau and the Labor Bureau for harboring them;

(15) to reduce working hours from ten to eight;

(16) to condemn the action of the government in moving villages out of oilfield area;

(17) to urge the Company to amend the bank regulations so as to include both deposits made under "B" or "C" whether or not the five-year period is completed;

(18) the pay and bonus from the "Rice Godown" to be given to the workers although they are on strike. The same to be disbursed on Sunday only at the BOC office;

(19) to return to the nationals all the oil wells and oil enterprises;

(20) to grant up to 3 months' medical leave on half pay;

(21) to form an executive body with the following people from the oilfield:

(a) U Aung Pe, (b) Thakin Kha, (c) Thakin Bo Tin, (d) Thakin Po Hla, (e) Thakin Lay Maung (Central Committee Dobama), (f) Thakin Mya (KMKC member), and (g) U Ba Hlaing Member of the House of Representatives for Labor Affairs.

[*Chauk Alok Thama Kyay Nyar Gyet* II, 1938.]

the BOC manager's office and waited for a reply. Equally expectant were the workers who had been gathering at their posts since 7 a.m. By 8:30 their hopes had been dashed to the ground. As no reply came, the leaders decided to hold another mass meeting the same day at U Po Chun Zat Yone [Ba Tin, 1964, 94].

While Thakin Kha addressed the 2,000 workers, a messenger arrived to announce that workers from the British Burma Petroleum Company (BBPC), and the Pyinma Development Corporation (PDC) had ceased working and were on their way to the meeting. The meeting was temporarily adjourned while the strikers from these two companies marched into the U Po Chun Zat Yone, holding the tricolor flag and shouting:

> "Master race we are, we Burmans!"
> "Strike! Strike!"
> "Firebrand! Firebrand! Burn! Burn!"
> "Triumph to the Revolution!"

The meeting confirmed the previous resolutions of October 31, 1937 and January 9, 1938 and passed a number of additional resolutions (see Document 4).

A similar meeting was held at Yenangyat at 8 p.m. the same day, and on the next day, January 11, 1938 the workers went on strike [Ba Tin, 1964, 96]. At midnight on January 12, the District Superintendent of Police, Mr. F.H.C. Mullerworth, proclaimed Section 144 and issued curfew orders for the Chauk area [Ba Tin, 1964, 98-99]. Mr. L. C. Glass, I.C.S., the deputy commissioner, issued an order to take effect in the Chauk oilfield areas, forbidding the bearing of arms and explosives under Section 12A (I) and 12A (I.B) I respectively, of the Oilfield Act [Ba Tin, 1964, 99-100].

These proclamations afforded a fresh reason for agitation. The Executive Committee met at 7 a.m. on January 15, 1938 and decided to hold a mass meeting in Yenangyaung at 7 p.m. the next day. The workers of Yenangyaung, in sympathy with their fellow workers at Chauk, declared a strike and marched, 3,000 strong, to the headquarters of the Workers' Association at Twingone [Ba Tin, 1964, 103-6]. In response, the authorities imposed a curfew and Section 144 which took effect on January 17, 1938 [Ba Tin, 1964, 106].

Thus far, the initiative in all activities had been taken by the Dobama Oilfield Workers' Association with the tacit approval of the Dobama headquarters. The first indication of interest taken by headquarters was a letter addressed to the secretary of the Chauk Dobama Oilfield Workers' Association requesting that a report on the situation be sent to them [Ba Tin, 1964, 107-8]. Heartened by this interest, the Dobama Oilfield Workers' Association issued a declaration promising joint leadership by the Dobama headquarters and the Dobama Oilfield Workers' Association in their struggle against the imperialist capitalists [Ba Tin, 1964, 109-10]. However, joint leadership turned out to be a farce. Actual leadership was exercised by the man on the spot. The fact that the Oilfield Workers' Association agreed to meet with Dr. Ba Maw, the prime minister, and Dr. Thein Maung, the minister of trade, disregarding a letter from Thakin Lay Maung forbidding such a meet-

DOCUMENT 4

ADDITIONAL RESOLUTIONS OF THE JANUARY 9 MEETING

(1) The meeting strongly urged the PBDC, the BOC, the Indo-Burmah Petroleum Company (IBP) and PDC to limit the working period to 8 hours a day and half a day on Saturdays;

(2) To offer the same pay scale as BOC;

(3) To build hospitals and open medical rooms for emergency cases;

(4) To build schools and extend free education to the children of the workers;

(5) To provide transportation facilities;

(6) To give double wages for overtime;

(7) To provide adequate electric lights in the homes of the workers;

(8) To build maternity shelters for workers staffed with qualified midwives.

[Ba Tin 1964, 95-96.]

ing, manifests the lack of coordination between the Oilfield Workers' Association and Dobama headquarters [Ba Tin, 1964, 120].

When the prime minister and his minister for trade came to the strikers the workers demanded retraction of Section 144 and the withdrawal of the curfew order. The ministers agreed on condition that the workers call off the strike. The BOC had refused to negotiate until and unless the workers resumed work [*Do Thamaing*, I, 1976, 243]. Thus a deadlock was reached which neither of the ministers could break, and so they left. However, after a careful study of the situation the government issued a joint communique undertaking

1. To withdraw the promulgation of Section 144 in the Yenangyaung municipal area.
2. To limit the curfew period from 10 p.m. to 5 a.m.
3. To withdraw all emergency police regulations.
4. To terminate the services of Special Police.
5. To enquire into excesses of police action.

The communique, then, asserted that, even before the strike began, at the government's insistence, the BOC had agreed to withdraw their notification and allow the workers to enjoy the original ten days' holidays. Should a worker so desire, he could use the additional three days as he pleased without needing to obtain Company permission. It further pointed out that under existing laws the cabinet had no power to force any company to comply with the demands made by the strikers. As mediators, they could only ask the companies to comply with legitimate demands. The ministers had done whatever was in their power; most of the demands had already been met and the ministers were convinced that other grievances would soon be rectified.

In explaining the deadlock, the communique stated:

> The Company has demanded that the workers resume their work before they give consideration to their demands. But the workers are adamant in their insistence that they will resume work only when their demands are conceded to. Although we have met several times, our attempts to discuss matters with them have failed. Thus, with both sides stubbornly holding their own positions, a deadlock is established.
>
> Because both sides are stubborn, no headway can be made to negotiate matters. As long as this deadlock remains, the government is in no position to give any concrete assistance. There is no law by which the government could force either party to give in. Although it is our sincere desire to help the workers to gain all their demands, and although we firmly believe that the companies would comply with most of the demands once the strikers resume work, so long as both parties remain stubborn, no action can be taken.
>
> However, if the present deadlock is removed, we are ready to help the workers to the best of our ability in securing their demands.

DOCUMENT 5

RESOLUTION OF THE JANUARY 20, 1938 MEETING

(1) To continue the strike till satisfactory compliance by the Oilfield Companies is given.

(2) To urge the clerical staff to join in the strike as the demands made by the workers are equally applicable to the clerical staff as well;

(3) To condemn the action of the Oil Corporation in employing outsiders in the posts fallen vacant due to the strike;

(4) To request all people concerned not to act as substitutes for those on strike, because the ten thousand strong strikers are sacrificing themselves for the benefit of posterity;

(5) To condemn the Government of Burma for taking sides with the Oil Companies, and to urge them to refrain from doing so;

(6) To appeal to the general public for help, as the strike now staged concerns not only the oilfield workers, but the whole country as well;

(7) To condemn the action of the government in threatening the peaceful demonstrators with a show of might through the military police;

(8) To deplore the action of the government for not standing by the strikers, as this concerns the whole nation;

(9) To urge the government to pass the Labor Protection Act which must be acceptable to the working masses;

(10) To remind the workers that the interests of the working masses and the capitalists always clash, and only by unity can the workers achieve victory over the capitalists, and therefore they should remain always united.

(11) To condemn the repressive measures taken by the government with regards to the freedom of speech and press, and strongly protest against the arrest of Thakin Tun Ok, secretary of the Central Dobama, under Section 144 A.

(12) To protest strongly against the collection of taxes in the areas affected by the floods, considering that the government had promised to waive capitation and Thathemeda taxes throughout the country for five years.

(13) To request the Government of Burma to suspend collection of taxes in Yenangyaung, Yenangyat, and Chauk while the workers are on strike.

[*Do Thamaing* (draft), undated (1968?), I, 173-74.]

Faced with this difficulty, the only course open for the government is to report to the Trade Dispute Act, and form either a Conciliatory Committee or an Enquiry Commission.

It would only be fair to warn the strikers that the outcome of such an action will not in any way be in excess of what we hope to acquire for the strikers through mediation, and that it will take considerable time before any settlement is reached.

Under the existing laws, the government is not under any compulsion to act according to the suggestions made by the Enquiry Commission.

This is an extremely important matter, both for the country and for the workers. Bound by our duty we have therefore placed before you in all sincerity, our endeavors, the possibilities, the impossibilities, and our assessments, so that the people might know the truth and reach a correct decision.

On January 24, 1938, the day the prime minister and trade minister arrived, a mass meeting was held at Yenangyaung Lebaw Kyaung, attended by over ten thousand people consisting of workers and Thakins. With U Ba Hlaing presiding, it passed 13 resolutions (see Document 5).

A similar meeting attended by both Indian and Burmese laborers, was held at U Po Chun Zayat the following day. The thirteen Yenangyaung resolutions were again passed, plus three additional ones. These were

> (14) Strongly to request the Government of Burma to withdraw Section 144, Police Act 30A, Oilfield Act No. 12A (1a1)(1b1), etc., proclaimed in Chauk and the surrounding oilfield area.
>
> (15) To protest against the imprisonment of five workers, including a lady, and demand their release.
>
> (16) To comply with the demands made by the workers to the Chauk BBFC and PDC together with those demanded to the BOC. [Ba Tin, 1964, 131.]

On January 26, 1938, the workers of Yenangyat held a similar meeting and added yet another resolution, to bring the total to seventeen:

> (17) To remove Mr. Brown, the Chief Driller, whose rude behavior and thoughtlessness is distasteful to the workers. [Ba Tin, 1964, 132.]

Thakin Lay Maung and U Ba Hlaing returned to Rangoon on January 27, and issued the following joint communique on January 30, 1938. The communique was addressed to the oil companies, the government, workers on strike, and to the general public. The following is a summary of its contents:

The oilfield workers' strike has spread from Yenangyaung, Chauk, Mulla, Yenangyat and has now reached Lanywa, and the total number of people on strike exceeds ten thousand. The only weapon with which to resist capitalism and bring it to terms is the united strength of the strike; the strikers are not criminals violating any existing laws. Therefore, dismissal of workers from their respective posts and the threat of dismissal and eviction from their living quarters, the presence of special and military police, denial of the right of assembly and speech, the curfew, and attempts to break the strike by illegal means, are all inhumane, unjust, and unlawful.

Oilfields in Burma are our heritage. The oil companies had usurped and monopolized this area for over fifty years with the help of the government. The workers are demanding reasonable rights. To ill treat them as if they are criminals verges on cruelty.

It is said that the demands made by the workers are unheard of even in England, and in the United States. But the workers there serve their own native employers. Besides, in a country whose climate tends to be extreme, the demand for 53 days' leisure a year is not unreasonable. If the European employers enjoy high salaries and live in luxury, is there any reason why such a privilege should be denied to the half-starved workers?

The Government of Burma, headed by its prime minister may have genuine sympathy for the workers, but as it is an institution which is aimed at protecting the interests of the capitalist minority, it is not surprising that it cannot stand up for the workers. Therefore, if the government is only capable of seeing to the interests of the capitalist minority, the country should have no confidence in such a government.

The demands made by the workers are legitimate ones. It is only because such demands were ignored that the workers are now peacefully demonstrating their discontent by striking. And as there is no danger of public disturbances, the proclamation of Section 144 should be lifted, and all other intimidatory tactics employed against its leaders withdrawn.

The general public should understand that the conflict in the oilfield area is not an isolated case of conflict between the capitalist and the oilfield workers. It concerns the rest of the citizens of Burma as well. If the workers are successful in their present conflict, this shall serve as a partial victory for all. Admittedly, the capitalist has mighty weapons, but none is mightier than the united strength of the workers. Therefore it is essential that in a drawn-out battle pitted against the capitalist, everyone should participate. This can be done by donating such essential commodities as food, rice, and money.

The strikers also should not be swayed by the words of either the companies, the government, or other agents. This strike is a matter of life and death for the workers. Of utmost importance is unity among the strikers.

All workers, regardless of their positions, are being subjected to the oppression of the capitalist employers. Therefore should the oilfield strikers emerge victorious, this will serve as a beacon for all workers. Therefore all-out support should be given to the strikers.

At noon on January 30, 1938, the central Dobama Executive Committee held its twenty-fifth meeting at its headquarters at 201 Lewis Street. After discussing the oilfield strike, the committee passed a resolution instructing country-wide branch organizations to give all-out support, both financial and moral, to the strikers. They also decided to call a general meeting in Rangoon, inviting all political parties and interested persons to discuss the oilfield problem and form a strike relief organization on a country-wide basis [Ba Tin, 1964, 141-42]. The same evening, the leaders held a general meeting at headquarters where Mr. Dada Jhanjee, president of the Indian Congress Party in Burma, served as chairman and Nagani Ko Nu as master of ceremonies.[4] The meeting passed a resolution to hold a mass meeting at Victoria Park (Fytche Square) on February 3, 1938 [*Do Thamaing*, I, 1976, 245].

At the February 3 mass meeting in Rangoon, Thakin Kodaw Hmine acted as chairman. In his presidential speech, he urged the people to give aid to the strikers. Then Thakin Lay Maung delivered a short speech, explaining the reasons behind the oilfield workers' strike. He told the audience that ten thousand workers were still on strike and that a large fund was needed to support them. He clearly pointed out the importance of the oilfield strike in the struggle to regain Burma's independence. The speech was translated into both Hindi and Urdu for the benefit of the Indian audience. Then a committee for strike relief was formed,[5] and Thakin Than Tun promised to collect funds in the city the following Sunday from 10 a.m. to 3 p.m. The meeting concluded at 8:30 p.m. with the Dobama Song played on the phonograph. On the same day a meeting of the Thakinmas on strike was held at Yenangyaung where they made appeals to the Buddhist clergy to support their cause.

---

4. The meeting was also attended by: Thakin Lay Maung, Thakin Ba Sein, Thakin Hla Baw, Thakin Ba Maung, Thakin Than Tun, Thakin Thein Aung, Thakin Aung Than, Thakin Thein Han, Lawkadan Ko Tun Hla, Mr. Raschid, Mr. Shukla, and Mr. B. N. Dass. [*Do Thamaing Ahtauk*, 1965, 31.]

5. Its members included Thakin Kodaw Hmine, Thakin Ba Sein, Thakin Ba Gwan, Thakin Hla Baw, U Min O, U Than Tun, U Ba Gyaw, U Nu, U Ba Cha, U Aung San, U Tun Hla, Mr. Rachid, Mr. Ganga Singh, Mr. Das, and Saw Taik Lyaung [*Do Thamaing*, I, 1976, 245].

On February 6, 1938, the governor of Burma issued a special gazette announcing formation of the Strike Enquiry Commission under Section 3 of the Trade Dispute Act. Its members were: Lt. Col. Urwin, labor minister; U Ba U, member of the Senate, and U Ba Yin, member of the House of Representatives [*Do Thamaing*, I, 1976, 245]. A meeting held to protest the commission at Lebaw Tazaung in Yenangyaung on February 13, 1938, was attended by over 5,000 workers, both Burmese and Indians, including many women. Thakin Lay Maung acted as the chairman and Thakin Kha served as the master of ceremonies. (See Document 6 for the resolutions unanimously passed at this meeting.) At the close of the meeting, a procession circulated through the town shouting slogans--"We do not want the Enquiry Commission" and "We have no faith in the Enquiry Commission." The 26th meeting of the central Dobama Executive Committee held in February, passed a resolution identical to resolution No. 3 passed on January 30, 1938, urging the Dobama branches to support the oilfield strike and to give the strikers aid. A memorandum of February 10, 1938 made an additional request that funds collected be sent straight to the Dobama Oilfield Workers' Association at Yenangyaung.

Not long afterwards, a notice, circulated in Rangoon, invited people from all walks of life to assemble at the Shwedagon on March 6, 1938 to support the strikers. The notice was addressed to "Friends, we Burmans, lords and masters," (Aswe do Dobama do Ashin do Thakin do) and it requested the people to assemble, discuss, and give support to the ten thousand strikers towards whom "the attitude of the Company is unbending, the Government is abetting the Company; and the police are oppressing." The grievances of the workers were given as:

(1) low wages;
(2) long working hours;
(3) (involuntary) overtime service;
(4) fixed pay with no increments;
(5) indiscriminate dismissals and demotions;
(6) poor living conditions;
(7) no adequate education system for workers' children;
(8) too few leave privileges (without pay);
(9) denial of privileges enjoyed by the workers in other countries; and
(10) no adequate medical care.

The pamphlet declared that the workers had resorted to strikes because the Company had ignored their "begging" to remedy their grievances. It further pointed out that the government and companies were all capitalists. The pressure to collect taxes was aimed at breaking the strikes. That was why repeated requests by telegram, letter, and by deliberations at the meetings, to suspend temporarily the collection of thathameda taxes had been ignored. Furthermore, not only were the strike leaders placed under arrest, the peacefully picketing womenfolk were also being brutally manhandled by the police. Then the pamphlet asked: "Are we going to be mere spectators? To help the oilfield workers now is everybody's concern. Everybody includes the hawker, the vendor, the ponycart driver, the lapidarist, the automobile driver, the mill hand, the farmer, the peasant, and the clerk. To be explicit, all workers of the Irrawaddy (Flotilla Company), Steel Brothers, IBP

DOCUMENT 6

RESOLUTIONS PASSED AT THE FEBRUARY 13, 1938 MEETING IN YENANGYAUNG

(1) To ignore the Strike Enquiry Commission when it opens at Yenangyaung on February 18, and to accord the same treatment to those who contact the said commission;

(2) To solve the present problem only through negotiations with the representatives chosen by the strikers;

(3) To demand the dismissal of the police commissioner who had insulted all women by his unsavory remarks;

(4) To stop paying taxes which are being forcefully demanded;

(5) To denounce the governmental action in charging Thakin Hlaing and Thakin Kha under Sections 124-a, 140, and 180.

[*Do Thamaing* (draft), undated (1968?), I, 192-95.]

(Indo Burma Petroleum [Company]), the British Indian Steam Navigation Company, the Rangoon Electric Tramways, the Bombay Burmah, Foucar, match factory, port, municipality, steamers, railways, banks, and all other salary and wage earners." The pamphlet further warned that-- "should the strike fail in the oilfield area, all the workers mentioned above will be subjected to increased restrictions and oppression."

The persons responsible for inviting the people to the mass meeting were listed as:

U Min O	--	President of the Oilfield Affairs Committee
Thakin Thein Maung	--	Secretary of the same committee
Thakin Saw Tun Hla	--	Member of the same committee
Thakin Than Tun	--	Member of the same committee
Ko Htein Win	--	Nagani
U Hla	--	Engineer (Ahlone)
U Kya	--	(The self-exiled Burman, now returned from England)

For further effect, the pamphlet bore a picture of a woman lying prone on the ground under the bludgeonings of a police baton charge.

As scheduled, at noon on Sunday March 6, 1938, a mass meeting was held at the Satuditha Zayat in the precincts of the Shwedagon pagoda [*Sun Daily*, March 7, 1938]. With Thamada U Soe Thein in the chair, Thakin Pe Than, who had arrived that morning from the strike camp, gave a full account of his personal experiences of police excesses in dealing with the women strikers, authenticating his statements with photographic evidence. Thakin Kha then explained that the adjournment motion in the House of Representatives regarding the oilfield strike had been rejected by the Speaker. Furthermore, Thakins were being accused of having instigated the workers to strike. In criticizing the Ba Maw cabinet he said that he had no confidence in a government which sides with the capitalists. He concluded his speech by roundly cursing the government [*Sun Daily*, March 7, 1938].

Resolutions were passed at the meeting:

(1) To demand abrogation of the Section 144;
(2) To honor the women who suffered ignominies at the hands of the police;
(3) To condemn the government for taking sides with the companies;
(4) To condemn the brutal and atrocious behavior of the police;
(5) To give all-out assistance to the strikers;
(6) To boycott BOC products. [*Sun Daily*, March 7, 1938.]

A committee to execute the resolutions was formed.[6]

---

6. Its members were: U Min O, Thakin Mya, U Ba Hlaing, U Aung Bala, Thakin San Tha Hla, Thakin Hla Baw, Ko Tun Sein, Ko Than Shwe, U Aung Myint, Amyotha Ko Thein, Ko Tun Aye, Thakin Ba Maung, Thakin Aung Sein, Thakin Thein Han, Thakin Ba U, U Hla, Ko Than Tun, Ko Htein Win, Thakin Ant Gyi, Thakin Thein Maung, Ko Kyaw Sein, and U Kyaw [*Sun Daily*, March 7, 1938].

After the meeting, Buddhist monks led a procession through the city. Starting from the Shwedagon pagoda they marched eastwards to the Royal Lakes, along the Zoo, then to the Upper Phayre Street, Little Sisters Road, Montgomery Street, Phayre and Dalhousie Streets, crossing the Sule Pagoda Road to the BOC headquarters on Merchant Street, along Mogul Street, Dalhousie Street, and Latter Street, then back to the pagoda. The marchers carried placards proclaiming: "Strike is the weapon of the workers" and "Destroy 144" and shouted "Downfall to the government," "Downfall to imperialism," "Help the Yenangyaung strike" [*Sun Daily*, March 7, 1938].

At the Lebaw Kyaungdaik in Yenangyaung, a meeting was held on March 17, 1938 from 1 p.m. to 5 p.m. attended by over one hundred representatives of the oilfield workers, three hundred women Thakins, and about 4,500 interested personnel [*Do Thamaing*, I, 1976, 245]. Thakin Lay Maung was elected chairman and Thakin Kha acted as the master of ceremonies. The meeting was declared open with the singing of the Dobama Song by Thakin Ba Han. Executive members for the All Burma Oilfield Workers' Organization were confirmed;[7] and ten resolutions were passed. Important among them were a resolution condemning the brutality of the authorities against the women picketers and one demanding the withdrawal of Police Act Section 30 and the banishment orders served on U Kwapeinda and Thakin Tin Hlaing at Myitkyina and Taunggyi respectively.

The strain, both financial and mental, of the long-drawn-out "battle" was beginning to tell on the leaders as well as the strikers. Thakin Ba Tin, the very leader who had instigated the strike, decided to negotiate with the Company authorities on his own initiative without informing his colleagues at central headquarters. He justified this action by rather contradictory statements. In his memoirs, *The Record of the Thirteen Hundredth Year Strife*, he recalled:

> Because we received no help from the Dobama Central Headquarters except verbal encouragement such as "Be united"

---

7. These were:

President	-- Thakin Lay Maung
Vice President	-- Thakin Ba Maung
Secretary	-- Thakin Pe Than
Joint Secretary	-- Thakin Hlaing
Treasurer	-- Thakin Ambrose*
Members	-- Thakin Po Hla Gyi
	Thakin Hta Gyi
	Thakin Ngwe Shan
	Thakin Mar
	Thakin Pe
	Thakin Thet
	Thakin Sein Kho
	Thakin Kha

[*Do Thamaing*, I, 1976, 245.]

*Probably an Indian Christian.

> and "unity means victory" . . . I decided to let the workers from BBPC, PDC, and IBP numbering some 2,500 return to work and with their [financial] aid to continue the "fight" against the BOC without obtaining the consent of the Executive and without informing them. [Ba Tin, 1964, 153.]

Yet, in a footnote to the letter sent to the warden, Burma Oilfield, at Chauk which he inserted in his memoirs, he had written:

> The reason I sent the [above] letter as an individual and not as the representative of the party was to save the organization from involvement. [Ba Tin, 1964, 155.]

In the abovementioned letter, Thakin Ba Tin asked for an interview to settle the strike problem. The request was readily complied with, and the meeting took place at the residence of the warden at 7 p.m. on March 30, 1938 [Ba Tin, 1964, 156].

The next day, the assistant warden forwarded the letters written by the managers of the BBPC, IBP, and PDC to Thakin Ba Tin. In his forwarding letter dated March 31, 1938 [Ba Tin, 1964, 166], he confirmed the promise given the previous evening to make the abovementioned companies raise their pay scale in conformity with that of the BOC and to concede to the demands made by the workers, as soon as they resumed work. The concessions made by the BBPC, apart from their pledge to raise the pay scale in accordance with the BOC standards, were:

> (1) Dispensaries will be opened and hospital facilities will be provided;
> (2) Daily transport will be provided for shopping at certain fixed hours;
> (3) All workers shall enjoy ten days religious holidays;
> (4) Should they work during religious holidays, overtime allowance (double) will be given;
> (5) No worker shall work more than eight hours a day;
> (6) Schools and teaching equipment and staff shall be provided;
> (7) A Workers Recruitment Center will be opened and shall accept the certificate of fitness issued by the government's medical officers;
> (8) No worker shall be victimized for having taken part in the strikes. [Letter dated: March 31, 1938, Ba Tin, 1964, 166-68.]

In the letter from IBP, the question regarding the school and its maintenance was clarified as:

> With regard to the education of the children of the employees, our former stipulation "that although the building shall be provided by us, the expenses for the equipment and maintenance should be borne by the workers" is now withdrawn and in its stead, we promise to provide the school, equipment, and salaries for the teaching staff. [Letter dated March 31, 1938, Ba Tin, 1964, 168.]

Other concessions were:

(1) Electric lights will be provided for the outside of the homes of the workers;
(2) All workers, except the watchmen, shall work only eight hours;
(3) A maternity shelter and a dispensary shall be provided;
(4) Besides the religious holidays, other leave privileges accorded by other companies shall be given;
(5) It is not the intention (of the Company) to make the worker work on religious holidays. However, should the necessity arise for him to do so, he shall be paid double for the period of the overtime served;
(6) No discrimination shall be attached for having participated in the strikes;
(7) The Company intends to raise the salaries of the workers as the other companies. However, such an increment shall take effect from the time the worker resumes his duties. [Letter dated March 31, 1938, Ba Tin, 1964, 169.]

The PDC promised to concede to the seven demands given by the IPB, and in addition, it pledged:

(8) To give transport facilities for shopping hours;
(9) To accept the certificate of fitness issued by the government medical officer as valid at the time of recruiting the workers. [Letter dated March 31, 1938, Ba Tin, 1964, 170.]

The concessions placated the workers from the BBPC, PDC, and IPB, who numbered some two thousand and who, looking forward to the privileges hitherto solely enjoyed by the workers of the BOC, left the strike camp in twos and threes to report for work [Ba Tin, 1964, 176]. Elsewhere, the workers were not that fortunate. Although the strike had entered its third month, because both sides were stubbornly clinging to their own demands, no headway towards conciliation had been achieved.

While the oilfield strike continued the Dobama led a mass rally on the first anniversary of Anti-Constitution Day [*Do Thamaing*, I, 1976, 261]. On April 1, 1938, at 8 a.m., a large crowd consisting of Thakins, Fabians, and Wunthanus assembled at the wedge-shaped open ground where Morton, Strand, and Dalhousie streets meet. Before they set out along Dalhousie towards Sule Pagoda Road, Thakin Hla Pe (Pinbyu) unfurled the "tricolor" amidst loud cheers of "Dobama," and Thakin Soe sang the Dobama Song. Thakin Nu explained the motive behind the demonstration, saying:

The demonstration is not only to protest against the Constitution, but also to express our contempt for its worthlessness. Many have been warned not to participate in the march lest they be beaten up by the police. But I pray that they shoot . . . torture can induce a strong desire for independence. I am ready to be the first one to face death. If it would mean betterment for the country, I am ready to face a worse fate than that.

The members carried placards with such slogans as:

> "Power for the proletariat";
> "Withdraw the special rights of the governor";
> "Withdraw the Senate";
> "Abolish the Act of Salary for the members of the House of Representatives";
> "Long live the Spanish government";
> "Arise all ye peasants";
> "Down with poverty";

and shouting:

> "Down with the capitalists";
> "Down with imperialism";
> "Down with the coalition government."

The demonstrators marched along Dalhousie, crossed Sule Pagoda Road, turned into Fraser Street and then along Canal Street back to the starting point at Morton Street. Before they dispersed, Thakin San Tun Hla, and Thakin Thein Maung gave short speeches [*Do Thamaing*, I, 1976, 261].

The Dobama conducted similar demonstrations at Bassein, Bogale, Letpadan, Mogaung, Monywa, Moulmein, Myaungmya, Paungde, Payangazu, Prome, Sagaing, Shwedaung, Taungdwingyi, Tharrawaw, Thongwa, Thonze, Toungoo, Yenangyaung, and Zigon. At Letpadan, after the ceremony, the monks recited the Paritta (Payeikkyi), a prayer usually reserved for exorcising evil spirits.

The Rangoon University Students' Union (RUSU) so far had not participated in the demonstrations, because April 1 fell during summer vacation. However, RUSU did show its contempt for the new Constitution, by flying the flag of the RUSU, the Fighting Peacock, at half-mast.

There were no demonstrations at the oilfield area, because Section 144 still prevailed there. On April 1, 1938, Thakin Ba Tin was served with an order forbidding him from speaking publicly within Magwe District for a period of two months or until the end of the strike. It read:

> Whereas there has been a strike in Chauk since 8-1-38 [January 8, 1938] and whereas many of the strikers are short of food, and whereas on 27-3-38 [March 27, 1938] you, Thakin Ba Tin made a violent and inflammatory speech to a large audience of strikers, and whereas there is a strong probability that you will address them again in the immediate future, and whereas I am of the opinion that if you speak it will lead to a disturbance of the public tranquility or a riot, and a danger to human life and safety, and whereas I think an immediate prevention of this is desirable, I hereby direct you to abstain from making any public speech within the Magwe District. This order will last until the end of the strike, or for two months. [*CM*, 8/1938.]

On the same day, at noon, the two representatives of the Dobama, Thakin Thein Maung and Thakin Hla Baw, approached the home minister at the Secretariat, to discuss with him the repressive measures taken by the government in Chauk, Yenangyaung, Syriam, and in Rangoon. The minister admitted his inability to interfere in the matter, maintaining that the authority to repeal the existing regulations lay not with him but in the hands of the judiciary. The Thakins informed the minister before they left of their intention to hold May Day Celebrations in Rangoon, Syriam, and the oilfield area [*Do Thamaing*, I, 1976, 264].

A month later, the Dobama organized the first May Day Celebrations held in Burma, in Rangoon, Syriam, and Yenangyaung. Due to the enforcement of Section 144, no celebrations could take place at Chauk. The Yenangyaung celebrations at Lebaw Kyaung, were on an impressive scale, and were attended by over 5,000 people. The meeting began at 1 p.m. and was followed by demonstrations at 3 p.m. Thakin Lay Maung acted as the chairman and the speakers for the occasion were Thakin Ba Maung, Thakin Hlaing, Thakin Pe Chit, and Thakin Soe. The chairman explained that, although the country was fifty years behind the times, by now celebrating May Day, Burma had joined the ranks of the workers of the world. He further explained that the Labor Bureau's repeated interference had delayed the establishment of labor organizations. Had a labor organization been established in advance, the strikers would have been financially well equipped and the strike need not have taken this long to succeed. The proposal to hold May Day celebrations in future, which was made by Thakin Ba Maung, vice-president of the Dobama Oilfield Workers' Association, was unanimously endorsed. At the close of the speeches, the demonstrators marched four abreast through the town shouting slogans:

> "Destroy capitalism";
> "Destroy the New Constitution";
> "Workers unite";
> "Abolish Section 60 Oil Fields Act";
> "Freedom of speech";
> "Freedom of assembly";
> "Freedom of the press";
> "Workers of the world unite!"
> "Triumph to the revolution";
> "Strike freely";
> "Picket freely";
> "All power be unto us--the workers";
> "Oilfields are for the workers";
> "Strike! Strike!";
> "Set up proletariat government";
> "Establish the era of the proletariat";
> "We do not want the labor bureau";
> "Company stores should be under workers' management";
> "Workers beware";
> "The country needs you!"
> "Fight to get all your rights";
> "Unite! Unite!"
> "We expect unity among all true Burmans."

During this period, the Dobama was active not only in supporting the oilfield workers both morally and financially and in revamping the Letyone Tat, but also in some cases their interests extended far beyond the normal round of activities. Such an occasion was the annual meeting of the Rickshaw Drivers' Organization held on May 15, 1938 at the Gaiety Cinema Hall in Rangoon. Serving as the chairman, Thakin Thein Maung stressed the need for a cordial relationship among the subject nations and urged the workers to join hands with the Dobama [*Do Thamaing*, I, 1976, 267].

In order to raise funds to meet the expenses of the strikers, the Thakin members of the Strike Relief Organization toured the countryside. Wherever they went, they not only appealed for funds, but they also spread anti-colonial sentiments. The strike also afforded them added scope to propagate their cause [*Do Thamaing*, I, 1976, 264]. Thus fresh adherents were added to the fold. New branch organizations were established at Amarapura, Mogok, Myaungmya Taungdwingyi, Thaton, and Wakema. At the same time they established branch organizations for the Letyone Tat at Kamonzeik, Nattalin, and Zalun [*Do Thamaing*, I, 1976, 267].

But for the oilfield workers themselves, the situation became worse. As daily wage earners without any savings to fall back on, the strikers held out under the greatest of financial strains. As days became weeks and weeks months, the conditions at the strike camp slowly deteriorated. To crown it all, there was a strained relationship among the Thakin leaders and a disagreement between them and U Ba Hlaing, a member of the House of Representatives who had constantly worked with the Thakins among the strikers. U Ba Hlaing finally broke away from the Dobama in mid-April 1938, and on the 17th of that month issued a public declaration explaining the reasons for his action. He published three statements accusing the Thakins of thwarting reconciliatory actions, and in a fourth charged them with "not devoting themselves to the interests of the strikers alone, but always working for the cause of the Dobama" [Ba Tin, 1964, 179-80].

The Ba Maw cabinet was at the time trying to make use of the Mamaka (Young Buddhist Monks). Led by U Pyinnyawuntha, fourteen monks arrived at Yenangyaung by bus on May 25, and put up at Seinban Kyaungdaik, the monastery of U Pandissa, a supporter of Dr. Ba Maw. They planned to hold a mass rally at the Yadanamyinsu pagoda at 3 p.m. but due to heavy rains, few people attended. Before an audience of only about thirty U Pyinnyawuntha declared that the monks had come to assist the strikers. Then U Teza took the platform to make a bold promise that the monks would lead the strike for three days, at the end of which they promised to secure at least half the strikers' demands. However, the news that they were stooges of Dr. Ba Maw preceded the monks and defeated their cause.

At this juncture a sympathy strike broke out among Syriam Refinery workers. Although the workers at the refineries are closely connected with the oilfield workers, the geographic distance had kept them from identifying themselves with the strikers. However, on June 27, 1938, 400 workers [*Do Thamaing*, I, 1976, 272] from the refineries at Syriam went on strike and within a few days their numbers swelled to over 1,200. When the news reached the oilfields that same evening it greatly heartened the people at the strike camp. With renewed vigor, over a thousand people rallied to an emergency meeting held by the Chauk Dobama Oilfield Workers' Association to welcome the news.

At 7 p.m. that evening the Dobama at Chauk held a special meeting attended by strikers and ten resolutions were passed. Six of these were repetitions of former demands and there were four new demands:

(1) To urge the government to take legal action against the BOC for evicting the strikers from their living quarters.
(2) To effectuate implementation of the pledge made by the oilfield warden.
(3) To give a loan of Rs. 150 to each worker and to lease free-grant land measuring 50 acres in the area where the workers reside.
(4) To warn the Company BOC that if no effective solution was found to settle the strike within seven days, workers now back at work would rejoin the strikers and renew their demands.

When the BOC ignored these demands, a further meeting at Chauk on July 2 passed a resolution to remind the BOC authorities that they should settle the strike through negotiations.

Meanwhile, the strike at Syriam was gaining considerable momentum. On June 30, when Dr. Thein Maung, the minister for trade, arrived at Syriam, over two thousand workers, both Indian and Burmese, met him at the jetty. The minister was greeted by the BOC officials as well as by representatives of the strikers. He told the strikers' representatives that he had come on an inspection tour and asked them to make the demands only after resuming their duties. Thakin Kha stated that such a suggestion was impracticable, and told the minister that the situation would worsen if he did not help to solve the problem. Then, Thakin Kha presented the following demands to the BOC authorities:

(1) To grant leave on medical grounds with full pay for one month, and half pay for two months.
(2) To reinstate the workers in their former positions on their return from medical leave.
(3) To give hygienic and spacious living quarters with facilities for light and water.
(4) To translate the Provident Fund regulations into Burmese.
(5) To extend the right to enjoy Provident Fund, both "A" and "B" categories to all workers whether or not they had completed five years of service.
(6) To extend the right to enjoy "A" category Provident Funds to all workers.
(7) To abolish the system of part-time and daily wages.

The outcome of the trade minister's visit to the troubled area in Syriam was formation of a Board of Conciliation on July 8, 1938.[8]

---

8. The notification, No. 114, Department of Commerce and Industry, Post and Telegraph Branch, dated July 8, 1938 reads:

Although no representative of the Dobama as such was included in the Board of Conciliation, the strike leaders at Syriam made no protests.[9] The meeting of the strikers held at Minkyaung on July 10, 1938, reached a decision to call off the strike for the time being.

A meeting at Chauk at noon of July 13, 1938 sent a resolution to the trade minister to put their grievances also before the Conciliation Board and to expand the board by including more representatives of the workers [Ba Tin, 1964, 1978].

On August 5, 1938, Thakin Ba Tin, Thakin Hlaing, and Thakin Ba Maung met and decided to send a representative each from Chauk and Yenangyaung to Thakin Kodaw Hmine, the President of the Burma Central Strikers' Association so that he could approach the authorities and present the strikers' case before the Board of Conciliation. The two representatives chosen were Thakin Hlaing and Thakin Pe Than [Ba Tin, 1964, 190]. At 2 p.m. on August 26, the Executive Committee members from Chauk, Lanywa, Yenangyaung, and Yenangyat met at Twingone Quarters in Yenangyaung to discuss what action should be taken if the Board of Conciliation refused to consider their case. With

---

Whereas a trade dispute exists between the Burmah Oil Company Limited, and a certain number of the Company's employees at Syriam, the Governor in the exercise of his powers under Section (3) of the Trade Dispute Act, appoints a Board of Conciliation constituted as follows:

Chairman	-- Senator U Thwin
Members appointed to represent the Burmah Oil Company Limited	-- Mr. H. Roper Mr. J. L. Buchanan
Members appointed to represent the strikers	-- U Ba, Clerk Mr. Narayam Singh
Secretary	-- Mr. E. C. Fuller, Deputy Commissioner

The Board shall endeavor to bring about a settlement of the dispute and for this purpose shall, in such manner as it thinks fit and without delay, investigate the dispute and all matters effectively the merits thereof and the rights thereof.

9. Both members appointed to represent the strikers in the Board of Conciliation, U Ba and Mr. Narayam Singh, were Thakins. In accordance with the declaration of its Constitution, the Dobama embraces in its fold, any person, regardless of caste, creed, or nationality, who genuinely serves the interests of the nation. Thus Mr. Narayam Singh, although an Indian, was endowed with the title of "Dobama." The first Indian to bear the title, however, was Thakin Sen Gupta. Thakin Narayam Singh was the second Indian Thakin and the third prominent one was Thakin Naidu, a peasant leader from Waw. Although Thakin Kha was a pure Indian, because he was a Burmophile bearing only a Burmese name, he ranks among the Burmese Thakin leaders. There are many other Indian Thakins besides the few mentioned here. [See Soe, 1966, 126-28.]

Thakin Po Hla Gyi as the chairman and Thakin Pe as the master of ceremonies the meeting passed three resolutions:

(1) [To request the people of] the country not to ignore the oilfield strikers who had been suffering for many months.
(2) [To inform the government that] should the strikers meet with any untoward incident, the government should be held responsible for it.
(3) To call a mass meeting of all laborers in the event of refusal by the Board of Conciliation at Syriam.

On September 6, 1938, the three representatives of the Burmah Oilfield Workers' Strike, Thakin Po Hla, Thakin Hlaing, and Thakin Ba, sent the following petitions to the Board of Conciliation at Syriam:

(1) To reinstate the strikers in their former posts.
(2) To reinstate in their former posts, the strikers who are compelled to draw money from their savings and salary [sic].
(3) To reimburse the daily wages of the strikers at Yenangyaung, Chauk, Lanywa and Yenangyat, Moola, and Syriam.
(4) When decisions regarding the demands are made by the Board of Conciliation, the same be notified to the respective strikers' associations.

On September 15, Thakin Kodaw Hmine sent a letter to the chairman of the Board of the Conciliation, regarding the oilfield strikers. The chairman gave the following emphatic refusal:

I am desired to say that this board has been constituted to settle the dispute between the BOC and certain of the Company's employees at Syriam only, and therefore, it is regretted that it is not within the province of the board to consider the grievances of laborers elsewhere. [Letter No. 1084/DOMP 2/38, September 20, 1938.]

The Board of Conciliation held its first sitting on September 15, 1938. Among the demands presented by the workers, demand No. 27 posed a problem. The representatives of the workers sought wages during the strike. Quoting a precedent from the 1921 strike at Syriam when no wages were cut, and pointing out that the salaries of high-ranking officials were being paid although they performed no work during the period of the strike, the representatives contended that wages of the striking workers should not be denied. In response the BOC issued a series of concessions on September 19, 1938 (see Document 7).

On October 1, 1938, a meeting at the residence of Thakin Kodaw Hmine, sought ways to settle the strike problem.[10] Participants reached a unanimous decision to make contacts with international politi-

---

10. Attending the meeting were Thakin Kodaw Hmine, Galon U Saw, Thakin Hla Baw, Fabian U Ba Khine, Deedok U Ba Cho, Thakin Tin Maung, Ko Than Tun, Thakin Hlaing, Thakin Po Hla Gyi, Thakin Aung San, Thakin Soe, and Thakin Thein Han.

DOCUMENT 7

BOC CONCESSIONS OF SEPTEMBER 19, 1938

1. (a) A worker on medical leave should draw half pay for the first seven days, and full pay for up to 90 days.

    (b) On resumption of his duties, although it is intended that he be allowed to return to his old position, should a permanent staff member have been substituted in his place, no such guarantee can be given.

2. Medical expenses at the Municipal Hospital for the worker will be given, though no such facility can be extended to his family.

3. The Labor Bureau established for the purpose of protecting the workers from maltreatment and corruption cannot be abolished.

4. Only a Medical Certificate issued by medical officers recognized by the Company shall be considered valid.

5. No further leave privileges can be given over and above the existing 37 days.

6. Allowances will be paid for overtime services.

7. The drivers shall work only eight hours a day.

8. Working hours prescribed by the Burma Labor Organization Act shall be observed.

9. Annual increments shall be granted to all workers, except the daily wage earners.

10. Full-time workers will be given a daily wage.

11. To raise apprentice staff to a permanent basis and the scale of pay cannot be guaranteed.

12. In recruiting new hands, preference will be given to the children of the ex-workers.

13. It has been the practice [of the Company] to fill vacant posts from among members of families of the workers.

14. The testers cannot be given the same privileges as the clerical staff.

15. Daily wage earners cannot be commuted to salary earners.

16. Enquiries concerning the dismissals can be made to the chief labor officers and labor managers.

17. No underpayment for the candle workers is made.

18. No responsibility can be given to abolish the system of retrenchment.

19. Monthly salary of the dispatchers cannot be raised more than Rs. 20.

20. No responsibility to raise the salaries of chauffeurs from Rs. 50 to Rs. 70 can be taken.

21. Whether or not the veto system should be abolished shall be considered.

22. Only those who complete five years' service shall be eligible to "A" and "B" categories of the banking system.

23. Loans shall be made available from savings.

24. Dismissal due to indebtedness will be considered [sic].

25. The Company refuses to consider the proposal made regarding the payment of pensions.

26. With regards to the living quarters, as previously stated on July 1, 1938, the problem of space still exists.

27. There is no precedent for a striker to be paid during the period of a strike.

28. With regard to the educational system, attention will be given to the advice given by representatives whenever suitable.

29. The Company recognizes only organizations which are duly registered.

30. The demands conceded to during the 1921 strike are attached.

[*Do Thamaing* (draft), undated (1968?), II, 157-59.]

cal organizations in order to consult with them on ways of breaking the dead-lock between the two thousand workers and the BOC authorities. On October 4, Thakin Kodaw Hmine, Thakin Hlaing, Thakin Po Hla, Thakin Pe Than, Thakin Hla Myaing, and Thakin Ba signed a public announcement stating that, although about ten thousand workers had returned to work, there still remained over two thousand on strike who insisted on demanding their rights. The Strike Relief Organization would raise funds by selling a booklet entitled *The Strike Campaign* (*Thabeik sir pwe*) by Thakin Po Hla Gyi at 4 annas each on October 8 and 9, at the Shwedagon pagoda.

The Board of Conciliation met for four days commencing October 18. During the session, the subjects discussed included bonuses, a provident fund, travelling allowances, terms for appointment of Europeans, leave privileges for workers, removal of tax on the free issue of candles and kerosene oil, hospital funds, building of schools, the formation of a workers' club, and dismissals of workers. None of the issues were decided in the worker's favor. Some issues were rejected and most were not discussed at all.

The leaders of the strike camps both at Syriam and the oilfield area were disappointed at the one-sidedness of the Board of Conciliation. At the meeting held at Lebaw Kyaung in Yenangyaung on October 23, 1938, over three thousand workers voted that the authorities form a Board of Arbitration to discuss the problems of all the oilfield workers. The Thakin leaders at the Central Headquarters were at the time engrossed in the split within their ranks.

So, the task of taking a new step to settle the oilfield problem fell to the "man on the spot." Once again, the prime mover in undertaking this monumental task was Thakin Ba Tin, who had first instigated the strike.

The news of the plans made by the peasants at Pegu to march to Rangoon to present their grievances to the authorities inspired Thakin Ba Tin to adopt a similar course [Ba Tin, 1964, 192]. This decision to march to Rangoon serves as a line of demarcation, dividing the oilfield strike into two distinct phases. The "long march" marked the close of the first phase of the strike which had broken out at Chauk ten months earlier on January 8, 1938 [Ba Tin, 1964, 194].

ii. *The Split in the Dobama*

By the time of the "long march" the smoldering dissension within the Dobama Asiayone, first discernible during its Third Annual Conference held at Prome in March 1938, had developed into a serious rift. This rift gradually widened, and despite several attempts at rapprochement, the yawning gap remained unbridged and the organization split into two factions. Although each of the splinter groups retained the original name of Dobama Asiayone, they came to be known by the names of their leaders as the Thein Maung faction and the Ba Sein faction.

The seeds of discord had first been sown more than two years before the Prome conference, when a small number of university students infiltrated into the organization early in 1936 as the result of a student strike. The strike had broken out on February 25, 1936, when

Rangoon University administrators punished the editor of the student magazine for protecting the identity of the author of an article entitled "Hell Hound at Large." The strike brought a number of university students into the Dobama. These newcomers were more radical in their outlook than the former Thakins. They were soon dubbed "leftist" by the older members, while the older members in turn were accused of being revisionists. According to the younger members, even the name Thakin and the Dobama Song reeked of fascist sentiments [Nyi, 1939]. Thus a factional struggle arose between the nationalist Thakins (who were later to join the Ba Sein faction) and the leftist-oriented Thakins with internationalist tendencies (who would become part of the Thein Maung faction).

The first clear sign of the split emerged during the presidential election at the Third Conference held at Prome on March 22, 1938. The Constitution of the Dobama, approved by the All Burma Executive Committee meeting held on January 29, 1937, required that the president for the ensuing year be elected before the conference. In accordance with the constitutional provision, Thakin Tun Ok was elected president for 1939. However, unfortunately for the Ba Sein faction, Thakin Tun Ok was arrested under P.C. No. 124(A) and was sentenced to one year's hard labor on January 16, 1938 for having delivered a seditious speech at the National Day rally on November 27, 1937. Thus the presidential chair fell vacant, and at the Prome conference a new president had to be elected. Thakin Thein Maung, the first president of the Dobama, and Thakin Nyi, who had been secretary the previous year, contended for the seat. Thakin Lay Maung, the outgoing president failed to observe the traditional neutrality of the Chair and took an active part in the election, casting his vote twice--as a participant, and when there was a tie, as chairman of the convention. After a heated debate, Thakin Thein Maung was elected president by a narrow margin [Maung Maung 1969, 59].

During Thakin Thein Maung's short tenure as president, Thakin Ba Sein was elected organizer and Thakin Nyi, his rival, an ordinary Executive Committee member. Then when Thakin Lay Maung took a leave, Thakin Nyi substituted for him as the secretary. The uneasy "alliance" thus formed did not last very long. Dissension was to erupt again on June 13, 1938 some three months after the conference, when Thakin Thein Maung dismissed Thakin Ba Sein and Thakin Kyaw Yin [*Do Thamaing*, I, 1976, 283].

This occurred during an attempt at reconciliation made by Shin Ariya and Thakin Aye at the residence of Thakin Kodaw Hmine on the night of June 12, 1938. Rebuffing this effort, Thakin Thein Maung personally served Thakin Ba Sein and Thakin Kyaw Yin with a written notice dismissing them and publicly sent the note to the press that very night [Central Dobama Memorandum, 20, June 1938].

Nevertheless, the Executive Committee made another attempt at reconciliation the next night, June 13, again at the residence of Thakin Kodaw Hmine. At this meeting Thakin Thein Maung objected to the presence of Shin Ariya and Thakin Kodaw Hmine on the grounds that they were not Executive Committee members, and he walked out of the room. Thakin Hla Baw, Thakin Tin Maung, and Thakin Thein Aung also walked out in sympathy with Thakin Thein Maung's protest. Thus the attempt to settle the dispute within the Executive Committee failed [Bilu, 1938].

On June 14, Thakin Mya called an Executive Committee meeting at the Dobama headquarters from which Thakin Ba Sein and Thakin Kyaw Yin were excluded. Thakin Thein Maung then proclaimed himself "Hitler-Dictator." The following day, June 15, further dismissals of Thakin Hla Pe (Pinbyu), Thakin Khin Aung, Thakin Aye, and Thakin Ba Gwan were reported by the newspapers. At the same time, Thakin Thein Maung refused to permit supporters of Thakin Ba Sein to enter Dobama headquarters [*Do Thamaing*, 1, 1976, 287].

With Dobama headquarters barred to them, the Executive Committee members who supported Thakin Ba Sein held an Executive Committee meeting at 8 a.m. on June 18, at the residence of Thakin Ba Gwan.[11] At the meeting which lasted for three hours, Shin Ariya acted as chairman and Thakin Nyi was secretary. The resolutions passed at the meeting were:[12]

1. To endorse unanimously the declaration issued by the Executive Committee (appended);
2. In due recognition of the decision made by the central Executive Committee to call the All Burma Committee meeting on July 16, 17, and 18, 1938, to convene the special meeting of the All Burma Committee jointly with the above in Tharrawaddy District.
3. To inform all members of the Dobama that until the decision of the aforesaid conference was published, no contact, financial or otherwise, be made to central Dobama headquarters at 201 Lewis Street in Rangoon, which was under the control of Thakin Thein Maung.
4. Meanwhile, all contacts had to be with the temporary headquarters, the address of which was soon to be announced.
5. To hold public meetings and publish declarations in order to make known to the public the unmannerly conduct and high-handedness of Thakin Thein Maung.
6. At the conference held at Prome, the decision was reached by which all members of the House of Representatives were to refrain from accepting a salary. It had been learnt that Thakin Hla Tin resigned so as to circumvent the above decision. It was further learnt that, although Thakin Thein Maung was fully aware of the above fact several days ahead, he kept the executive members in the dark about it. Besides, till the very last day on which Thakin Hla Tin drew

---

11. Members present at the meeting were: Thakin Ba Gwan, Thakin Aye, Thakin Ba Sein, Thakin Kha, Thakin Aung Than, Thakin Hla Pe, Thakin Nyi, Thakin Khin Aung, Thakin Kyaw Yin and Shin Ariya. The guests of honor were Thakin Thin, president of Ryapon Dobama (a member of all Burma executive), Thakin Shein, secretary of the Pyapon district Dobama (a member of all Burma executive), Thakin Pe Than (Chauk), Thakin Hlaing (Yenangyaung), Thakin Tin Oo (Pyinmana) and YMB Saya Tin.

12. Minutes of the meeting held at Thakin Ba Gwan's residence on June 16, 1935 (in Burmese).

his salary, he had kept silent. It was clearly evident that Thakin Hla Tin was dismissed only when further shielding was impossible and his dismissal then made public. Furthermore, it was learnt that although Thakin Hla Tin had placed his resignation days before it was announced in the papers, Thakin Thein Maung wired for him to attend the meeting. Even after the announcement was made in the papers regarding the resignation, Thakin Thein Maung wired Thakin Hla Tin for financial aid. Judging by these actions it was evident that Thakin Thein Maung and Thakin Hla Tin were of the same mind. It was suggested that all members be notified about the above case with the notice under the caption "The Violation of the Resolution passed at the Conference, aided and abetted by Thakin Thein Maung," and to remind Thakin Mya, leader of the KMKC to make an endeavor to abrogate the Salary Act, in accordance with the decision reached at the meeting held in August. In accordance with the resolution passed by responsible Executive Committee members, all financial matters were to be referred to the treasurer, Thakin Ba Gwan, 37 Aneintpaing Street, Kemmendine.

The accusations levelled at Thakin Thein Maung, endorsed by the above meeting were signed by the following Thakins belonging to the Ba Sein faction: Thakin Hla Pe, Thakin Ba Gwan, Thakin Aye, Thakin Khin Maung, Thakin Nyi, Thakin Kyaw Yin, Thakin Ba Sein, Thakin Thin, and Thakin Aung Than. The pamphlet, entitled "The accusations against Thakin Thein Maung," contained seven charges:

1. In disregard of the ruling mentioned in the Minutes No. 3 that the decisions of the Executive Committee members must be sought in all matters during the interim period between the formulation of the old and new Constitutions, Thein Maung feigning ignorance had taken the law into his own hands and thus attempted to destroy the organization.

2. Disregarding the statutes of the Constitution, he took the law into his own hands and created turmoil. If he was ignorant of the fact that he possessed no dictatorial power, it was an indication that he was unfit to take charge of the organization; if on the other hand he was not, then, although he was fully aware of his limitations, he was deliberately violating the rulings of the Constitution, thereby creating a scandal, detrimental to the interests of the organization.

3. Whether knowingly or unknowingly, Thakin Thein Maung had overstepped his limits and, without consulting his Executive Committee, he had on his own initiative not only terminated the services of Officer for Publicity Thakin Ba Sein, General Secretary Thakin Nyi, Thakin Aung Than, and Thakin Kyaw Yin, but had also prevented them from entering the premises by blockading the way with his followers, who were well armed, and used the headquarters premises at will by keeping the keys with him. Such behavior was unworthy of a politician.

4. In order to perpetuate the organization and safeguard its prestige, the executive members attempted to conduct negotiations (to reconcile the two). Thakin Thein Maung disregarded such efforts and proclaimed himself Hitler, the Dictator--and prevented entry to the headquarters by those whom he disliked. Besides driving out Thakin Khin Aung and Thakin Aung Than, both Executive Committee members, from the premises, he publicly announced the fact through the newspapers. The prevention of Executive Committee members entering the headquarter premises amounted to an insult, leveled not only at the members of the Executive Committee, but also at the whole organization, because the Executive Committee members were elected by the All Burma conference.

5. Thakin Thain Maung claimed that the dismissal of Thakin Ba Sein and other Executive Committee members was carried out in view of the impending danger to the organization. Yet he could not produce proofs to support his accusations. Therefore, his actions in the eyes of the general public amounted to disruption of the organization. Thus he shook the stability of the organization from its foundations.

6. Thakin Thein Maung's intention to monopolize the association became apparent with his most recent behavior. But his intention had been a long-standing one. This could be discerned from the fact that he had registered the Office Stamps in his own name some two years previously. Therefore, it was evident that he intended to monopolize the association. If he could not do so, he would create obstacles and set up a rival establishment. Finally, if all his intentions failed, he aimed at jeopardizing the work of the organization by sabotage. Now his actions clearly showed these intentions.

7. In order to diminish the prestige of the organization and discredit its name, Thakin Thein Maung flaunted the authority of Shin Ariya and Thakin Kodaw Hmine. That was proof enough of his intention to destroy the organization.

The pamphlet concluded: "With the hope of perpetuating the life of the organization and with loyalty to it, these accusations are presented to the All Burma Executive Committee meeting so that befitting action can be taken against Thakin Thein Maung who has committed the abovementioned serious crimes." [*Do Thamaing*, I, 1976, 287-89.]

Thakin Thein Maung, too, submitted his charges against Thakin Ba Sein to the All Burma Executive Committee [Thein Maung, 1938b]. Briefly they were:

1. Thakin Ba Sein had diligently alienated Thakin Ba Thoung from Dobama activities.
2. U Soe Thein was similarly alienated.
3. Thakin Han and his wife were also alienated.
4. Several attempts, though unsuccessful, were made to alienate Thakin Thein Maung.

5. Thakin Ba Sein worked diligently to bring about misunderstandings between important central Dobama leaders like Thakin Tun Ok, Thakin Lay Maung, and Thakin Thein Maung.
6. He caused mutual suspicion between Thakin Chan Tun and Thakin Han.
7. He directly or indirectly discredited Thakin Thein Maung in order to undermine his leadership.
8. He accused, without any proof, President Thakin Thein Maung of not being sincere to the Dobama cause.
9. While he was in jail, Thakin Ba Sein demanded that Dobama should request the authorities to set him free; when Dobama refused to do so, he had his wife carry out the negotiations to free him.
10. He took bribes in naming two persons as KMKC candidates in the election.
11. Instead of taking risks in fighting for workers' demands, etc., Thakin Ba Sein was always in favor of appealing to or negotiating with the authorities.
12. Attempts were made not to accept new blood (like Thakin Nu, Thakin Than Tun, Thakin Soe, Thakin Aung San, and Bilatpyan Thakin Kyaw) in the central Dobama.
13. Thakin Ba Sein had a printing and publication business of his own, though he purposely misled people into believing that it was a Dobama concern.
14. Thakin Ba Sein asked money on loan from Dobama sympathizers and when it was refused he quarreled with the person who thus denied him help.
15. He ignored the importance of the oilfield strike and even tried to break it.
16. Thakin Ba Sein made a personal approach to Dr. Ba Maw and promised not to criticize the prime minister and his cabinet.
17. He sent information of the contents of the Dobama Constitution before it was confirmed to Dr. Ba Maw who was an arch enemy of Dobama.
18. Information from him led to arrests of several Dobama leaders, including Thakin Tun Ok.
19. Similarly, Thakin Kodaw Hmine was arrested through Thakin Ba Sein's information.
20. Long before he became a Thakin, he was, as a student of Judson College, asked by the Civil Intelligence Department of Police, to spy on student activities and he received a monthly salary of Rs. 75. It was believed that he was a similar kind of stooge among the Dobama. [*Do Thamaing*, I, 1976, 286-87.]

The last was a very serious charge, but Thakin Thein Maung could not produce any evidence to support it. It seems that the nineteen other charges were made to provide circumstantial evidence for the final and vital charge of naming Thakin Ba Sein as a British spy. On the other hand, Thakin Aye, who tried to refute the charges on behalf of Thakin Ba Sein, could not say anything against any one of these twenty charges, though he emphasized the point that Thakin Thein Maung had no power to expel any member of the All Burma Executive Committee [*Do Thamaing*, I, 1976, 289-91].

Despite the ill-feeling between them, Thakin Thein Maung and Thakin Ba Sein, in the presence of Thakin Kodaw Hmine, agreed to call an All Burma Executive Committee meeting on July 3, 1938 with the sole purpose of settling their dispute [Central Dobama Memorandum No. 321, June 25, 1938]. With the accusations and counter-accusations being printed in pamphlets and circulated among the rival factions, it is small wonder that this executive meeting, held at the Moulmeim Zayat at the Shwedagon pagoda took place in a very tense atmosphere. Before the meeting, some members of the Ba Sein faction placed a box of swords at the meeting place. Thakin Ba Sein distributed tricolor armbands to members of his faction so that, should it become necessary to eliminate their rivals, they would not mistake each other. A hideous drama was prevented through the compassion, farsightedness, and audacity of Shin Ariya of the Ba Sein faction. Before anyone realized how close was the danger, Shin Ariya firmly seated himself on the box in which the arms were hidden, thus preventing a massacre and bloodbath on the platform of the Shwedagon pagoda. If Thakin Thein Maung's faction had been annihilated that day, the course of the history of the Dobama would have been entirely different. So would the course of Burmese history itself.

The meeting was declared opened at 1 p.m. and was attended by over forty delegates from the districts. As it was held exclusively for the purpose of settling the Thein Maung-Ba Sein dispute, no reporters were admitted and amplifiers were not used. Photographers however, were permitted to attend. Thakin Kodaw Hmine acted as chairman and Thakin Hteik Tin Kodawgyi as master of ceremonies. In his short presidential speech, Thakin Kodaw Hmine explained the purpose of the meeting. He then told the delegates that, should a split occur, he would not take sides, but would tender his resignation from Dobama. He then urged them to assume the role of jurors. Thakin Kodaw Hmine attributed the cause of discord to outside influences, mentioning as an example a derogatory account of himself published by someone connected with Dr. Ba Maw. He urged both the Thakin leaders to bury the hatchet and work in the interests of the organization [*Do Thamaing*, I, 1976, 284-85].

There is no record of the discussion of the accusations and counter-accusations at the meeting, which passed five resolutions:

1. That the All Burma Committee delegate the power of arbitration to settle the Ba Sein-Thein Maung dispute exclusively to Thakin Kodaw Hmine. Proposed by Thakin Saw Gyi and seconded by Thakin Ant Gyi;

2. That a pledge to abide by the decisions of Thakin Kodaw Hmine without reserve be signed by Ba Sein and Thein Maung in the presence of the present congregation. Proposed by Thakin Hla Baw and seconded by Thakins Min Gaung and Aye;

3. That the Executive Committee of the central organization and the All Burma Executive Committee also pledge to abide by the decisions of Thakin Kodaw Hmine. Proposed by Thakin Shein and seconded by Thakins Pu and Khin Aung;

4. That full authority be delegated into the hands of Thakin Kodaw Hmine. (Until the convention of the annual conference, Thakin Kodaw Hmine was to perform all functions of the organization in collaboration with the Executive Committee members of the central Dobama.) Proposed by Thakin Pu and seconded by Thakins Shein and Tun Khin.

5. That having delegated full authority into the hands of Thakin Kodaw Hmine, his decisions should be accepted as final, and whomsoever he considered to be in the wrong and then punished accordingly, should give a written pledge that no rival party would be formed using the name of the Dobama or a similar one. Proposed by Thakin Pe Than and seconded by Thakin Ant Gyi. [*Do Thamaing*, I, 1976, 291-92.]

The first four resolutions were endorsed unanimously, but Ba Sein objected vehemently to the fifth. Only when it was pressed by all at the meeting did Ba Sein relent, so that the resolution was endorsed unanimously. In his closing speech, Thakin Kodaw Hmine called himself "Dictator" (Arnashin) and promised not to favor either Thein Maung or Ba Sein and to help the continued existence of Dobama. Thakin Kodaw Hmine's speech was followed by speeches from U Sandawbatha (Bagaya Sayadaw), U Ketu (Twante Kyaung Sayadaw), U Wilatha (Panswe Sayadaw), and U Kwapeinda. At 5 p.m. the meeting concluded with the singing of the Dobama Song twice--first on the Moulmein Zayat and then again when the delegates assembled outside the Zayat before they dispersed [*Myanma Lu Nge Kyway Kyaw Than*, I, ix, 41].

Although the meeting was brought to a successful close without any mishap and the appointment of Thakin Kodaw Hmine as arbitrator augured well for the future, dissension was soon to break out again. This time it was over the election of new Executive Committee members for the central organization, to replace those who had been demoted to the status of ordinary members. Exercising the powers entrusted to him as arbitrator, Thakin Kodaw Hmine passed the following judgments on August 18, 1938:

1. In the light of the present situation, the accusation made by Thein Maung against Thakins Ba Gwan, Aye, Hla Pe, and Khin Aung that they harbored thoughts of setting up a rival organization is not considered to be of a serious nature, they are to be reinstated in their former posts.

2. The accusations against Thakins Nyi and Aung Than, that they were slack in the discharge of their duties, is also considered not to be of a serious nature; they are to be reinstated after being warned that in future, they conduct their affairs with assiduity.

3. (a) The accusations against Thakin Kyaw Yin are that during the election campaign, he delivered a speech for a candidate belonging to another political organization and that he was involved in a program to set up a rival organization. It is considered that his actions were merely governed by financial stringency. As his actions made him unworthy of the high position as an Executive Committee member, he reverts to being an ordinary member.

(b) The accusations leveled against Ba Sein are of an ominous nature. If the accusations are to be accepted as truth, there is no one more dangerous than Ba Sein. However, since it is not possible to verify the authenticity of the charges, there remains the benefit of doubt. Therefore, if he is allowed to hold a responsible post, the stability of the organization is considered to be at stake. Therefore, until the convening of the next conference, he reverts to being an ordinary member.

(c) With regard to Thein Maung, the first problem is to decide whether as president of the organization, he is empowered to take a dictatorial attitude. It must be admitted that there is no such precedent. If the organization is faced with immediate danger and the delay caused by consultation with the Executive Committee members should result in a catastrophe, his actions would be justified. Since there is no evidence of immediate danger threatening the organization, the hasty action of Thakin Thein Maung is uncalled for. Besides, there is no tangible proof to show that he is completely free from harboring thoughts of causing schism within the organization, Thein Maung is to give up his presidential post and remain as an ordinary member until the coming annual conference.

The above decisions shall be considered final. In order to make the remaining adjustments and set up a temporary executive body to function until the annual conference, all remaining Executive Committee members are requested to relinquish their duties within seven days. [*Do Thamaing*, I, 1976, 291-95.]

The new temporary Executive Committee members were:

President	-- Thakin Hteik Tin Kodawgyi
Vice President	-- Thakin Hla Baw
General Secretary	-- Thakin Nyi
Treasurer	-- Thakin Ba Gwan
Komin Kochin	-- Thakin Tin Maung (Pantanaw)
Letyone	-- Thakin Hla Pe (Pinbyu)
Organizers	-- Thakin Khin Aung, Thakin Nu, Thakin Aung San, and Thakin Thein Aung (Ahlone)
Workers	-- Thakin Hla Pe (Calcutta)
Auditor	-- Thakin Mya
Others	-- Thakin Ba Maung (Moulmein), Thakin Chan Tun and Thakin Aung Than

[*Do Thamaing*, I, 1976, 296.]

However wise the decisions of the arbitrator, Thakin Kodaw Hmine, the removal of the two belligerent leaders from the executive body did not destroy the root cause of the hostility between the two groups. In fact, the inclusion of the new members to the Executive Committee proved more disastrous than the previous situation. It only further aggravated the existing antagonism.

Prior to the elections to the central body, Thakin Nu, Thakin Aung San, Thakin Hla Pe, Thakin Ba Maung, and Thakin Chan Tun were ordinary members. According to the Constitution of the Dobama, only the members of the All Burma executive were privileged to be elected as members of the central Executive Committee. Therefore, the faction which favored Thakin Ba Sein considered such election to be improper. But bowing to the supreme authority of Thakin Kodaw Hmine, they refrained from voicing their dissatisfaction [Nyi 1939]. Their feelings, however, were not long concealed and suppressed. To inform Dobama members of the latest development and activities of the organization, a bulletin had been published by the new president, Thakin Hteik Tin Kodawgyi. Newspapers had then published a declaration announcing that Thakin Thein Maung, Thakin Ba Sein, and Thakin Kyaw Yin had been demoted to the level of ordinary members and as such, the central organization held no responsibility for their actions. At a meeting held at the headquarters of the Dobama on October 12, 1938, a dispute arose over this item, with Thakin Aye voicing strong objections to it. After a heated argument Thakin Aye withdrew his objection [Do Thamaing, I, 1976, 299].

At this same meeting, a second argument arose when a proposal was made to expel Thakin Aung Than for withholding the documents regarding the conferences. Thakin Thin argued that Thakin Aung Than should be served with a seven days' ultimatum demanding an explanation why he was withholding the documents, and that he should be expelled if he was found guilty. Thakin Hla Pe, on the other hand, was of the opinion that Thakin Aung Than was an executive member, elected by the conference and therefore deserved milder treatment. If he were found to be at fault, the worst one could do to him was to demand his resignation within seven days. In the midst of the heated argument, Thakin Hla Baw picked up a lantern and threw it at Thakin Hla Pe. Tempers were so inflamed by then that the meeting had to be called off, although it was originally planned to last two days [Do Thamaing, I, 1976, 302].

When the matter was reported to Thakin Kodaw Hmine that very night by Thakin Ba Gwan, Thakin Hla Pe, and Thakin Thin, Thakin Kodaw Hmine told them to form a new Executive Committee and prepare a list of appointees. Later when the prepared list of seventeen members (which included Thakin Tun Ok, Thakin Lay Maung, Thakin Aung San, Thakin Nu, Thakin Hla Pe [Calcutta]) was presented, Thakin Kodaw Hmine told the three that he preferred to convene a conference. He also told them to ignore the normal procedure of calling the All Burma Committee, a day ahead of the actual conference. There and then they decided on the date, place, and time of the conference and sent an announcement to the press, together with a decree that no Executive Committee meeting was to be held until the conference. The conference was scheduled for November 23 and 24, 1938 at Panswe Kyaungdaik, Thonze in Tharrawaddy district.

The Thein Maung faction objected to the idea of hastily summoning the conference. As soon as the plan become known, Thakin Hteik Tin Kodawgyi pleaded with Thakin Kodaw Hmine to rescind the order. The notice, however, had already gone to the press, and Thakin Kodaw

Hmine made no attempts to retrieve it. Then, Thakin Nu and Thakin Aye were sent for, and, in the presence of Thakin Kodaw Hmine, one last attempt was made to reconcile the warring factions. Thakin Nu, who had joined the ranks to serve as mediator, made known his intention to align himself with the Thein Maung faction. Thakin Kodaw Hmine, realizing the futility of his endeavors, wrote an announcement of his resignation and sent it to the press through Thakin Nu. The announcement appeared in the newspapers of October 17, 1938. Thus, with the mediator having finally given up all hopes of rapprochement and having resigned, no further attempts at reconciliation were made. An irrevocable split between the two factions, was finally assured when Thakin Kodaw Hmine joined the faction led by Thein Maung, so that it sometimes was known as the Hmine faction.

This split in the Dobama became public when the Thein Maung faction refused to attend the annual conference, sponsored by the Ba Sein faction, which was held at Panswe on November 23 and 24, 1938. This conference is an important milestone in the history of the Dobama, not so much because of the deliberations and resolutions passed at the conference, but because it was not, as in the past, attended by all leaders. From this date the activities of the Thakins must be studied in two separate parts and it should be borne in mind that the Dobama activities mentioned in this chapter after the above date were those of the Thein Maung, or Hmine, faction.

iii. *The Second Indo-Burmese Riot*

It will be recalled that the first Indo-Burmese riot of 1930 ushered the Dobama into the arena of Burmese politics. The Dobama's first manifesto had borne the dedication "to those who gave up their lives during the Indo-Burmese riot" (Appendix I).

At the time of the second Indo-Burmese riot in July 1938, however, the unity that had existed for nearly a decade within the Dobama was in the process of breaking up. Therefore, the Dobama's reaction to the second Indo-Burmese riot verged almost on indifference. Although there were cases of Thakin involvement in the riots, Dobama members participated as individuals and not as a body.

This singular attitude of the Thakins is attributable to many factors. Outstanding among them are the change in their political outlook and their involvement in the oilfield strike. It will be recalled that from the very outset, although their song and slogans strongly expressed national sentiments, the Dobama had never been intensely nationalistic. Even their very first manifesto, dedicated to those who died during the riot of 1930, had refrained from attacking Indians as a body. One of its injunctions was "Do not hate the Indians but love one another more." Eight years after the first incident, with much of the initial nationalist tendency replaced by a wider internationalist outlook, the noncommittal attitude of the Dobama can be appreciated. Besides, the riot took place while the oilfield strike was still raging. The ratio between Burmese and Indians among the workers at the oilfields was roughly 7:5, as seen in Table 2.

TABLE 2

RACIAL COMPOSITION OF OILFIELD WORKERS [Soe 1966, 133]

Calendar Year	Burmese	Indians	Others	Total
1931	8,649	7,424	321	16,394
1932	7,726	6,401	203	14,330
1933	6,719	5,862	66	12,647
1934	7,143	5,943	67	13,153
1935	7,103	5,525	82	12,710
1936	7,803	6,121	91	14,015
1937	7,955	5,631	72	13,658
1938	7,277	5,231	71	12,579
1939	8,270	5,250	86	13,606
1940	9,013	5,771	71	14,855

No data regarding the racial composition of the strikers are available. A large contingent of Indians, both Hindu and Muslim, participated as oilfield marchers. The proportion of Indians among those strikers under the guidance and leadership of the Dobama may have been near their ratio among the workers as a whole. Above all, within their ranks the Thakins had a good many Indians. Prominent among them were Thakin Sen Gupta and Thakin Narayan Singh. It is therefore possible that the attitude of the Dobama towards the second Indo-Burmese riot was noncommittal.

The circumstances in which the two Indo-Burmese riots were precipitated were also different. While the first broke out as the result of an emotional outburst from unlettered and ignorant classes of manual laborers of both nationalities, the second one resulted from a religious controversy. Among the instigators were freelance writers, a moulvi, a supporter of the Islamic faith, a press owner, and some fanatical Buddhist monks. A vehement press campaign launched against the publication of a certain book, the tardiness of the governmental authorities in proscribing the same, and the anti-Indian climate created by the press at the time, account for the outbreak of the second Indo-Burmese riot.

In order to appreciate the public reaction to the riot, the socio-economic conditions prevalent at that time must be briefly surveyed. During the 1920s there had been heavy Indian immigration which had tapered off at the end of the decade. The first Indo-Burmese riot of May 1930 spurred a large exodus. For three years the figures for Indian immigration decreased considerably, but over the next few years they rose once again. Furthermore, since the early years of the annexation Indians had cooperated with the British in dominating the Burmese economic scene. From petty traders to merchant princes, from laborers to professional and high-ranking officials, Indians had an upper hand. Besides, the majority of the absentee landlords in Burma then were the Chettiars of South India, who were mainly money lenders. Through usury, much of the paddy lands had changed hands. In 1937, out of 11,201,766 acres of agricultural land in lower Burma only 5,895,749 were occupied by actual cultivators, while 989,419 acres were in the hands of resident non-cultivators and 4,316,598 acres were in the hands of non-resident non-cultivators. In the thirteen principal rice-growing districts in Lower Burma, the Chettiars had occupied 6 percent of the total occupied area in 1930, while in 1937 they occupied 25 percent. Demands for the introduction of Land Alienation and Tenancy Bills were not yet seriously taken up by the government. Since 1891, when Mr. Smeaton, the then Financial Commissioner of British Burma first made an attempt to introduce such a bill, there had been efforts, the latest of which were the Treasury Bill and the Land Alienation Bill of 1938, neither of which was on the Statute Book at the time of the incident [*IRRIC* 1939, 13].

For a good many years before the outbreak of the incident the need to ward off this "Indian peril" had been repeatedly stressed in the vernacular papers such as *The Sun Daily*, *The Saithan*, and *The New Light of Burma* [*IRRIC* 1939, 34-38]. Besides, there was also the social problem. What inflamed the minds of the Burmese people most was the marriage question. Mixed marriages between an Indian male and a Burmese female, and the subsequent inheritance and divorce problems created a great deal of hostility towards the Indians. In the eyes of the Hindus, by endogamus principles, no marriage outside the caste was considered valid, and since conversion to the Hindu faith was also impossible, the Burmese partner of any Hindu was in an unlawful situation. Thus the offspring of such a liaison were illegitimate. Muslims accept conversion. But to become a lawful, legally wedded wife of a Muslim, a Burmese woman was compelled to renounce the religion of her forefathers, embrace a new one, and adopt a new name in the process. Therefore, when a Burmese woman married a foreigner, she lost not only her racial identity, but also her religion. On the other hand the "marriage" between a Burmese male and an Indian female seldom occurred.

The offspring of the liaison between Hindu and Burmese is called "Kalai," whereas the progeny of a Muslim father and Burmese mother is known as "Zerbadi."[13] In the beginning, these Zerbadis tended to identify themselves with the people of their father's race. However, in later years, they preferred to be called "Burmese-Muslims," and it is by this name that they are now known.

One of the popular songs, sung during this period, composed by YMB Saya Tin indicates the people's awareness of the danger of "Indianization" in Burma. One line in the song suggests the cause of an average Burman's resentment of his Indian neighbor.

---

13. The derivation of the word "Zerbadi" is obscure. Arab traders who visited Burma, Malaya, Sumatra, Java, and other places in Southeast Asia called these countries "Zerbad," that is "lying under the wind." Hence they called anybody living in these places Zerbadi and probably through some mis-information the Burmese termed people of Islamic faith living among them Zerbadis.

> Exploiting our economic resources and seizing our women, we are in danger of racial extinction. [Shwe Thway, 1965, 150.]

The immediate occasion for the outbreak of hostilities between the two communities, however, was the publication of a novel, *The Abode of Nats* by one Maung Htin Baw. Two thousand copies were printed at the Aung Myingyin Press in 37th Street, Rangoon, in July 1938. The books were distributed in the districts on July 9 and were on sale in Rangoon on July 14. Within ten days of its publication, 1,350 copies were sold [*IRRIC* 1939, 5-6].

The popularity of the book, however, lay not in the penmanship of the author. The trouble was caused by the inclusion of some extracts from the *The Teachings of a Moulvi* (*Maw 12 wi Yogi Aw Wada Sadan*) by one Maung Shwe Hpi, as an appendix with the following comment:

> It is most earnestly asked that this sort of book should be stopped and action taken with regard to these books which have already been distributed . . . the books which have been published to disparage our religion, our "Paya," our Community, and our Pagoda. [*IRRIC* 1939, 8.]

The Buddhist monks took up the author's suggestion very seriously, followed by agitation by the Mamakas supported by the press. On July 26, 1938, as scheduled, a large crowd of people, both clerics and laity, assembled at the Shwedagon pagoda. Out of ten thousand people, about fifteen hundred were Buddhist monks. The meeting lasted from about 1 p.m. until 3:45 p.m., and was presided over by the Thadu Sayadaw as chairman, and Tharrawaddy U Nyeya as master of ceremonies. Among those prominent at this meeting were the executive members of the General Council of the Thathana Mamaka Young Monks' Association, Rangoon, representatives of the Thayettaw Kyaungdaik, a number of representatives of the Dobama, representatives of *Sun Daily*, *The New Light of Burma*, and *The Progress*. Some twelve speeches were delivered at the meeting. The speeches which were violent and abusive, focused on Burmese-Muslim marriage [*IRRIC* 1939, 12-13].

At the close of the meeting, at about 3:45 p.m., U Kumara of the Thayettaw Kyaungdaik, the president of the Rangoon Central Thathana Mamaka Young Sanghas' Association organized the audience into a procession to march along the Shwedagon Pagoda Road to the Soortee Bara Bazaar. In a belligerent mood the procession marched along the Shwedagon Pagoda Road ransacking the wayside stalls, wrecking the rickshaws and halting two trams, Nos. 60 and 68, to strip off their sidebars to use as weapons. But they harmed no one. When the procession reached the crossing of China and Canal Streets, it was confronted by a small contingent of police--fifteen Indian constables, twelve British sergeants, and one inspector under the command of Mr. W. H. Tydd, the Assistant Commissioner of Police.

Some people in the procession started throwing stones at the upper story of the Bazaar, and Mr. Tydd ordered his small force to charge the crowd. People began running helter-skelter. During the melée which lasted about three or four minutes, some people including some monks were wounded. However, none were killed at the Soortee Bara Bazaar [*IRRIC* 1939, 23-24]. Thus the first clash of the Indo-Burmese riot occurred between the Burmese and police rather than between Muslim and Buddhist fanatics.

The rioting raged in Rangoon for a week. By August 1 it had died down there but terrorism had spread to the districts. By August 17 it was officially announced that the rioting had ended. However, fresh incidents broke out in Rangoon on September 2, lasting until September 9 [*IRRIC* 1939, 41-42]. The areas most affected by the riots were along the Irrawaddy from Shwebo to the delta and along the railways from Mandalay to Rangoon. Deaths totalled 1,227 with about three million rupees worth of property destroyed at Rangoon, and over two million in the districts [*IRRIC* 1939, 281-84].

iv. *The Breakdown of the Oilfield Strike*

The second Indo-Burmese riots broke out at a time when the Dobama was in the process of going through the most crucial period of its history. The oilfield strike, to which it was lending its leadership and patronage, had already entered its seventh month, and as yet no tangible response to the strikers' demands or any settlement of the dispute was in sight. The majority of the strikers were discouraged, and with dissatisfaction slowly worming its way into the strike camp, disintegration set in.

The second phase of the oilfield strike began with the decision to make the "glorious march" of the thousands from Pegu to Rangoon on November 14, 1938 (Ba Tin, 1964, 194) and ended with the "inglorious retreat" by the few stragglers in July 1939.

The second phase differed greatly from the first in scope as well as in intensity. While the first served as a gentle prelude to a more important event, the second, in contrast, was boisterous, bitter, bellicose, and brutal. The first phase was confined to the oilfield workers, pure and unalloyed. The second encompassed not only workers but also students, peasants, and monks.

The severity of the governmental reaction also was proportionate. During the first phase relatively few agitators, instigators, strikers, and picketers were imprisoned. In the first three months only forty-four were arrested in connection with the strike, including twenty-five women. Thakin Tun Ok was also arrested during this period. This, however, was not in connection with the oilfield strike, but for the speech he delivered on the National Day, November 27, 1937. He was sentenced to six months R.I. under Section 124(A) on January 16, 1938 [*Myanma Lu Nge Kyway Kyaw Than*, I, v, March 15, 1938, 12]. There were even fewer subsequent arrests. Thakin Lay Maung was arrested on June 28 under Section 124(a), 153(A), and U Arsaya, a Mamaka monk was arrested under Section 107 at about the same time. Thakin Kha was arrested on July 6, 1938 under the Telegraph Act No. 29, and Maung Tin and Maung Thin under 436-120(A) and the Police Act 54 on July 9, 1938. Other arrests were in connection with the Indo-Burmese riot.

The decision to make the long march to Rangoon was reached at a meeting held by a group of Thakins at Chauk on November 14, 1938.[14] These Thakins held mass rallies at Yenangyat, Lanywa, Chauk, and Yenangyaung on November 24, 25, 26, and 27 respectively to arouse public enthusiasm.[15] On November 29, 1938, the eve of the march, Thakin Ba Tin boldly announced at a meeting in Chauk that the march was to be staged in order to place the difficulties of the striking workers before the authorities [Ba Tin, 1964, 197]. Three resolutions were then passed.

(1) To urge the governmental authorities to secure for them [the strikers] the demands made to the respective oil companies. To withdraw the capitation tax and refund what had been levied during the past fifty years.
(2) All strikers, including the clerical staff, were to stage a long march and personally present the above resolutions to the authorities in Rangoon.
(3) To request the marchers to continue peaceful and law-abiding practices throughout the long march as they had done since the outbreak of the strike on January 8, 1938. [Ba Tin, 1964, 203.]

At the close of the rally, the speaker insisted that individuals consider carefully before deciding to join the march. Those who joined the march were advised to bring in a bag only such bare necessities as a change of clothes, a blanket, a water bottle, and an identity card [Ba Tin, 1964, 202]. A witness recalled the events of this fateful day in these words:

> Today is the noble day. The day on which, one thousand strong, oil strikers with the flame burning in their hearts ignite the torch of freedom and set free the country which has been in an ignoble state of slavery for the past sixty years. [Ba Tin, 1964, 203.]

---

14. They assigned responsibility for specific tasks in the following manner:

Organization	-- Thakin Ba Tin (Chauk)
Accommodation	-- Thakin Khin, Thakin Toe, and Thakin Tun Kyaw (all of Chauk)
Discipline	-- Thakin Po Hla, Thakin Ba Maung (Yenangyaung), and Thakin Pe Gyi (Yenangyaung) as the Commander (Tatbo)
Medical Aid	-- Thakin Pe (Lanywa) and Thakin Kyaw
Collection of Funds	-- Thakin Maung Gyi (Chauk)

15. The mass rallies at Chauk on November 26, 1938 and at Yenangyaung on November 27, 1938 made the decision to march to Rangoon (*Do Thamaing*, II, 1976, 335).

At 6 a.m. on November 30, 1938, in front of the Chauk Dobama office all was in readiness. The tricolor flag with its inlaid emblem of the hammer and sickle fluttering in the morning breeze rested lightly on the shoulder of the standard bearer. Then to the soft strains of the Victory Drum (Aung Si) the strikers marched four abreast with sedate steps. Southwards they marched while the onlooking Thakinmas shouted in unison:

Victory to you! Victory to you!

and thrust bunches of Thabye (Eugenia) leaves into the outstretched hands of the marchers. In response the marchers raised their arms and shouted:

Burning torch! Burning torch!
May its light shine throughout Burma

While the strikers marched along in a militant manner, flanking the roadsides were another set of marchers made up of their wives and children, who were in no way militant. One moment in tears and the next smiling, they marched alongside their loved ones. The fathers bade fond farewell and the children waved. With smiles alternating with tears, the wives looked on this human drama full of pathos [Ba Tin, 1964, 205]. (One is reminded of the tearful parting of Hector from Andromache in Homer's *Iliad*.)

According to Thakin Ba Tin, on December 2, 1938, the central Dobama sent telegrams to Thakin Maung Gyi of Chauk and to Thakin Soe Nyunt of Yenangyaung Workers' Association forbidding the marchers from proceeding. After showing the telegrams to Thakin Ba Maung and Thakin Pe Gyi the two leaders burned them. Thus the march continued. On the same day Mr. T.S.S. Kingson, the oilfield warden, made a similar attempt to stop the marchers [Ba Tin, 1964, 206], and had his attempt succeeded, the course of the oilfield strike would have been greatly altered, as would the general historical trend of the country itself. The human tide, which could have been stopped at the 40th milestone, surged forward, and there was no further chance to stop its onrush until it reached its destination in Rangoon, some 400 miles away. Consequently the whole country was thrown into a frenzy of strikes and demonstrations which ultimately culminated in the downfall of the Ba Maw cabinet, as one of the leaders had predicted on the eve of the historical march [Ba Tin, 1964, 202]. At 10 a.m. on December 4, 1938 as the marchers were partaking of their midday meal at Magwe the series of arrests began. The first victims were Thakin Ba Tin and Thakin Khin. Later in the day U Wayama Thami, U Ganda, U Zawtika, Shin Ananda, Thakin Po Hla Gyi, Thakin Ba Maung, and Thakin Pe Gyi were arrested under Section 107 [Ba Tin, 1964, 210]. If intimidation was the purpose of the arrests, they were partially successful--for of the 1,500 marchers who had gathered at Magwe that morning only 1,200 were still present at the time of dinner, and by 7 p.m. when the mass rally began only 1,100 remained [Ba Tin, 1964, 210]. However, at a meeting held at Medi monastery that night the stalwarts who remained vowed to undergo even a hunger strike until their leaders were released [Ba Tin, 1964, 211]. When all attempts to dissuade the marchers had failed, the authorities at Magwe declared Section 144 to be in effect from midnight of December 4, 1938 [Ba Tin, 1964, 212].

Whatever the initial attitude of the central Dobama towards the march, the arrests of its leaders and the hunger strike staged for their release made it impossible for the organization to remain aloof. Therefore, a meeting of the central Executive Committee, convened the same night, decided to make an all-out effort to break the hunger strike and to take the lead in bringing the marchers to their destination. Thakin Tun Khin was immediately dispatched to the scene [*Do Thamaing*, II, 1976, 337]. When he arrived at Magwe, on December 6, 1938, he pointed out the ineffectiveness of the hunger strike at this juncture and urged the participants to change their tactics and instead engage in civil disobedience by defying Section 144 [Ba Tin, 1964, 212].

As a mark of defiance to the proclamation of Section 144, fifteen marchers in groups of five paraded through the town, beating a gong and announcing the meeting planned for 7 p.m. that evening [Ba Tin, 1964, 212]. At the close of the meeting at 10:30 p.m. on December 6, 1938, Thakin Tun Khin and Thakin Maung Nyo were arrested under Section 107. Other Thakins arrested that night were Thakin Kyaw Din, Thakin Thein Maung, Thakin Mar, and U Damma. Thakin Lwin, arriving the next day, was also taken into custody [*Do Thamaing*, II, 1976, 339]. Those arrests were soon to cause much sturm und drang.

The first group to be swept into this storm were the students. Their entry into the turmoil was not accidental, as it was made to appear at the time, but was planned and calculated, as will soon become evident.

The repeated arrests of the Thakin leaders heading the oilfield march necessitated the creation of a loose corps of leaders known as "Bos"[16] whose task was to bring the marchers safely to Rangoon. On December 8 a meeting of the central Executive Committee was held at 7 p.m. at the Dobama headquarters, 277 Phayre Street. It was attended by Thakin Hteik Tin Kodaw Gyi, Thakin Than Tun, Thakin Hla Pe, Thakin Hla Maung, and a few others who had enlisted as Bos. Two student leaders, Ko Ba Hein and Ko Ba Swe attended this gathering on invitation from Thakin Hla Pe (Letya) [Ba Hein, 1938, 30].

It was neither necessary nor expected that the students would immediately enter the struggle. The Dobama's desire was merely to create an illusion of student-worker unity [Ba Hein, 1938, 33]. When discussions were held to find the best possible means to implement their plan for the safe conduct of the marchers, a decision was reached by which Thakin Pe Than, Thakin Soe, and Thakin Htein Win were to be dispatched to Magwe where the marchers were temporarily halted. In the event of their arrest, the two student leaders, Ba Hein and Ba Swe, were to take the lead in bringing the marchers safely to Rangoon

---

16. *Bo*, a notice signed by Thakin Than Tun, Thakin Hle Pe, Thakin Soe, Thakin Ba, Thakin Hlaing, Thakin San Tun Hla, Thakin Ba Tha, and Thakin Ba Yin issued on December 6, 1938 calling for "enlistment" of "Bos" warned the people that the Thakins would not be responsible should tardiness in enlistment deprive the people of the chance of serving the country (Thein Maung, 1938a, 26).

[Ba Hein, 1938, 3]. The student leaders had valid reasons to be present in the oilfield as the student strike at Yenangyaung was still unsettled. Using student unrest as a pretext, Ba Swe and Ba Hein arrived on the scene. Thakin Htein Win, Thakin Soe, Thakin Pe Than, and the two students sought an interview with the commissioner to demand the withdrawal of Section 144. When no response came, they decided to defy the restrictions and proceed with the march [Ba Hein, 1938, 37).

At 7 p.m. on December 11, 1938 all five of them were arrested under Section 107. At midnight, Section 144 was proclaimed. All roads leading to Natmauk, Taungdwingyi, and Magwe were blocked, except for the return route to Yenangyaung [Ba Tin, 1964, 216]. However, undeterred by the arrests or by the blockade, and in defiance of the proclamation of Section 144, the marchers continued their journey. To prepare themselves for the unknown, they first participated in a ceremony at 5 a.m. to pledge observance of the Five Precepts, and an hour later, funeral rites were performed. Few witnessing such a melodramatic scene were able to restrain their tears [Ba Tin, 1964, 217].

As soon as the funeral rites were over a search party comprising one police inspector and about fifty policemen searched the marchers for hidden weapons. Not finding any, they left. However, at 7 a.m. as the marchers set out, two abreast, they were confronted by a police officer accompanied by U Pe, the township officer. He tried to persuade the marchers to retrace their steps, saying that they would starve on the way. The leaders replied that they had been starving for the past year and death was no stranger to them. Besides, they preferred death to slavery and misery. Then, defying death at gunpoint, they marched on. Just then, at a given signal, the police began to beat the marchers, who in retaliation at once fell upon the police. The truncheon-bearing police were suddenly withdrawn and police with guns stepped in to disperse the crowd. But as police and marchers were so intermingled, shooting became impossible. Therefore, mounted police were brought to the scene. No sooner had the mounted police charged, than these slogans resounded from the defenseless marchers:

>Failure means death and burial, yet the throne
>   itself is reward for success and survival;
>To be born is to die;
>Show your valor when faced with danger;
>Victory shall be ours.

In the ensuing commotion a student, Maung Tin U, and about thirty companions ran to the prison to report the situation [Ba Tin, 1964, 218]. Directed by one of the leaders, Thakin Khin climbed on to the rooftop of one of the prison buildings and read aloud the following message issued on December 11 by Thakin Ba Tin:

Dear Victorious Death-defying Comrades,

>It is your bounden duty to defy Section 144 and to set out at 6 a.m. and reach your destination. Everyone is mortal, and to be born and to die is nothing strange. No one is born twice. Death can come in many ways. Death can claim you in your own bed. You shall die as fate de-

crees. Of the various modes of meeting death, the most
noble one is to die defying the imperialists who have taken
away our King and have subjected us to slavery.

Oh valiant ones, on this your day of battle, like true
heroes may you be able to march without trepidation and
attain the flower of victory. [Ba Tin, 1964, 219-20.]

The prison sentry, seeing Thakin Khin on the rooftop, raised the alarm. At once, the mounted police who were trampling over the marchers rushed to the prison and surrounded it. While their attention was diverted, the marchers proceeded again unhampered along the road to Rangoon [Ba Tin, 1964, 220-21]. On January 8, the first anniversary of the oil strike in Chauk [Ba Tin, 1964, 240], twenty-six days after they had set out from Magwe and forty days after they left Chauk, and after stopping at twenty towns and nine villages, the marchers arrived at Rangoon. Along the four hundred mile route, the strikers were shown utmost hospitality and kindness. Wherever they stopped, not only were they given food and drink, but they were also greeted with dances and musical entertainment. In some places medical facilities were provided. At Shwedaung, each Tatbo was presented with a length of Pinni and at Gyobingauk over sixty bamboo helmets and leather slippers were received as donations. Monetary gifts also flowed in. At Shwedaung, a generous couple gave an anna to each of the marchers, which cost them seventy rupees and eight annas [Ba Tin, 1964, 226-27]. The marchers received contributions totaling Rs. 2,408, 1 anna, 9 pies and their expenses incurred on the way Rs. 1,027, 1 anna, 3 pies.

At all the stops, the local Dobama branch took the lead in welcoming and entertaining the marchers. As soon as Thakin Po Hla Gyi's telegram announcing the decision to set out on the long march arrived at the Dobama headquarters on November 30, 1938, the central body was thrown into a frenzy of activity. Their initial reaction was to forbid the march, and a telegram was sent to that effect [Ba Tin, 1964, 206]. However, news of the arrests at Magwe greatly disconcerted the Dobama leaders in Rangoon. On December 5, Thakin Tun Khin was sent to Magwe to investigate, and on the same day a notice was issued to the general public inviting "Bos" to lead the marchers [Ba Tin, 1964, 202]. The immensity of their task is well manifested in their pledge:

(1) I promise to lead either the oilfield strike "army" or the peasant "army" or both to Rangoon.
(2) My task will only end when in Rangoon the meeting of the workers and peasants is completed and the marchers have dispersed.
(3) Whatever difficulties I may have to face, I shall not retreat but I shall (only) go forward till my task is over.
(4) I shall never cause the disruption of the march either by deportment or by deed. [Thein Maung, 1938a, 29.]

The first to enlist from the district was Thakin Mya Thwin, the president of the Dedaye Dobama. The names of fourteen other volunteers were submitted to Thakin Than Tun and Thakin Hla Maung, officers-in-charge of recruiting [Do Thamaing, II, 1976, 338]. The first "Bo" to be sent to Magwe was Thakin Pe Than. The next to be selected for the honor were Thakin Soe and Thakin Htein Win [Thein Maung, 1938a, 52].

In order to form a Reception Committee to receive the marchers and provide them with accommodation and other facilities during their stay in Rangoon, a mass meeting was held on December 7, 1938 at the U Ba Yi Zayat on Shwedagon attended by various political parties and associations. The meeting elected Ledi U Zadila as the patron, with Thakin Hteik Tin Kodaw Gyi as president, and Thakin San Tun Hla and Thakin Than Tun as secretaries. The meeting also formed a Reception Committee,[17] as well as several sub-committees for medical care, providing food, and collecting funds (Thein Maung, 1938a, 33-34].

The resolutions passed at the meeting were:

(1) To applaud the zeal of the marchers.
(2) To condemn the government for various detentions under Section 107.
(3) To demand that the government refrain from interfering with the marchers and set free those held under detention.
(4) To commend the hunger strikers for their spirit.
(5) To request the marchers to abandon the hunger strike and proceed with the march, because the arrests of the leaders were aimed at jeopardizing the march.
(6) To applaud the volunteers (both male and female) who had enlisted as Bos to lead the marchers. [Thein Maung, 1938a, 35.]

The meeting also applauded the peasants who were marching on their way to Rangoon to demand the convening of a special session of the House of Representatives to pass the Land Alienation and Tenancy Acts. The meeting entrusted Thakin Aung Bala with the task of filing a suit against U Po Sa, District Magistrate, Rangoon, for indiscriminately issuing Section 144 in the Rangoon area (*Do Thamaing Ahtauk*, 1965, 77].

The central Dobama held a meeting at their headquarters on December 12, 1938 attended by Thakin Hteik Tin Kodaw Gyi, Thakin Hla Baw, Thakin Mya, Thakin Than Tun, Thakin Ba U, and Thakin Hla Pe (Letya), which lasted from 8 p.m. until after midnight. Resolutions passed there were:

(1) To condemn BOC, etc. for unfair treatment of the workers and the government for its arrests, and to urge the companies to reinstate the strikers in their former positions.
(2) To demand the release of all those arrested.
(3) To present the above demands to the premier in Britain and the leader of the opposition in the British Parliament, Labor Department of the League of Nations at Geneva, All India

---

17. This consisted of Thakin Hteik Tin Kodaw Gyi, Thakin Htein Win, and Ye Maung Maung Nyo, U Tun Sein, Thakin Ba Tha, Thakin Khin Maung, Ko Ba Swe, Thakin Maung Gyi, and Thakin Kyaw Sein.

Labour Organization, and to the international press. [Thein Maung, 1938a, 46.]

A manifesto was also issued, which included the following important points:

> The proletariat in Burma are [well aware of all labor movements of the world] . . . The strikes staged by the factories in the neighborhood of Rangoon during recent years and the strike of the oilfield workers for eleven months . . . augurs great events for the country.
>
> We are aware that very soon Burma will be free, but at present the government is using every possible means to break the power of the proletariat. Let us run forward and face these now and strive towards independence. [Thein Maung, 1938a, 49-50.]

The manifesto concluded with the following maxims:

> Be it failure, be it success, To defend, we must fight our best;
> Don't get killed with your back to the foe;
> Noble is he who takes the blow to the chest.

On December 23, 1938, Thakin Kodaw Hmine, Thakin Mya, and Dr. Thein Maung, the minister for trade, met the marchers at Paungde [Ba Tin, 1964, 227]. The next day, the first batch of Thakins arrested under Section 107 were released [Ba Tin, 1964, 231]. On January 5, 1939, Thakin Lay Maung met the marchers at Htaukyant [Ba Tin, 1964, 236]. On January 6, at about 1 p.m. from atop the clock tower of Insein Jail, Thakin Ba Hein greeted the procession with the Dobama Song. In the refrain he was joined by all the marchers [Ba Tin, 1964, 237]. The president of the Dobama, Thakin Hteik Tin Kodaw Gyi welcomed the marchers from Mingaladon [Ba Tin, 1964, 237].

While the oilfield marchers were preparing to enter Rangoon, there was yet another set of marchers trudging along the same route. They were the peasant marchers of Waw, Thaton, and Pegu, numbering over 1,000. Led by Thakin Ba Than, president of the Thaton Municipality [*Do Thamaing*, II, 1976, 364-65], they had come to demand the introduction of the Land Tenure and Land Alienation Acts [*Do Thamaing*, II, 1976, 340]. Their sole grievance was their abject poverty and their sole aim was to present their case before the authorities. The flood and storms of 1937-1938 had played havoc with their crops and most petty farmers were reduced to farm laborers on their own fields. Their scheduled country-wide Peasant Conference planned by an eight-member committee for the Shwedagon on December 19, 1938 had been thwarted by the declaration of Section 144. When Section 144 was rescinded through the efforts of Thakin Aung Bala, on January 3, 1939 the eight-member committee of Waw peasants once again took up their cause with renewed vigor.

In fact, the march of the peasants began on December 29, 1938 when one hundred peasants from Thaton, and three hundred from Theinzeik set out along the motor road to Bilin. They were a thousand strong when they set out from Waw for Pegu on January 4. On the sixth morning they were once again on the road to Rangoon. It was this peasant "army" which converged with the workers' "army" at the junction of Prome, Hledan, and Insein roads and University Avenue on the morning of January 8, 1939. The peasant "army" 1,000 strong had within its ranks about two hundred monks and about one hundred women.

The entry of these "armies" into Rangoon was spectacular. The reception party and the general public had been foregathered in front of the University Dammayone since early dawn. While the tricolor of the Dobama Asiayone fluttered in the morning breeze, alongside other flags, the stirring strains of the Royal Drum played by the Yekyidaw Wut Athin filled the air with expectancy and festivity.

As soon as the "armies" arrived at the road junction, the thunderous cry of "Dobama! Master race we are, Dobama!" "Triumph to the Revolution" threatened to rend the very skies [*Do Thamaing*, II, 1976, 368]. At 8:30 a.m. the procession began in an orderly fashion. The following groups participated:

(1) Seven heralds holding pots of Eugenia;
(2) Pilots on bicycles;
(3) Standard bearers;
(4) Shwedagon Yegyidaw Wut Athin chanting Paritta;
(5) Yetat (Rangoon) playing bands;
(6) Reception Committee members;
(7) Peasant "army";
(8) Oil workers' "army";
(9) Rangoon bus employees;
(10) Lapidarists (Sanchaung);
(11) Voluntary Fire Brigade (Yegyaw);
(12) Voluntary Fire Brigade (Kandawgalay);
(13) Galon Tat;
(14) Bama Letyone Tat;
(15) Suratee Bazaar, Kemmendine Association;
(16) Youth (Kemmendine);
(17) Burma Independent Party (Women);
(18) Members of other parties and organizations;

and lastly, the general public [*Do Thamaing*, II, 1976, 368-69]. Arriving at Hanthawaddy Road, they turned towards the cemetery to lay wreaths at the grave of the fallen student leader Bo Aung Gyaw, who had died in the cause of the oil strike marchers on December 20, 1938.[18] At the cemetery, speeches were delivered by Thakin Po Hla Gyi and Thakin Tun Sein. Marching along the Kemmendine Strand, Shan, Hume, and Ahlone Suburban Roads, the marchers reached the reception area at Ahlone Park, where breakfast was served. At 2:30 p.m. they were joined by 3,500 workers from Syriam who were waiting along Godwin Road. Passing the Myoma School, the student strikers camping there gave them a rousing welcome [*Do Thamaing*, II, 1976, 369-70]. From Godwin to Ahlone Roads they marched past the statue of

---

18. See below pp. 111-14 on Aung Gyaw's death.

U Wisara, finally arriving at the southern entrance of the Shwedagon at 5 p.m. [*Do Thamaing*, II, 1976, 370].

Although the marchers had reached their destination, the strife was not over. The march served only as a prelude to greater upheaval, for the subsequent disturbances all stemmed from the oilfield strikers' march. Ba Hein denied that the student upheaval was caused by the arrests of the students alone. He attributed it to the students' pledge made in the statement issued by the Student Council on November 3, 4, and 5, 1938, that the students would agitate throughout the country for freedom [Ba Hein, 1938, 41].

The news of the arrests of the student leaders at Magwe on December 11, 1938 was received with great concern by the student body in Rangoon. Representatives from various schools in Rangoon, and the Executive Committee members of the All Burma Student Union (ABSU) met on December 12, 1938 [Thein Maung, 1938a, 68-71]. At 7 p.m. the next day, a large crowd of students congregated at Rangoon University Student Union (RUSU). The executive members of Student Unions wore black armbands and outside the building, the student flag, Thuyegyi Aunglan, flew at half mast, while posters bearing the following slogans were erected within view of everybody:

> Live dangerously!
> We want the reckless ones!
> Be brave!
> Unity for prosperity throughout the land!
> Down with imperialism!

At 7:30, the meeting protesting the arrests of the two student leaders was declared open by the master of ceremonies, Ko Aye Kyaw, while the vice-president of RUSU took the chair. The speakers for the occasion were Barrister U Kyaw Myint, Thakin Nu, Fabian U Tint Aung, Thakin Hla Pe, Tetphongyi Thein Pe, Barrister U Myint Htoo, Mr. C. C. Khoo; and monks from the All Burma Mamaka Association [Thein Maung, 1938a, 70-71].

Two resolutions unanimously passed at the meeting were:

1. The meeting strongly urges that Section 23(7) proclaimed in Mandalay, and Section 144 in Rangoon and other cities be withdrawn immediately.
2. To release RUSU president Ko Ba Hein and secretary Ko Ba Swe who are being detained under Section 107, and to stage a three-day token strike. [Thein Maung, 1938a, 75-77.]

On December 14, 1938, a special meeting of the students from various schools in Rangoon was held at 4:30 p.m. on the Shwedagon pagoda. Besides the students,[19] members of the Dobama, the Rate and Taxpayers' Association, and the general public participated, totalling

---

19. These were from the Myoma High School, Pazundaung Teachership Training Municipal School, Lanmadaw Municipal Middle School, Khitthit Normal School, Kandawgale Municipal School, Methodist High School,

ten thousand [*Do Thamaing*, II, 1976, 348]. Thus the people in Rangoon successfully defied Section 144.

The student flag was displayed together with the Dobama tricolor and the Dobama Song and Bamazani (Bama Zarni) song were sung. The slogans shouted at the occasion were blood curdling.

> Victory to the revolution!
> Burn firebrand, burn!
> Arise rebels, arise!
> Death to Dr. Ba Maw!
> Down with capitalism! [*Do Thamaing*, II, 1976, 348.]

By a unanimous vote, the vice president of RUSU, Ko Hla Shwe, was elected chairman and the secretary of RUSU, Ko Aye Kyaw, master of ceremonies. Ko Thein Aung, the speaker for the occasion, an Executive Committee member of RUSU, announced that the aim of the meeting was to explain why students should help workers and peasants against capitalism. The students had been forbidden to get involved in political affairs on the grounds that their concern was to learn and to pass their examinations. The students claimed that they could not possibly remain indifferent when their "parents," the workers and peasants, were being ill-treated. So they had sent out some of their leaders to help the workers, and they considered arrest of their leaders as an act of provocation. Pointing to student activities in other parts of the world, their spokesman said that the entry of Burmese students into politics was in fact very much behind that of the others. He then made a direct attack against the coalition government of Ba Maw [Thein Maung, 1938a, 82-83]. The RUSU meeting passed five resolutions (see Document 8) and at the close, enrollment for "Bos" was announced. Of the 56 enrolled to lead the marchers, there were three women, one, a university undergraduate and a resident of Inya Hall. It was announced that two university students, Ko Hla Myat Soe and Ko Chit Hlaing would leave Rangoon that very night to serve as "Bos." Then the meeting was brought to a successful conclusion at 6:45 p.m. [Thein Maung, 1938a, 92-93].

The next day, December 15, the students engaged in civil disobedience. In order to defy Section 144, the All Rangoon Students Union arranged to meet at 4 p.m. at Myoma High School. The students lined up four abreast and divided into small contingents, with a leader heading each contingent. Marching at the head of the column were Ko Htay Myaing (Dagon Taya) and an Executive Committee member of the Students' Union, Ko Kyi Maung. Holding aloft the Red Flag with hammer and sickle, the leaders led the students first along Commissioner Road, shouting slogans:

> We want no (restricting) laws!
> Withdraw Section 144!
> Down with capitalism!

Pegu Karen Middle School, Cushing High School, Rangoon Government High School, St. John High School, University College, Judson College and Medical College.

DOCUMENT 8

RESOLUTIONS OF THE RUSU MEETING OF DECEMBER 14, 1938

(1) The meeting condemned the authorities for enforcing:

    (a) The amended Section 23(7) of 1932 at Mandalay.
    (b) Section 144 restricting the movement of the oilfield marchers.
    (c) Section 144(d) promulgated in Rangoon and other suppressive laws proclaimed in other cities.
    (d) As the above restrictions are contradictory to personal liberty, the meeting demands the withdrawal of the above restrictive laws and the freeing of all citizens detained under the above laws.

(2) The meeting strongly warned that no such suppressive measures be repeated.

(3) Immediate freeing of the student leaders who had been detained under Section 107 on the allegation that they had incited the oilfield workers.

(4) The above action is an insult to all students in Burma and if the above demands are not conceded to and should the student tempers get out of control, the meeting clearly announced that the students shall not be held responsible for their actions.

(5) The following representatives are elected to form a student body to work in conjunction with ABSU:

Ko Thaung Sein	-- St. Johns
Ko Tin Maung)	
Ko Chit)	-- Methodist
Ko Hla)	
Ko Nyunt Maung	-- Kandawgale
Ye Ye Tauk Ko Than Tin	-- Myoma
Ko Hla Shwe	-- Government High School
Ko Kvin Swi	-- Pazundaung Municipal
Ko Tin Aye	-- Lanmadaw
Ko Hla Nyunt	-- Khitthit Normal
Ko Aye	-- U Nyi Pu School
Ko Hla Han	-- Medical College

[Thein Maung 1938a, 90-91 and *Do Thamaing*, II, 1976, 350.]

as they passed through the city. Crossing the Sule Pagoda Road they marched along Montgomery Street until they reached Lakekan Park at Pazundaung. Despite the threatening armored police vans, the marchers reached their destination without any untoward incident [Dagon Taya, 1967, 172]. They had successfully defied the much hated Section 144.

A similar protest procession was staged by Galon U Saw on December 19. At 3 p.m. a gathering, numbering some 10,000[20] assembled at U Ba Yi Zayat at the southern entrance to the Shwedagon [Thein Maung, 1938a, 140]. After short speeches by U Saw and his two lieutenants, U Ein and U Ba Ohn, explaining their reasons for defiance, the procession set out along Shwedagon Pagoda Road, Canal Street, Morton Street, Dalhousie Street, Sule Pagoda Road to the Rangoon Corporation where the crowd was dispersed [Thein Maung, 1938a, 141]. The significance of their demonstration is that, however short the duration, it was the first and last occasion when the Galon and the interests of the Dobama became one. The slogans shouted by the marchers are indicative of this brief fraternity. They included:

> Master race we are, hey we Burmans!
> Burn, firebrand, burn!
> We don't want Section 144!
> Defy! Defy!
> Arise! Galon, arise!
> Strike! Strike! [Thein Maung, 1938a, 141.]

Apart from the specific mention of "Arise! Galon Arise!" it will be noticed that all the other slogans were those coined by the Dobama. However, the fleeting moment of seeming collaboration soon passed. Galon U Saw was only capitalizing on public sentiment for his own personal gain. In his closing speech before the crowd dispersed, he belittled the Ba Maw cabinet by saying: "Don't be too critical of Ba Maw--have sympathy for him. He is not our rival. He is only a very insignificant creature. Our attack is not against him, it is against the British Government which is manipulating him" [Thein Maung, 1938a, 150-51].

For his seditious speeches, U Saw, leader of the Myochit Party, his second-in-command, U Ba Ohn and U Ein, B.A., D.D., the member of the House of Representatives for Henzada, were placed under arrest under Section 37(2) and the Rangoon Police Act 40, on December 22, 1938. After a brief trial, they were sentenced to pay a fine of Rs 100 each or two months' imprisonment [*Do Thamaing*, II, 1976, 355]. Amidst the shouts of "Do Galon! Dobama!" the trio were led away [Thein Maung, 1938a, 150].

On December 17 a group of young journalists[21] met at Dobama Publishing House, 196 Montgomery Street, and discussed public con-

---

20. U Saw with about 500 of his followers walked in defiance of Section 144, from the Shwedagon to the City Hall on December 19, 1938 (*Do Thamaing*, II, 1976, 355).

21. They were Aung Thein (Mya Daung Nyo); Chin Sein (Dagon); Chit Maung (Myama Alin); Chit Maung 2 (Let yay to); Hla Bu (Dagon); Hsu

frontations against oppressive laws. After some discussion, they decided to join the Dobama in its current activities [Thein Maung, 1938a, 165]. Thakin Than Tun, in his capacity as general-secretary of the Dobama, extended a cordial welcome to the young journalists and invited them to work alongside the Thakins at the Dobama headquarters every day between 5 and 6 p.m. A meeting of journalists and publishers from many newspapers[22] held at 12:30 p.m. in Rangoon on December 18, 1938, also supported activities against imperialism [Thein Maung, 1938a, 166]. On December 19, the day Galon U Saw organized the demonstration in defiance of the Section 144, ABSU sent an ultimatum to the authorities declaring that, if the government did not comply with their demands (to withdraw Section 144 and release the student leaders) by 4 p.m. that day, further steps in civil disobedience would be taken [Thein Maung, 1938a, 138].

At 11 p.m. that night, a secret meeting was held at the RUSU building, attended by the Executive Committee members of the student unions and a few trusted student leaders. The only two outsiders at that meeting were Thakin Hla Pe (Bo Letya) and Tetphongyi Thein Pe. Various suggestions for disruptive activities were discussed. It was decided not to conduct public meetings at road junctions on the grounds that these would cause a traffic jam. Finally the leaders agreed to a suggestion made by Tetphongyi Thein Pe, who had been briefed by U Chit Maung, the chief editor of the *Weekly Thunderer* ([Journal] Gyane Gyaw Ma Ma Lay, 1953, 260). His plan was to surround the Secretariat [Dagon Taya 1967, 174].

During this action Ko Aung Gyaw, a student leader, was fatally wounded; he died on December 22 [*RSIEC* 1939].

The students fled helter skelter, but as soon as the panic subsided, Ye Ye Tauk Ko Than Tin of the Myoma High School reassembled them and led them back to his school in an orderly fashion, where they awaited further orders from their leaders [*Do Thamaing Ahtauk*, 1965, 67].

Myiang (Hse Thann); Htoo; Kyaw Sein (Thakin); Lun Maung (Maymyo Maung); Maung Maung (Myama Yok shin); Maung Maung Pye; Myo Nyunt (Toe tet); Ohn Pe (Tet Toe); San Ngwe (Dagon); Soe Myint (Toe tet yay); Saw U; Thein (Toe tet yay); Thein Han, Thakin; Thein Maung, Thakin; Thein Pe (Tet Phongyi); Thin (Yodaya); Tin Maung (Tekkatho Htin Gyi); and Tun Shwe (Nagani).

22. These included: Kyipwayay (The Prosperity); Khitsan; (The Modern); Hse Than (The Ten Million); Toli Moli (The Titbit); Toetet Yay (The Progress); Do Letyon, Sit Twe (The Right Hand of Ours, Akyab); Do Lok Tha (Our Workers); Bandula; Bwin Bwin (The Candid); Maw Kaw Bandaik (The Bank of Mawkaw); Zeya (The Triumph of Burma); Myama Taya, Mandalay (The Burma Star, Mandalay); Myama Tar Wun (The Burma Task); Myama Yok Shin (The Burma Films); Myama Alinn (The New Light of Burma); Myama U Zun (The Burma Leader); Yakhaing Pyi Thadinza (The Arakanese Newspaper); Yok Shin Theippan (The Scientific Filming); Shwe Dah Bo (The Master of the Golden Sword); Hla Tun Phyu, Alon (The Hla Tun Phyu Press, Alon); Thahaya (The Fraternity); Thida Aye (The Cool Water); Thuriya (The Sun); Thuriya Mandalay (The Sun, Mandalay); and Arzani (The Hero).

On arriving at the RUSU the first action of the student body was to hold a meeting to condemn the imperialist government and the coalition cabinet led by Dr. Ba Maw. On December 22 the vice-president of ABSU, Ko Hla Shwe, issued a notice urging all schools in the country to call a strike as a gesture of protest against the student's death and the arrests and injury caused to the other students. The notice further urged that all schools remain closed until ABSU issued further orders [Hla Shwe 1939]. The ABSU also issued a set of demands.

(1) that all those arrested and detained in connection with the oilfield marchers and the student agitation be released;
(2) that the restrictive laws and the emergency act issued by the governor be withdrawn;
(3) that the government refrain from taking action against the students or teachers involved in the strike;
(4) that examinations be held three months after the strike was called off. [*Do Thamaing Ahtauk* 1965, 69.]

The Dobama's immediate concern at the death of Ko Aung Gyaw was to arrange for a funeral befitting a martyr. He was the first student to have actually shed his blood for the sake of the country. The manner of his death was profoundly imprinted on the minds of the youthful leaders, both students and Thakins. The Rangoon District Dobama and some interested members of the public met at the Dobama office at Phayre Street at 9 p.m. on December 23 to discuss the arrangements for Ko Aung Gyaw's burial [*Do Thamaing*, II, 1976, 359]. A funeral committee was formed, and it decided on twelve steps:

(1) Instead of taking the body back to his native village of Minywa in Mezaligon, in the interests of the country to bury him in Rangoon. The task of obtaining such permission from his relatives, was entrusted to Ashin Kyaw, uncle of the deceased, and Thakin Kun his old school master.
(2) The students desired the body to lie in state at the RUSU building and the townspeople preferred the Zaduditna Zayat at Shwedagon, while the Myoma students wished to have it at their own school. Ashin Kyaw was asked to obtain the consent of all three parties for the choice of the Myoma School.
(3) Eulogies were to be conducted every night till the day of the burial.
(4) To request the newspapers to give adequate coverage to Ko Aung Gyaw.
(5) To distribute obituary notices to every nook and corner.
(6) To request all pedestrians, motor cars, pony carts, and rickshaws to suspend all movement on the day of the funeral, and all newspaper offices, bazaars, and firms to remain closed.
(7) To bury the body at Kyandaw Cemetery and deliver a funeral speech there. For the above, Thakin Aung Bala was given responsibility.
(8) To fly flags at half-mast on the day of the funeral.

(9) To erect a statue either of bronze or stone at a suitable place and inscribe an epitaph "Ko Aung Gyaw who met a violent death at the hands of the police."

(10) To enlarge photographs of Ko Aung Gyaw and display these pictures at Political Associations, Public Buildings, and especially at Schools and Student Unions.

(11) Every year, the 2nd day of the waxing moon of Pyatho to be set aside as "Ko Aung Gyaw Day." On that day to hold public meetings, fly flags at half-mast, and suspend all business activities.

(12) The 14th waxing moon of Nadaw, the day on which the students shed their blood, to be observed as "Student Persecution Day."

Seventeen "B" class prisoners including Thakin Lay Maung and U Arsara went on a hunger strike on December 22 for many grievances, among which was the brutal beating of the students who had protested in an orderly manner against the oppressive laws. On the same day, Ko Ba Swe, Ko Ba Hein, Thakin Soe, Thakin Pe Than, and Thakin Htein Win, were transferred from the Magwe jail to Insein jail. On the way they smuggled out a message to Ko Hla Shwe, that "Since yesterday morning we have been on a hunger strike."

On December 24, Thakin San Tun Hla, the secretary of the Rangoon District Dobama was arrested under an emergency act of the governor as he accompanied the student leaders to the mortuary to take away the body of Ko Aung Gyaw.

The funeral was held on December 27. At 2 p.m. the cortege left the RUSU precincts [*Do Thamaing*, II, 1976, 359]. The distance between the campus and Kyandaw Cemetery is less than half a mile, yet it took the hearse nearly four hours to reach the burial ground, because the sympathetic mourners lined the roadside so densely. When the cortege reached Kyandaw, it was almost dark, and the place was so crowded that many were forced to turn back since they could not reach the burial site [Gyane Gyaw Ma Ma Lay 1953, 265].

Myoma Saya Hein gave the graveside eulogy. On behalf of the entire nation, Ko Aung Gyaw was awarded a posthumous title of Nemyo Thiha Thura with the following message:

Dear Comrade Martyr,

From this day, as long as Burma remains in the world, you shall be remembered by us, as the first officer in the vanguard of our fight for freedom.

The sound of the baton with which the merciless police hit you shall serve as a clarion call, forever prompting us to enter the fight for freedom.

Just as your passive forbearance sent you to the land of death, so shall our future activities bring about self-government to Burma.

Your noble death which resulted from passive resistance to oppressive measures shall serve as a good omen, for the country towards its goal for independence.

> The flame ignited by your nobleness, persevering zeal, fortitude, selflessness, and the sacrifice of your life shall forever burn within the hearts of our entire nation.
>
> Victory to the Revolution! [*Do Thamaing*, II, 1976, 360.]

Then his bereaved mother, Daw Kyawt, started to deliver a speech:

> My son had not even a needle as a weapon. Yet the government has brutally beaten him to death. How can I ever forgive . . .

This she said with sobs interrupting every few words. Then, overcome by emotion she fainted so the speech remained unfinished [Dagon Taya, 1967, 188].

Then Ko Aye Kyaw, secretary of RUSU read a message from Ko Ba Hein and his colleagues in prison. In their pride in Ko Aung Gyaw who had fulfilled his task as a Burman, they pledged to fight for freedom even in the face of the hangman's noose. The death of Aung Gyaw would pave the way for Burma's independence.

Then Ko Hla Shwe delivered a short speech made famous by its opening words, "Oh, you Ba Maw Government" (Hey! Ba Maw Asoya). He was shaking with emotion as he delivered the speech. The last speaker was Thakin Hla Maung, who explained to the audience how student support of the oilfield strike had resulted in such a tragedy.

Then the expulsion order, Ameint Sar, was read and to a bugle's sad and haunting strains, the coffin was slowly lowered into the grave. So ended the burial services for the first victim of the Thirteen Hundred Years' Strife. Eighteen more were soon to follow in his steps, seventeen from Mandalay and one from Allanmyo. However tragic the incident, neither the students nor the members of the Dobama were able to dwell long upon it. Their attention was immediately drawn back to the oilfield marchers who were soon to enter Rangoon.

On the day of the funeral, the marchers had entered Gyobingauk. There the mantle of leadership was transferred from the shoulders of Thakin Tun Sein and Thakin Tin Oo of the Rangoon District Dobama who had so far led the marchers, onto the willing shoulders of Thakin Po Hla Gyi, recently released from detention at Magwe [*Do Thamaing*, II, 1976, 362]. Under his able leadership, the marchers arrived without further mishap at the steps of the Shwedagon pagoda on January 8, 1939. Their arrival is significant not only because it epitomizes Dobama leadership in the affairs of workers and peasants, but also because of the subsequent events which were to rack the whole country for almost another year and bring in their wake the fall of the Ba Maw coalition government.

During the marchers' encampment at Shwedagon two organizations were formed, affiliated to the Dobama. Establishment of the All Burma Peasants' Organization and the All Burma Workers' Organization took place on the same day, January 9, 1939, the second day after the peasants and workers arrived at the Shwedagon. Three weeks later, on January 29, a third organization, the Burma Independence Women's

League, was formed as a protest against the government for its general suppression of all political organizations and especially the persecution meted out to the Dobama members encamped at the Shwedagon pagoda [*Do Thamaing*, II, 1976, 393].

At Shwedagon the Dobama had their headquarters at the Moulmein Zayat, the Reception Committee at U Ba Yi Zayat, the clergy at U Ba Yi Zayat, the oilfield marchers at the Zayats situated at the northeastern side of the middle terrace, the peasants at the Zayats on the southeastern side of the middle terrace, and the suicide squad at the Zayats adjacent to theirs. The open space between U Aye Maung Zayat and U Ba Yi Zayat formed the rallying grounds. The student strikers remained at the Myoma High School. The Executive Committee of the central Dobama took upon itself responsibility for the entire movement and assumed leadership in politically significant matters. The Reception Committee, composed of all parties, assumed charge of accommodation, food, and hygiene, and extended its services to the student strikers wherever necessary. The Letyone Tat served as scouts. The Ba Hnin First Aid Corps and the Burmese indigenous medical team were responsible for the health of the strikers [*Do Thamaing*, II, 1976, 371-72].

On the second day after the arrival of the strikers a mass meeting of the peasants was convened at 10:30 a.m. at the Shwedagon pagoda. Thakin Mya, the member of the House of Representatives, served as the chairman and Thakin Hla Maung as the master of ceremonies. Thakin Lay Maung spoke of how the Dobama was acting for the benefit of the peasants and how only peasant leadership could serve the interests of the peasants. Fourteen resolutions were passed at the meeting before formation of the All Burma Peasants' Organization was announced [*Do Thamaing*, II, 1976, 375-79].

The resolutions passed at the meeting concerned, primarily, agricultural problems. The first of them condemned the coalition government for its delaying tactics regarding passage of the Land Alienation Act, and the Tenancy Act.[23] The task of presenting amendments which would benefit the peasants was entrusted to the Executive Committee members of the newly formed peasants' organization. The second resolution suggested a standardization of weights and measures for agricultural products. The third insisted on translation of the Loan Act into Burmese, and the fourth demanded the withdrawal of the Village Act of 1886 which prevented the cultivator from living on his cultivation plot throughout the year. The fifth resolution demanded that old rental debts be waived and cultivators not be subject to arrest during the period they were engaged in cultivation. The sixth resolution urged that land be given to those who actually worked on the land, and the seventh that taxes derived from the land be used for the sole purpose of uplifting the cultivator. The eighth resolution demanded the right of a peasant to catch fish in the paddy or marshy area in his own land. The ninth resolution condemned the government for not using the 150 million rupees derived from the sale of rice some twenty years ago for the benefit of the peasants and farmers. This amount, together with

---

23. Both Land Alienation Act and Land Tenancy Act were enacted in 1939. But due to the outbreak of World War II they were not enforced in practice.

the interest, should be used for the sole benefit of the peasantry. Resolution ten proposed the following measures to lighten the peasants' burden of heavy debt:

(a) a peasant protection organization to be set up at governmental expense;
(b) the peasantry to be saved from the clutches of usurers and capitalists, with laws restricting such practice promulgated;
(c) to prevent land from falling into the hands of capitalists, a law to be promulgated which would prevent transaction on the sale of land owned by the peasantry;
(d) laws to be promulgated serving only the interests of the land owners.

The eleventh resolution expressed the fear that the abrogation of the Thathameda and Capitation Taxes would deprive many people of the right to vote and insisted that universal manhood suffrage be introduced. The twelfth resolution established the All Burma Peasants' Organization, to be directed by the Executive Committee composed of representatives of all districts, and elected officers to the temporary Executive Committee.[24] The thirteenth resolution expressed the prayers of the participants for the repose of the soul of Aung Gyaw. The fourteenth resolution demanded exemption from taxation in the Pakkoku District where crops had been destroyed by repeated floods [*Do Thamaing*, II, 1976, 375-79].

The same afternoon a meeting was held at 3:30 p.m. (January 9, 1939) at the Shwedagon pagoda. (For resolutions passed at the meeting see Document 9). At the close of the meeting, the All Burma Trade Union Congress was formed. Its avowed aims were complete independence for the country and the predominance of the proletariat. The following executive members were appointed to office with explicit authority to expand the organization at will:

Thakin Thin (Chauk)
Thakin Po Hla Gyi (Chauk)
Thakin Ba Maung (Yenangyaung)
Thakin Hlaing (Yenangyaung)
Thakin Sein (Yenangyaung)
Thakin Ngwe Shan (Lanywa)
Thakin Hla Myaing (Syriam)
Thakin Hla Thoung (Motor Vehicles, Rangoon)
Thakin Thein Maung (Motor Vehicles, Rangoon)
Thakin Shwe Yin (Lapidiary, Rangoon)
Thakin Ba Thwin (Lapidiary, Rangoon)
Thakin Tin (Thilawa Refinery)
Thakin Chit Maung (Thilawa Refinery)
Thakin Sint Thein (Rangoon Electric Tramways)
Thakin Dagon Saya Tin (Film Industries, Rangoon)

---

24. Thakin Mya was elected president, with the other members being Thakin Khin Aung; Thakin Than Tun; Thakin Aung San; Thakin Hla Baw; Thakin Tin; Thakin Thein Pe; Thakin Soe Min; Thakin Ba Thaw; Thakin Kyaw Lu Gale; Thakin Hla Tun; and Thakin Ba Nyein.

DOCUMENT 9

RESOLUTIONS PASSED AT THE JANUARY 9, 1939 MEETING AT THE SHWEDAGON PAGODA

(1) To demand reinstatement for the oilfield strikers.

(2) To endorse the demands made by the Rangoon Electric Tramways Company employees.

(3) To endorse the demands of the bus drivers.

(4) To endorse the demands of the workers from the Mogok area.

(5) To expose the grievances, and in conjunction with the other trade unions from Europe and India, condemn the capitalists.

(6) To improve the lot of the workers in Burma, the following rights were declared justifiable:

    (a) A minimum salary of Rs. 45;
    (b) Forty-four working hours per week;
    (c) Fifty days' leave on full pay;
    (d) Right to join labor organizations;
    (e) Free participation in politics;
    (f) Workers not to be dismissed without a reason given;
    (g) Provision of airy and spacious accommodations.

[*Do Thamaing*, II, 1976, 379-81.]

Thakin Kyaing (Hackney Carriages, Rangoon)
Thakin Thein Maung (Hackney Carriages, Rangoon)
Thakin Lay (Mandalay)
Thakin Than Pe (Thayetmyo)
Thakin Ba Aye (Allanmyo)
Thakin San Kyaw (Setsan, Rangoon)
Thakin Lwin (Kyaukanyaung, Rangoon)
U Ba Khine (Fabian)
Thakin Thein Maung Gyi (central Dobama)
Thakin Lay Maung (central Dobama)
Thakin Hla Pe (central Dobama)
Thakin Hla Baw (central Dobama)
Thakin Than Tun (central Dobama)
Thakin Soe (central Dobama)
[*Do Thamaing*, II, 1976, 380.]

On the day that the two organizations were formed, the Dobama issued a manifesto known as the *Treatise on Revolution* (Ayaydawbon Sadan) which defined the causes of the prevailing turmoil. The manifesto attributed its main cause to the 1935 Constitution. Recalling the protests and critiques the Dobama had made when this Constitution was introduced, the manifesto claimed that their predictions had come true. Problems of agriculture, illiteracy, suppression of individual freedoms, of the press, of speech, of assembly were all attributed to the Constitution. The rise in the crime rate and unemployment problems in general were, the pamphlet claimed, but a few of the ills that the Constitution had brought in its wake. The manifesto urged all-out efforts to annihilate the horrors that the Constitution represented. The manifesto further exhorted all members of the House of Representatives to resign, thus preventing establishment of a new government, and to form themselves into organizations which would facilitate the leadership of the proletariat and the peasantry. Students, workers, and peasants should unite and help one another. The womenfolk should raise their political consciousness and work hand in hand with the downtrodden masses. In the event of war, the people should not give aid to the British government and should boycott all foreign goods, as a means of undermining colonialism. The final exhortation was for people to join the Dobama and form branch organizations at all levels and send delegates to the mass meeting to be held at the Shwedagon pagoda the next day January 10, 1939.

The meeting which opened at 2 p.m. was attended by over 10,000 delegates from all over the country--workers, peasants, students, monks, and laymen [*Do Thamaing*, II, 1976, 381]. The first resolution passed there called for strong antigovernment measures. It stated:

In order to protest against the existing Constitution and any other which may be given by the British Parliament, the following programmes are to be adopted:

(a) To refuse all posts within the House of Representatives;
(b) All members of the House of Representatives and District Council members to resign immediately;
(c) To boycott all British goods;
(d) To demand all workers in Burma to strike

The central committee of the Dobama was entrusted with the task of implementing this resolution. (For other resolutions passed at this meeting, see Document 10.) The meeting closed at 7 p.m. and was followed one hour later by a strikers' meeting, also at the Shwedagon, with Thakin Lay Maung in the chair. By a unanimous vote, this meeting issued an ultimatum to the authorities, stating that unless their demands were met by January 15, a general strike was inevitable.

The president of the British Chamber of Commerce suggested on January 11 that the Dobama be proscribed. The strikers promptly held a meeting on January 12 to condemn his attitude. As expected, the authorities did not respond to the ultimatum. Therefore on January 16, after weighing all possibilities, the central Executive Committee of the Dobama issued a manifesto for all work to cease throughout the country beginning on January 18, 1939. (See Document 11.)

From the time the oilfield marchers and the peasants arrived at the Shwedagon, local workers from various factories and warehouses had gone on strike, prompting the Dobama headquarters stationed at the Shwedagon to issue a notice on January 12 requiring that from January 15, all those who wished to strike must obtain prior sanction of the Dobama [*Do Thamaing*, II, 1976, 385].

Despite such restrictions, workers from thirty-two factories and business concerns went on strike during the period between January 9 and February 28, 1939. The grievances and problems differed with each individual group, yet the basic demands were almost identical. These demands were for fair wages, better working conditions including reduced working hours, adequate accommodations, ample leave privileges, pensions and gratuities, freedom of speech, of press, right of assembly, and right to join the trade unions.

In the early dawn of January 23, the police raided the headquarters of the Dobama at the Shwedagon [*Do Thamaing*, II, 1976, 389]. At 4 a.m. Mr. Prescott, the deputy commissioner of police, accompanied by three magistrates, U Nyi Peik, U Ba Saing, and U Shwe Tin, and one hundred armed police ransacked the place and confiscated documents and office equipment. The following leaders were arrested: Thakin Hteik Tin Kodaw Gyi, Thakin Aung San, Thakin Than Tun, Thakin Thin, Thakin Ba Tha, Thakin Tun Sein, Thakin Hla Thoung, Thakin U Arsaya, Thakin Aye Kyi, and Thakin Hla Pe. Simultaneously the headquarters at Phayre Street, the residences of Thakin Kodaw Hmine and Thakin Nu were also ransacked. Deedoke U Ba Choe was arrested at his residence in Yegyaw Quarters [*Do Thamaing*, II, 1976, 389].

The raid had the required effect. It prevented the country-wide general strike. However, its side effect was to create a general state of unrest. The main cause of this unrest was not the raid itself, but the manner by which it was conducted. It will be recalled that the strikers and the Dobama headquarters were encamped at the Shwedagon, a place deemed the holiest of sacred places in the entire Buddhist world, a place where the sacred relics of the Lord Buddha were believed to be enshrined in the vault hidden beneath the pagoda. Therefore to walk shod in the precincts was not only sacrilege but it was a hideous crime. To protest this sacrilege performed by the police when they entered the shrine with footwear, the strikers held an emer-

DOCUMENT 10

FURTHER RESOLUTIONS AND MEASURES PASSED AT THE JANUARY 10, 1939 MEETING

(2) In order to establish Komin Kochin Government after the "ousting" of the 1935 Constitution, large scale organizations of workers, peasants, students, Letyone, women and monks were advocated.

(3) Recognition of the demands made by the All Burma Meeting of the workers, peasants, and students as justifiable.

(4) The wars waged by the capitalists are for the expansion of imperialist interests. Therefore, non-participation in war efforts, either monetary or otherwise is stressed. Besides, it was urged that all-out efforts for the immediate cessation of hostilities be made and for the supremacy of the proletariat be striven for.

(5) In order to make known the affairs of Burma to the world at large, a Foreign Affairs Bureau be set up and collection of funds be made to subsidize the said bureau.

(6) The taxes collected are being used, not for the protection of the general public, but to suppress them. The yearly admittance to the prison totalled 70,000, those sentenced to death are 110 and 1,200 are given punitive lashes. These data prove the above accusation to be justifiable.

In order to reduce crimes, the meeting declared that the following measures should be adopted:

(i) Strict prohibition of intoxicants;
(ii) Provision of adequate means for livelihood;
(iii) Provision of a "master" education system (as opposed to the system of a "slave" education).

[*Do Thamaing*, II, 1976, 380-81.]

DOCUMENT 11

MANIFESTO ISSUED BY THE DOBAMA, JANUARY 16, 1939

The oppressive measures of the capitalists and the government representing the capitalists have become unbearable so that we are now forced to wreck the Constitution which is the instrument of oppression. This, we have done with the sanction of the All Burma Emergency Political meeting. We have reached an agreement that four methods be employed in wrecking the Constitution. They are:

- (a) to refuse ministerial posts,
- (b) to resign membership of the House of Representatives,
- (c) to boycott all British goods; and
- (d) to stop all work throughout the country.

Of the four methods, the fourth one is considered the most effective in subduing the capitalists, who are suppressing us, and the government which they represent.

The wealth of the capitalists is dependent upon minerals and mineral oils. The only weapon against the capitalists is the strike. As soon as a strike is staged the government is bound to suppress the strikers by intimidation and by promulgation of Sections 144, 107, 108, and 109.

The authority of the government is enforced through an effective communications system. The road, rail, and river communications all serve the authorities' purpose. To wreck this network of communications and cripple the actions of the government, post and telecommunications, road, rail and river transport must all cease.

We must endeavor to bring all activities to a standstill. A general strike must be launched with a definite date and duration specified.

- (a) All hands from factories such as match, rope, aluminum, oil, timber, and rice mills to cease work.
- (b) All markets and bazaars to suspend sales.
- (c) Workers from capitalist concerns such as BOC, and Steel Brothers to cease work.
- (d) All stevedores to cease work.
- (e) All transport workers, bus, trolley, pony-cart, rickshaws, and trams, to cease functioning.
- (f) Workers from all public communications, such as trams, steamers, post and telegraphs to cease work.
- (g) All government workers to refrain from work.
- (h) All armed forces and police to cease work.
- (i) All electric employees to cease work.
- (j) All cooks and servants to cease work.

The above is our program. We are confident that the imperialist government will cease to function once all workers join our strike.

The actual date for ceasing work shall be notified later. Then at a given signal, all must cease work.

[*Do Thamaing*, II, 1976, 386-87.]

gency meeting at the Shwedagon on January 23, with Sayadaw Ledi U Zadila in the chair [*Do Thamaing*, II, 1976, 389]. Earlier in the day, the strikers had shown their disgust and contempt by abstaining from eating and smoking. The Dobama leaders elected new Executive Committee members to replace those arrested:

>President   -- Thakin Hla Baw
>   (in place of Thakin Hteik Tin Kodaw Gyi);
>Vice President   -- Thakin Lay Maung
>   (in place of Thakin Hla Baw);
>General Secretary -- Thakin Tin Maung
>   (in place of Thakin Aung San);
>   Thakin Mya Thein
>   (in place of Thakin Thin);
>   Thakin Kyaw Thein
>   (in place of Thakin Than Tun);
>   Thakin Ohn Myint
>   (in place of Thakin Tin Maung);
>   Thakin Khin Maung
>   (in place of Thakin Lay Maung).
>[*Do Thamaing*, II, 1976, 391.]

The meeting was opened at 2:30 p.m. by the Dobama Song recital. The Sayadaw in his presidential speech stated that:

>The arrests of the Thakin leaders and the confiscation of documents and office equipment can be considered as a mere routine activity of the police. But to enter the pagoda precincts without removing footwear is a violation of religious freedom and an affront to all Buddhists; therefore it can neither be condoned nor forgotten. Furthermore, to protect religion is not the task of the laity, but it is the sacred duty of the cleric.

The footwear problem escalated anti-imperialist sentiment and drew the monks closer to the strikers. At the meeting, the formation of the Assembly of the Workers on Strike was announced, with Thakin San Ya, the leader of the Dawbon Dockworkers as its president; Thakin Min Maung, leader of the General Electric Company, and Thakin Thoung Shwe, leader of Steel Brothers clerical strike, as secretaries; Thakin Lay Maung as adviser and director; and with Thakin Mya, Thakin Po Hla, Thakin Hla Maung, Thakin Soe, Thakin Ba Tin (Sandoway), and one or more representatives from each group of strikers [*Do Thamaing*, II, 1976, 390].

At the meeting held the following day, eight representatives from the oilfield marchers--Thakins Po Tha, Ngwe Shan, Po Hla Gyi, Toke Gale, Thet, Tun Kyaw, Ba Maung, and Ambrose--were added to the ranks of executive members. Thakin Ambrose was elected joint secretary and Thakin Tin Aung and Thakin Than Pe assigned as secretarial assistants, and Thakin Lay Maung, Thakin Mya, and Thakin Thein Maung were entrusted with the task of negotiating with the employers [*Do Thamaing*, II, 1976, 391]. The "Assembly of the Workers on Strike" was organized into two chambers. Thakin Lay Maung, Thakin

Mya, Thakin Thein Maung, and those whom they chose to nominate as members constituted the upper chamber, and the assembly was to be guided by the Dobama in political matters [*Do Thamaing*, II, 1976, 391]. On January 25 at 3 p.m. the strikers held a mass meeting on the Shwedagon pagoda premises, with Thakin Po Hla Gyi in the chair and Thakin San as the master of ceremonies. To protest the injustices the meeting declared that from January 26 the strikers would observe a fast [*Do Thamaing*, II, 1976, 391].

An emergency meeting of journalists was held at *Myanma Alin* Press on the same day. The editors of *Saithan, Deedok, Tet Khit, Thuria Myanma Alin, New Burma, Toe Tet Yay,* and *Zani* unanimously endorsed the condemnations of the arrests and the defiling of the sacred grounds. The Rangoon Sangha Aphwegyoke conducted another mass meeting on January 26 at 2:30 p.m. at the Shwedagon. Sayadaw Ledi U Zadila took the chair, with the president of the All Burma Thathana Mamaka Aphwegyoke, U Teikkhawuntha as the master of ceremonies. After condemning the authorities for violating the sacred ground and for arresting the Thakin leaders, the meeting demanded repeal of the law which allowed military personnel to wear shoes on the pagoda in time of emergency. By another resolution, the Pagoda Trustee Board was given the task of settling the "shoe question" and should the Board fail to accomplish the given task, some bodies of Buddhist monks would be assigned this responsibility.[25]

One of the political organizations that came into existence during this year of tribulation was the Burma Independent Women's League (Bama Pyi Lut Lat Yay Amyo Thamee Aphwe), also known as the Freedom League. It was formed in Rangoon on January 29, 1939 with the aim of wrecking the Constitution and fighting for freedom by all non-violent means [*Do Thamaing*, II, 1976, 392]. An invitation signed by forty-eight politically minded ladies was sent out, and a mass meeting was held at the Shwedagon pagoda on January 28. The meeting was inaugurated with the Dobama Song sung by Thakinma Ma Khin Hla. With Daw Ant in the chair, Khin Mya (Khin Myo Chit) acted as the master of ceremonies. The meeting adopted resolutions: to wreck the 1935 Constitution; to take action against those who were perpetuating the Constitution; to strive for the formation of the Komin Kochin form of government; to boycott foreign goods; to sacrifice their lives in the interests of race and religion; to make a record of the persecutions against the students; to stand united to defend the organization should the government persecute it; and to move a motion of non-confidence against the coalition government. At the close of the meeting Daw Hla May (wife of Doedok U Ba Choe) was appointed president, Ma Khin Mya (Khin Myo Chit, vice president of the Executive Committee), with representatives of the various wards in Rangoon as members [*Do Thamaing*, II, 1976, 393].

---

25. These were: Thathana Malawithawmana Aphwe, Thathana Mamaka Young Monks Association (Thayettaw Kyaungdaik), United Thayettaw Kyaungdaik Aphwe, Tharrawaddy Monk Association, The Wunthahitakari (West), The Thathana Wunthayekhita (East), Thathana Withutimahawepulla Aphwe, and the Thathana Saung Ahpwe.

On January 24, the five-thousand strong strikers who remained at Chauk held a demonstration in support of the strikers assembled at Rangoon. When the police employed force to disperse the crowd they injured over fifty men and women [*Do Thamaing*, II, 1976, 392]. When news of this incident arrived at the Shwedagon strike camp, the Assembly of Workers on Strike organized a meeting which was held on January 27 at 2 p.m. with Sayadaw Ledi U Zadila as the chairman and Thakin Po Hla Gyi as the master of ceremonies. The meeting vehemently condemned the police violence and urged the Assembly of Workers on Strike to support the strikers, both in money and in kind, should the strike intensify due to police excesses. Then, the audience silently paid tribute to those who had sustained injuries at Chauk by standing to attention while a black flag with skull and crossbones fluttered in the breeze and the band played softly.

On January 30, at Allanmyo a mass demonstration was staged to protest the arrests of Thakin Ba San, leader of the strike camp at Allanmyo [*Do Thamaing*, II, 1976, 394]. Led by Thakin Ba Aye, students and workers clamored for the release of Thakin Ba San. When the procession reached the front of the police station, the police charged into the crowd and arrested nine Thakins and seven other demonstrators. The marchers retaliated against the police batons by throwing stones. The mounted police were also brought in to disperse the crowd. During the melée about sixty were wounded. One demonstrator, Ko Ba Po, was hit by a police officer, and when he retaliated by hitting the officer with a prop which he hastily pulled from under a nearby bullockcart, he was shot. Denied medical attention at the Civil Hospital at Allanmyo he was taken to the Thayetmyo hospital. Having lost much blood during the journey, he succumbed to his wounds, dying soon after he arrived at the Civil Hospital. His body was carried across by boat to Allanmyo, accompanied by a fleet of boats filled with mourners. In midstream, one of the boats collided with the *Ananda*, a steamer owned by the Irrawaddy Flotilla Company, and capsized, drowning eleven of the mourners. The body of Ko Ba Po was cremated and his ashes are enshrined near the Kuthinayon pagoda. The tomb now bears the legend "The Martyr of the Thirteen Hundredth Year Ko Ba Po" [*Do Thamaing*, II, 1976, 396].

At this time, students of the university, colleges, and schools all over the country were on strike. From the day of the Secretariat incident the student strikers in Rangoon had encamped at Myoma High School. Because the strike occurred over the Christmas holidays, the school authorities gave the students a free rein for some time. However, when the holiday period came to a close, the Department of Public Instructions issued orders that all schools must reopen by the second or third of January 1939 [*Do Thamaing Ahtauk*, 1965, 70].

On January 2, 1939, at 1 p.m., while the student strikers were holding a meeting at the Municipal School at Pazundaung, Rangoon, police officers called Ko Hla Shwe away from the meeting and arrested him. Ko Thein Aung took his place and conducted the meeting as scheduled, but otherwise student activities came almost to a standstill.

On January 19, a mass meeting of parents was held at the Myoma High School. Attended by over one thousand people from all walks of life, the meeting passed four resolutions.

(1) That the parents considered student action protesting against the government suppression to be laudable.
(2) The student protest was justified, and the meeting pledged to give all possible help to them.
(3) Until the demands made by the students were met on no account would the children be sent to school.
(4) The meeting condemned the brutal action of the coalition government and the British government in causing death and injury to the students.

The "Dictator" (Hla Shwe) issued two "orders" for the currency office to be picketed and for a hunger strike to be staged. When put up to the Executive Committee, the majority sided with Ko Thein Aung in considering these steps to be too drastic and too dangerous. Instead, they called a meeting of the students' council at 10 a.m. on January 30. Held at the Myoma Assembly Hall, it passed a number of resolutions [*Do Thamaing Ahtauk*, 1965, 71]:

(1) To demand the release of all people arrested for activities involved with the oilfield marchers, and withdrawal of all restrictive laws.
(2) To secure immunity for those students and teachers involved with the student strike.
(3) To demand formation of a Board of Enquiry, comprising members representative of the general public to examine the Secretariat incident.
(4) To make the above demands known to the entire nation.
(5) To stage protest demonstrations throughout the country.
(6) To make known the approval of the students to adopt the following methods to wreck the Constitution of 1935:

   (a) To cause the downfall of the coalition government.
   (b) To refrain from accepting posts after causing the downfall of the coalition government, and continue to wreck the Constitution.
   (c) To patronize homespun cloth.
   (d) To refrain from using British goods except when absolutely necessary.

While the council meeting was in progress, Ko Hla Shwe was released on bail, and arrived to insist upon the picketing and a hunger strike [*Do Thamaing Ahtauk*, 1965, 72]. Ko Thein Aung who from the start had objected to these proposals as too drastic, and had feared that they might result in a wholesale massacre, remained adamant in his refusal to consider them. Thereupon, Ko Hla Shwe threatened to return to jail. Therefore, after consultation with the Executive Committee members, the council agreed to stage a hunger strike.

Thus, on February 7, 1939, all the student strikers from Rangoon who were not camping at the Myoma strike camp were summoned, and a mass hunger strike was staged. They did this to show their contempt for the governmental authorities who were treating the student issue with calculated indifference. On the eve of the hunger strike Thakin Thein Maung headed a delegation from the Assembly of Workers on Strike to meet Dr. Ba Maw, Dr. Thein Maung, and U Ba Win at the residence of the premier in Park Lane. Thakin Thein Maung informed the premier that, due to the increased tempo of anti-government sentiment among the people, members of the House of Representatives would be compelled to move a motion of no confidence against the coalition government should the situation remain unchanged. He also pointed out that the students had decided to go on hunger strike, and the only remedy to prevent the fall of the coalition government was to meet students' and strikers' demands. Thakin Thein Maung further urged the premier to go against the wishes of the governor by issuing orders to settle the student strike through negotiations.

On the second day of the hunger strike, the parents met at the Shwedagon pagoda. They endorsed the students' demands and pledged to assist them. A committee of the thirty-eight was formed for the implementation of the above aim. However a similar meeting, held by the members of the Dobama at the Shwedagon on February 8 decided to urge the students to call off the strike, and they persuaded the students to abandon their hunger strike on the evening of February 8 [*Do Thamaing*, II, 1976, 398].

Probably as a measure to prevent the hunger strike from spreading throughout the country, the authorities at Mandalay arrested three student leaders and two monks at dawn on February 8. The student leaders arrested were Ko Chan Tun of the Central National High School, Ko Kyi of Paukmyaing monastic school, and Ko Ko Lay of High School. The monks arrested were members of the Young Monks Association, U Awbatha and U Thumana of Nan Oo Taik [*Do Thamaing*, II, 1976, 399]. Prior to the arrests, the newspapers had carried a blank form headed "Notification No. 36 of the All Burma Student Union." Presumably the authorities took the blank as a sign of subversive activities to be perpetrated by the students and they made the arrests as a preventive measure.

However, this action was to prove fatal. The arrest of the monks and student leaders so infuriated the people in Mandalay who had thus far remained apathetic, that a mass rally protesting the governmental action was called for the next day.

The President of the Young Monks' Association, U Kalayana, acted as the chairman and U Tun Maung, a school master from the Central National High School, served as the master of ceremonies at the mass meeting in the Eindawya at 1 p.m. on February 9. The meeting passed a number of resolutions protesting the wearing of footwear in the pagoda and supporting the students' demands. It also called for a boycott of foreign goods. (For the resolutions passed at this meeting, see Document 12.) As it was then getting late, the demonstration was postponed until 11 a.m. on the following day [*Do Thamaing*, II, 1976, 401].

At that hour, monks, students, bazaar sellers, and the people of Mandalay, together with those from the nearby towns of Madaya, Kyaukse, Amarapura, and Sagaing assembled at the Eindawya. At 1 p.m. under the direction of U Kalayana, Saya U Tun Maung announced the commencement of the demonstration and advised the marchers to observe strict discipline.

The young monks bearing the tricolor flags led the crowd in an orderly procession [Maung Maung 1969, 57]. At about 2 p.m. as they

DOCUMENT 12

RESOLUTIONS OF THE FEBRUARY 9, 1939 MEETING

1. (a) The wearing of footwear on sacred ground is distressing to the minds of all Burman Buddhists, and it is urged that a law forbidding footwear in the pagoda precincts be promulgated by the authorities. The proposal was made by U Kumara, a member of the Young Monks' Association, and seconded by U Maydaka of Khinmakan and was unanimously endorsed.

   (b) At dawn on February 8 when arresting U Thumana, C.I.D. Inspector David entered the Sankyaung Taik without removing his shoes. It is demanded that strict disciplinary action be taken against him. It was proposed by U Nyaneindawbatha (the Iron Fist) and was seconded by U Kumara.

2. (a) The city-wide meeting in support of the All Burma Student Assembly demands that a Board of Enquiry Commission be formed without delay to enquire into the death of Ko Aung Gyaw and the injury sustained by over two hundred students on December 20 at Rangoon.

   (b) The meeting approves of the demands made by the All Burma Student Assembly.

   (c) The meeting agrees that the above demands be fully explained and printed by the district (student) unions and distributed throughout the country.

3. To march in procession at the end of the meeting.

4. The meeting without any reserve affirms that the present Constitution not only fails to serve the interests of the peasants, workers, and the proletariat, but promotes dissension among the people.

   (a) To strive for the collapse of the coalition government. The resignation of its cabinet, or to cause its downfall through a no-confidence vote.

5. Since the occupation of the country by the British government, all industries and homecrafts have suffered neglect and become a lost art. All people in Burma are now dependent upon imported goods and the nation's wealth has flowed into foreign lands. To remedy this unequal balance of trade, all Burmans are (i) to patronize Burmese owned shops, (ii) to patronize home made goods, (iii) students are to promote a country-wide boycott of foreign made luxury goods.

   The meeting agrees to entrust the task of determining what goods are to be classified as luxury goods to the executive committee of ABSU.

6. For effective implementation of the above aims, the meeting entrusted the executive committee of RUSU and ABSU with full authority.

[*Mandalay Ayaydawbon*, 1939, 12-13.]

reached 26th Street, they were confronted by Mr. H. N. Lett, deputy commissioner, and Mr. C. H. Raynes, the district superintendent of police, who ordered them to disperse [*Do Thamaing*, II, 1976, 401]. The monks remained in their positions to await further orders from their leader, U Kalayana, who at that moment, was still at Eindawya advising the remaining demonstrators to march in an orderly manner. C.I.D. police officer Mr. David repeated the order to disperse three times. After that the squad fired at the demonstrators. Six monks from the vanguard fell on the spot, but the two standard-bearing monks in the center kept their flags aloft. The army then arrested seven monks. During the ensuing melée thirteen of the demonstrators were wounded and seventeen were killed. The seventeen who died were: U Pandita, U Pyinnyazawta, U Wepulla, U Zanita, U Arlawka, U Kelatha, U Ketu, Bo Ba Htay, Bo Hla Maung, Bo Tin Aung, Bo Mu, Bo Tun Aung, Bo Aung Htoo, Bo Khin Maung, Bo Tun Ei, Bo Ba Tun, and Bo Khin Maung (alias) Shwe Yoe. Among them, Bo Tin Aung, was a mere boy of thirteen. Seven monks were among the dead and four among the wounded [*Mandalay Ayaydawbon*, 1939, 18-19].

The next day, the police arrested the president of the Young Monks Association, U Kalayana, and the student leaders Ko Maung Ko and Ko Aung Kyaw. The following day they were tried, together with four students and two monks, and four of them were sentenced to a year's imprisonment while U Kalayana and Ko Aung Kyaw were sentenced to two months each [*Do Thamaing*, II, 1976, 403].

An impressive funeral was given to the martyrs massacred on February 10, sixteen of whom were then entombed at Thagywezu on February 17 [*Mandalay Ayaydawbon*, 1939, 42-47]. Maung Khin Maung, who died a week later was also buried there on February 27, 1939 [*Mandalay Ayaydawbon*, 1939, 55]. The most outstanding feature of the funeral arrangements was the draping of the coffins with the peacock flags and the tricolor Dobama standards. The flags were placed across one another, the peacock flag placed vertically over the coffin and the tricolor draped over it [*Mandalay Ayaydawbon*, 1939, 45]. Hteik Tin Kodaw Gyi, the president of the Dobama, was among the distinguished individuals attending the funeral and delivering addresses. Other Thakins who came from Rangoon were Thakin Thein Han, Thakin Hla Baw, Thakin San Mya, Thakin Myat Tun, Thakin Tin U, and Thakin Ba Kun [*Mandalay Ayaydawbon*, 1939, 44]. U Kumara read the speech on behalf of U Kalayana while Ko Maung Ko, leader of the Mandalay Student Union, and Ko Thein Aung of ABSU gave speeches [*Mandalay Ayaydawbon*, 1939, 48-54]. Just as the death of the student leader Ko Aung Gyaw had caused a great furor, the deaths of these seventeen martyrs rocked the country and shook the coalition government to its foundations.

On February 12, an unprecedented mass demonstration took place in Rangoon. The marchers, walking four abreast, stretched for two miles. The demonstration was preceded by a mass rally at the Shwedagon where the following resolutions were passed:

1. The meeting applauded those who had given up their lives and those injured during the February 10 demonstration at Mandalay and proposed a two-minute silence as a mark of respect to them.

2. If the authorities failed to comply with the demands made by the students before nightfall, (a) All students from Government and Government-aided schools were to withdraw themselves, (b) All school teachers were to resign, (c) Private Anglo-Vernacular and Vernacular schools were to be set up without delay, (d) For the implementation of the above aims the Independent Women's League was to take full responsibility.
3. All possible aid was to be given to the students in their future struggle and if needs be to give up their lives for the student cause. [*Do Thamaing*, II, 1976, 404.]

The Dobama seized the opportunity to turn the fury of the embittered people against the coalition government. It was a fortunate coincidence for them that the parliamentary session was scheduled to be held on February 16. They planned a multiphase demonstration.

1. All houses were to fly black flags commencing from 9 a.m.
2. Tin cans were to be beaten from 9 a.m. to 10 a.m. as a means of exorcising the coalition government.
3. While beating the tin cans people were to shout in unison "Down with the coalition government."
4. At 11 a.m. sham coffins marked as the coalition government or the effigies of the coalition cabinet members were to be burnt.
5. All shops and all public vehicles were to stop their normal course of work till the fall of the coalition government.
6. After the final exorcising (No. 4) all activities (other than No. 5) were to resume as usual. [*Do Thamaing*, II, 1976, 406.]

The Thakins claimed that the embittered people followed their instructions throughout the country. When the motion of no-confidence was moved in the House of the Representatives, on February 16, 1939, the coalition government fell, with 70 supporting the motion, 37 protesting and 11 abstaining [*Do Thamaing*, II, 1976, 407].

The next step of the Dobama was to prevent formation of a new government. A mass rally was held at Rangoon on February 20 at the City Hall, with Thakin So in the chair and U Khin Maung, the secretary of the Kemmendine Bazaar Association, as the master of ceremonies. The object of the meeting was to protest the Constitution and urge that no members of the House of Representatives accept office. On February 21 the central committee of the Dobama issued a directive to all district organizations that they

(a) hold mass rallies, public demonstrations, and announce non-acceptance of office;
(b) condemn those who accept office; and
(c) that the respective constituents refrain from supporting those who accept office and focus their attention on those who plan to form a new cabinet. [*Do Thamaing*, II, 1976, 408.]

Despite their protests and endeavors, however, U Pu formed a government. The U Pu government's first successful achievement was to break the student strike. On the night of February 26, the president of ABSU, Ko Hla Shwe, met with U Pu at the residence of U Thwin and reached an agreement that the students would call off the strike and that the authorities would form an enquiry commission to investigate the Secretariat incident. The government agreed that no action would be taken against the student leaders and the oilfield strike marchers. The date for the examination of the University and High Schools was set for three months from when the strike was called off [Do Thamaing, II, 1976, 409]. The announcement appeared in the newspapers the following day, greatly surprising the entire nation.

The most shocked and infuriated of the strikers encamped at Shwedagon and the student strikers at Myoma High School was the student leader Ko Than Tin who had accompanied Ko Hla Shwe to the negotiation talks with U Pu. Two days later, at the Myoma strike camp meeting held on February 28 at noon, he admitted having fallen asleep during the talks. He rallied students to shift their camp to the Shwedagon pagoda.[26]

As a counter measure, ABSU held an emergency Executive Committee meeting on the same day, February 27, and issued a statement dismissing Ko Than Tin from the Executive Committee and denying all responsibility for his actions. There was an immediate attempt at reconciliation with the student leaders. A parents' meeting was held which entrusted the liaison task to Myoma Saya Hein, Tetkatho Hsu Myaing (Dagon Taya) Daw Mya May, and Daw Khin Hla. This group succeeded in bringing about an understanding. In the presence of Thakin Ba Gyan of Minbu, at the residence of Daw Mya May, the president of the Independent Women's League, Ko Than Tin pledged to abide by the decisions of the student council and Ko Hla Shwe rescinded the dismissal notice served on him.

On March 8 the student council held a meeting at the RUSU building attended by over one hundred student delegates. With Ko Ba Hein in the chair, and Ko Ba Swe as the master of ceremonies, the meeting opened with the Dobama Song. In his presidential speech, Ko Ba Hein stressed the importance of preventing the establishment of a rival student organization. When Ko Hla Shwe moved and Ko Thein Aung seconded a resolution reaffirming the end of strike, Ko Than Tin objected, and his objection was seconded by Ko Maung Maung Hla and Ko Ye Myint. Ko Than Tin explained that he objected to calling off the

---

26. Those who supported him were students from Cushing High School, led by Ko Aye Kywe, Ko Kyi Lwin, Ko Tin Hla, Ko Aye Maung, Ko Chit, and Ko Kyi Lin; St. John students led by Ko Thaung Sein, Ko Nyi Lay, and Ko Hla Aung; Methodist students led by Ko Thaung Sein and Ko Hla Kyi; Lanmadaw Municipal students led by Ko Hla Nyunt, and Ko Tin Aye; students from the Pazundaung Teachers' Training Municipal School; students from U Nyi Pu Kemmendine Teachers' Training School led by Ko Shwe; and students from U Po Ain Municipal School [Do Thamaing, II, 1976, 410].

strike out of sympathy for the peasants and workers. He further clarified his claim by saying that:

> We have stood in their vanguard and to abandon them now would be sheer cruelty. Besides, our demand for the withdrawal of the Constitution is still unheeded, and the restrictions over individual liberty still prevail. It is true that the examinations are soon to be held, but we have not gone on strike for educational gains. We had plunged ourselves into politics. If it had been suggested that the strike be called off at Ko Aung Gyaw's death, I would not have objected, but now seventeen more have lost their lives and to call off the strike now is sheer folly.

With 87 for, 27 against, and 2 abstaining, the proposal for calling off the strike was finally confirmed [*Do Thamaing*, II, 1976, 411]. Thus the student strike which had begun on January 8, 1939 over the arrest of the two student leaders, Ko Ba Hein and Ko Ba Swe, came to an abrupt end exactly two months later.

The student support had greatly enhanced the popularity of the strikers. Students are not a class by themselves. As they are the sons and daughters of the nation, their entry into the strike automatically brought closer contact between the strikers and the populace. The fall of the Ba Maw cabinet had been the direct result of the massacre at Mandalay, and the massacre had its roots in the arrests of the students. Therefore, although the period of the students' strike was short, it had an immense effect upon the political scene.

The manner in which Ko Hla Shwe conducted himself in reaching the agreement to call off the strike calls for strong censure. He seems to have been carried away by his popularity. In this extremely important action, the decision should not have been his alone. The outcome of the votes taken at the student council on March 8 does indicate that he might have had majority support had he but asked for a vote. Yet this cannot be safely assumed, for the two situations differ a great deal. The decision made at the student council was whether or not to confirm the resolution already made. That vote was not taken to decide whether or not to call off the strike. The withdrawal of the students from the strike camp greatly weakened the entire movement. One last stand was to be made before the strikers' anger petered out and they returned home, a sad, dejected, and depressed band of stragglers, a far cry from the glorious marchers who had entered Rangoon on January 8.

On March 12 Thakin Po Hla Gyi and about one hundred strikers left the Shwedagon pagoda on the pretense of going to pay homage at the Botahtaung pagoda. After spending the night at the pagoda near the docks, they began at dawn to picket the entrance of the Dunnedaw BOC and IBP (oil conservatories) petrol dumps. Simultaneously, about one hundred strikers led by Thakin Hla Kywe, and another hundred led by Ko Ba Ba picketed the Rangoon Electric Tramways bus and trolley godowns respectively, while the tram godowns at Kyaukmyaung, and the Adamjee Match Factory at Pathein-nyunt were also picketed [*Do Thamaing*, II, 1976, 423]. At about 7 a.m. the picketers were rounded up and taken to the Barr Street lock-up. The city's transport was crippled for one day, but it resumed the next day. The sight of the buses so infuriated the people that many men and women joined in with the strikers in picketing and blockading the routes taken by the RET vehicles. This picketing continued till March 16, when the picketers allowed themselves to be carried away to prison shouting: "Master race we are, we Burmans! Mother gave us life! Prison will give us rice!" They were detained for about a month, and when they were set free, the authorities provided the marchers with rail transport back to the oilfield [*Do Thamaing*, II, 1976, 424].

On April 27, the Adamjee Match Factory was once again picketed by fifty women under leadership of Thakin Thein Maung. The following day, Thakin Ohn Khin, leader of the Steel Brothers' clerical strike, staged a week's hunger strike, stationing himself at the entrance of the Adamjee Match Factory. Meanwhile, most oilfield strikers had returned home at government expense. On May 5, 144 oilfield marchers, led by Thakin Ba Tin and U Damma, returned home by train, in carriages specially reserved for them. They were each given Rs. 6 and 12 annas for the fare and Rs. 3 for other expenses. Po Hla Gyi, who had earlier been sent home, returned to Rangoon on April 29 and for a while staged a one-man silent protest. All communications with him had to be made in writing [*Do Thamaing*, II, 1976, 420].

On May 10, about 200 strikers conferred and decided to refuse traveling aid from the government and returned home on foot. Their planned itinerary was to walk along the rail track to Pegu, from thence to Meiktila, Kyaukpadaung, and back to the oilfield area. Four guides were elected to act under the direct supervision of Thakin Po Hla Gyi. They left the Shwedagon strike camp and, stopping at Ngadatkyi, Shwephonebwint, and Botahtaung pagodas to pay homage, they finally reached Kodatkyi on June 1 [*Do Thamaing*, II, 1976, 427]. Two days later, they held a mass meeting. After receiving a final blessing from the town elders and performing burial rites they pledged to go on a hunger strike to the death if their demands were not met. They demanded that the government appoint a board of negotiators for the peaceful settlement of the dispute between the strikers and the oil companies; that the oil companies give a written guarantee that, from the date the companies accepted arbitration, all strikers would be reinstated in their old posts; and that the general public permit their death, as they would certainly die should their demands be denied [*Yenan tat tha Athuba*, 1939]. The threat was not carried out. Thakin Po Hla Gyi who had donned the robe during his brief sojourn at the Kodatkyi, shed his robes on June 17 and gave a farewell speech. The same evening he and his followers left for the oilfield by boat. The workers' council and the rest of the strikers also faded away and thus the famous oilfield strike came to an inglorious end sometime in July [*Do Thamaing*, II, 1976, 428].

CONCLUSION

All the events that took place during the Year of Strife were of colossal dimensions. Within its short span there occurred a countrywide upheaval caused by the oilfield strike, student unrest, racial riots, and the split within the ranks of the Dobama itself. Of these events, the split in the Dobama is the most significant. Its repercussions upon the country are still being felt today, more than four decades after the event.

Although the first signs of disintegration were discernible at the Prome Conference held on March 22, 23, and 24, 1938, it reached its irrevocable and unredeemable final stage when the Panswe Conference was held exclusively by the Ba Sein faction on November 23 and 24 of the same year. The ineffectiveness of the reconciliatory efforts had been apparent since the meeting of the All Burma Executive Committee held at the Moulmein Zayat on the Shwedagon pagoda on July 3, 1938.

The cause of the split stemmed from both personal incompatibility and differences in political outlook. The spirit of unity which prevailed among the Thakins even during the so-called "period of unity" had been superficial, the temporary result of confronting a common enemy. Beyond their shared aim of complete independence for Burma, there was little evidence of any single-mindedness among them. Because their ideology was fluid and its interpretation flexible, for some time the differences in their outlook were not perceptible. Only when a policy was defined did these differences become pronounced. Yet personal incompatibility rather than ideological divergence was most responsible for the wide rift, which after several abortive attempts at reconciliation, culminated in so irrevocable a split that neither the national crisis of the countrywide strike staged by workers and students, nor the advent of the war itself could completely bridge the cleavage.

As already stated, the predominant factor which contributed to the split was personal incompatibility. The charismatic nature of Burmese politics is well expressed in an old Burmese adage that "a sermon is acceptable when preached by someone dear." The split within the ranks of the Dobama clearly conforms to this adage. The very nomenclature by which each faction came to be known following the split, and the accusations and counter-accusations they leveled at each other bespeak its charismatic nature.

Long afterwards, when contesting for a seat in the Lower House on a democratic ticket from Tharrawaddy District in 1960, Thakin Ba Sein was to claim on the title page of his propaganda brochure that he had championed the cause of "steering Burmese politics from left to right and from wrong to right" [Ba Sein 1960]. In explaining the reason for the split then, he recalled that it was a difference in ideology that had caused the rift. In his brochure he wrote:

> The Thein Maung faction harbored such elements as Thakin Soe, Thakin Than Tun, and Thakin Nu who were strong adherents of Socialism. On the other hand [he] Thakin Ba Sein did not accept such ideologies but employed a few tactics which were instrumental in his fight against the British.

This, however, was not correct. In a conference it held on April 20, 1940 at Pyapon the Ba Sein faction resolved that its ideology was socialism [Ba Sein 1943].

Thakin Nyi of the Ba Sein faction gave a more lucid explanation of the split. He said that Fabians headed by Dedok U Ba Cho tried, through Ko Nu (Thakin Nu), to merge Fabians and Thakins. This overture failed as Thakin Lay Maung, Thakin Ba Sein, Thakin Tun Ok, and Shin Ariya turned down the Fabian suggestion that the Thakins relinquish their cherished affix, change the name of Dobama Asiayone, and boycott Japanese goods. (A Chinese businessman who accompanied Deedok U Ba Cho, had promised a large sum of money if the Thakins agreed to boycott Japanese goods.) Thakin Nyi further observed that the newcomers--the university students who had joined in 1936--with a smattering of knowledge of leftism claimed to be socialists, denouncing the current Thakins as fascists and alleging that the Dobama Song itself was imbued with imperialism. They then added "This is Our Land," "This is Our Country," as an embodiment of nationalism and suggested that such usages be abandoned [Nyi 1939]. Nyi then added:

> Just as the Lord Buddha had warned that "My religion would be destroyed by my own followers," aware that only its members could destroy the Dobama, stooges of U Saw, Fabians, and writers, were placed within the ranks; thus disharmony ensued among the colleagues who had faced poverty, and persecution selflessly. [Nyi 1939.]

Thakin Nyi claimed that the acceptance of these "stooges" into the party, without the probationary membership advocated by the Thakin Ba Sein faction, was the primary cause of the disunity.

Its secondary cause, according to Thakin Nyi, stemmed from the salary question; that is whether or not the Komin Kochin members in the House of Representatives should accept a monthly salary of Rs. 250. The Thein Maung faction favored acceptance of a salary, while the Ba Sein faction objected to it on the grounds that the Draft Act which sanctioned the disbursement of salaries to the members of the House of Representatives was aimed at perpetuating the new Constitution. It will be recalled that the Prome Conference unanimously passed a resolution to adopt the principle of non-acceptance of salary. Accepting the salary, therefore was considered a flagrant violation of the principle laid down by the highest authority of the party itself [Nyi 1939].

On the other hand, the Thein Maung faction attributed the cause of the split to a difference in outlook between "a group of educated personnel who possess wide knowledge and faresightedness and an uneducated group who lacked foresight" [Thein Maung 1938b].

Despite these contentions from participants on both sides we still maintain that, judging from the available documents, it was the personal incompatibility between the two leaders, Thakin Thein Maung and Thakin Ba Sein, that was the chief cause of the split. When certain motives and activities of Thakin Ba Sein became intolerable to Thakin Thein Maung in his capacity as president of the central Dobama, he dismissed Thakin Ba Sein and another executive member, Thakin Kyaw Yin, without consulting other executive members. This dismissal of Thakin Ba Sein and Thakin Kyaw Yin was the immediate cause of the split.

It is sheer irony that the last gathering of the Thakin body should have taken place at the sacred grounds of the holy Shwedagon pagoda, where one evening in July eight years earlier they made their first public appearance with the recital of the Dobama Song. It is still more ironical that, in response to public entreaties, the Dobama Song was sung twice on July 22, 1930, and that on July 3, 1938 it was again sung twice, although this time for no apparent reason. Although later attempts were made at a rapprochement, the destiny of the split was sealed during that meeting. There is no record to show that Thein Maung faction was aware then or now of the violent preparations made then by the Ba Sein faction (see above p. 90). The incident has been mentioned in this study only to show the intensity of the feelings of hostility, with the hope that this may, to some extent, explain why attempts at rapprochement failed.

How far the accusations and counter-accusations were correct, and how far they were imaginary is also not possible to ascertain. No concrete evidence is available either to confirm or deny them. A careful study of the evidence, however, showed that neither faction disproved or denied the charges leveled against it. Therefore, if their silence is to be considered as tacit confirmation, it appears that both parties were guilty--Ba Sein for his weaknesses and Thein Maung for his high-handedness.

With the exception of the charge against Ba Sein that he divulged the contents of the Constitution to the premier and home minister, and that his attitude was partial in securing release of the Thakins imprisoned in various jails, all other accusations leveled against him were of a personal nature. Nevertheless they touched upon his integrity as a leader so that, unless they were refuted, they remained serious. Thein Maung should have given Ba Sein a chance to explain his position before initiating drastic measures against him.

The accusations levelled against Thein Maung boiled down to two--first, his close association with such personalities as Thakins Aung San, Nu, Hla Pe (Calcutta), Deedok U Ba Cho, and Fabian U Ba Khine, and, second, his tacit approval of Thakin Hla Tin's acceptance of a salary given by the government. The salary problem was rather hard to explain. With respect to the first charge, time has proved that the influx of "new blood" provided the Burmese political scene with some illustrious figures. The most outstanding of these are Thakin Aung San and Thakin Nu. The former as Bogyoke Aung San became a father symbol, respected and revered by the entire nation, and Thakin Nu became the first premier of independent Burma.

However, blinded by emotion and enmity, the Thakins chose to part company rather than strive to reunify their movement. Thus a chapter of a united effort among the Thakins came to an inglorious close in the eighth year of the Dobama's existence. And the chasm still remained unclosed more than forty years later.

BIBLIOGRAPHY OF REFERENCES ABBREVIATED IN TEXT

Aung Myin--Aung Myin Gyaung Thadinza [The Success Daily].

Ba Hein 1938--Ba Hein, *Kyaung Tha Mya Ayaydawbon* [Students' Movement], Rangoon, Nagani Sar Ok Taik, 1938.

Baho Akhun Htan 1965--*Baho Akhun Htan Ahpwe Thamaing* [History of the Tax and Rate Payers' Central Association], Rangoon, Rangoon Siyinzu Dobama Asiayone Thamaing Pyuzuye Ahpwe, 1965.

Ba Khine 1964--Ba Khine, Fabian, *Myanma Pyi Naingngan Ye Yazawin* [The Political History of Burma], Rangoon, Pagan Sar Ok Taik, 1964. (Reprint.)

Ba Maung 1975--Ba Maung, Thakin, *Wanthanu Ayaydawbon Thamaing 1906-36* [History of the Nationalist Movement in Burma, 1906-36], Rangoon, Ta Thet Tar Sarpe, 1975.

Ba Sein 1943--Ba Sein, Thakin, *Thakin Mya Lut Lat Ye Kyo Pan Hmu* [Thakins' Struggle for Independence], Rangoon, Taing Pyi Pyu Ponhneik Taik, 1943.

Ba Sein 1960--Ba Sein, Thakin, *Ba Sein, Aung San, Nu, Than Tun, Soe Do Hnint Bama Naingngan Yay Dwin Myi Tho Thabaw Kwe Lwe Hke Tha Nee* [Antagonism between Ba Sein and Aung San, Nu, Than Tun and Soe in Burmese Politics], Rangoon, Bama Ponhneik, Taik, 1960.

Ba Thoung 1940--Ba Thoung, Thakin, *Yenan* [Oil], Rangoon, Hpyant Chi Yay Ponhneik Taik, 1940.

Ba Tin 1964--Ba Tin, Thakin, *Htaung Thon Ya Pyi Ayaydawbon Hmat Tan* [The Record of the Thirteen Hundredth Year (1938) Strife], Rangoon, Myawadi Ponhneik Taik, 1964.

Bilu 1938--*Bilu The Kya Shay Lu Yaung Ma Hsaung Naing* [An Ogre could not assume the Guise of Man for Long], 1938.

BLP/FHR, 1937--*Burma Legislative Proceedings of the First House of Representatives*, I, i-ii, 1937.

Chauk Alok Thama Kyay Nyar Gyet II, 1938--*Chauk Myo Bama Pyi Yenan Myay Dobama Alok Thama Asiayone Hma Htok Pyan Kyay Nyar Gyet Amat II* [Declaration II of Labor Organization, Chauk, Oil Field, Burma], Yanangyaung, Baho Mandaing, 1938.

CM 7 1935--*Criminal Miscellaneous Case No. 7 of 1935*, Office of the Subdivisional Magistrate, Yenangyaung, 28 March 1935.

CM 8 1938--*Criminal Miscellaneous Trial No. 8 of 1938*, Office of the First Magistrate, Chauk, 1 April 1938.

Dagon Taya 1967--Dagon Taya, *Dagon Taya Thu ei Kabya* [An Autobiography with an Appreciation of his own Poems], Rangoon, Pagan Sar Ok Taik, 1967.

Daung Hpatsar Thit III 1924--*Daung Dazeik Myanma Hpatsar Thit* III [The Peacock Brand New Burmese Reader III], Rangoon, British Burma Ponhneik Taik, 1924.

Desai 1959--Desai, W. S., "Review of Cady: *Modern Burma*," *Indian Quarterly*, Vol. 15, No. 4, 1959.

Do Nyi Largan 1939--*Dobama Asiayone Pye Nyi Largan E Khan Aphwe Hnok Hset*, Rangoon, Dobama Ponhneik Yaik, ?1939.

Do Pyandan III [Dobama Bulletin], 1938.

Do Thamaing 1976--*Dobama Asiayone Thamaing I & II* [History of the Dobama Asiayone I & II], Rangoon, Sarpe Beikman, 1976.

Do Thamaing Ahtauk 1965--*Dobama Asiayone Thamaing Pyuzuye Ahtauk Ahta Pyu Sadan* [Source Material of the History of the Dobama Asiayone], Rangoon, Rangoon Siyinzu Hsaing Ya Dobama Asiayone Thamaing Pyuzuye Aphwe, 1965.

Do Sadan 1933--*Dobama Thadinzin Hmattan* [The Dobama News Weekly], I, i-xii, January 21, 1933-April 22, 1933.

EDB 1956--*The Economic Development of Burma*, Rangoon, Rangoon University Economics Department, 1956.

FRRIC 1939--*Final Report of the Riot Inquiry Committee*, Rangoon Government Publications, 1939.

Hla Shwe 1939--Hla Shwe, *Amha Daw Bon, Kyaung Tha Thabeik Hlan 8 Mat 1939* [Hla Shwe's Mistake in Calling Off the Students' Strike, March 8, 1939], Rangoon, Ye Ye Tauk Than Tin Gaing, 1939.

IRRIC 1939--*Interim Report of the Riot Inquiry Committee*, Rangoon, Government Publications, 1939.

Gyane Gyaw Ma Ma Lay 1953--Journal Gyaw Ma Ma Lay, *Thu Lo Lu* [There was No One Like Him--Biography of her Former Husband], Rangoon, Lawki Ponhneik Taik, 1953.

Khin Zaw 1965--Khin Zaw, Thakin, *Pyi Thu Lok Tha Kyaymon* [A Mirror of the Labor Movement in Burma], Rangoon, Sarpe Beikman, 1965.

Komin Kochin I, 1936--*Komin Kochin Sardan Amhat I* [Manifesto No. 1 of the Komin Kochin Party, ?1936], Myingyan, Mingala Yaung Shein Ponhneik Taik, 1936.

Komin Sarzu I, 1936--*Komin Kochin Te Daung Mhu Sarzu Amhat I (Dodika)* [Collection of Records No. 1 on the Komin Kochin Party Establishment: About Ourselves, 1936], Rangoon, Bama Art Ponhneik Taik, 1936.

Mandalay Ayaydawbon 1939--*Mandalay Ayaydawbon Nepyidaw Lut Lat Yay* [Mandalay Incident--National Independence Movement at the Former King's Capital], Mandalay, Mandalay Thuriya Thadinza Ponhneik Taik, 1939.

Maung Maung 1969--Maung Maung, Dr., *Burma and General Ne Win*, Bombay, Asia Publishing House, 1969.

Maung Thuta, "Sayagyi Thakin Kodaw Hmine," 1971--Maung Thuta (Bomhu Ba Thaung), *Sar Hso Daw Mya Ahtokpatti* [Biography of the Writers], Rangoon, Zwe Sarpe, 1971.

Myanma Alin Ne Sin Thadinza [The New Light of Burma Daily].

Myanma Lu Nge Kyway Kyaw Than 1938--*Myanma Naingngan Lon Saing Ya Lu Nge Mya Athin Gyi Tet Lu Do ie Kyway Kyaw Than I Htoke Pyan Kyay Nyar Gyet Sadan Amhat I* [Declaration No. I of All Burma Youth League Organ], Rangoon, Myanma Zeya Ponhneik Taik, 1938.

Nyi 1939--Nyi, Thakin, *Thakin Ayaydawbon Thakin Yaung Thakin War Mya Hnint Thakin Masit Thakin Mahnit Do ie Taik Pwe Sadan* [Factional Struggle Among Thakins--An Exposition on Pseudo Thakins], Rangoon, Shwe Pyi Nyunt Ponhneik Taik, ?1939.

Overstreet & Windmiller 1959--Overstreet, G.D.F. and M. Windmiller, *Communism in India*, Los Angeles, University of California Press, 1959.

RSIEC 1939--*Report of the Secretariat Incident Enquiry Committee*, Rangoon, Government Publications, 1939.

Shwe Thway 1965--Shwe Thway, *Y.M.B. Thakin Tin Ahtokpatti* [Biography of Y.M.B. Thakin Tin], Rangoon, Pinma Yezi Sarpe, 1965.

Soe 1966--Soe, Maung, *Aindiya Myanma Hset Hsan Yay Thamaing* [Burma-India Relations], Rangoon, Sarpe Beikman, 1966.

Sun Daily [*Thuriya Ne Sin Thadinza*].

The Sun Magazine [*Thuriya Maggazin*].

Thakin Kodaw Hmine 1936--Thakin Kodaw Hmine, *Khway Gandi* [A Treatise on Dogs], Rangoon, Amyo Tha Sar Ok Taik, 1936.

Thein Maung 1938a--Thein Maung, Thakin, *Ta Htaung Thon Ya Pyi Ayaydawbon I* [The Movement of 1938, I], Rangoon, Toe Tet Sar Ok Taik, 1938.

Thein Maung 1938b--Thein Maung, Thakin, *Thakin Ayaydawbon Hnit Amyo Tha Thakin Thein Maung ie Tin Pya Gyet* [Thakin Factional Struggle and My Views], Rangoon, Dobama Sar Ok Taik, 1938.

Thit Lwin 1967--Thit Lwin (Ludu), Maung, *Htaung Thon Ya Pyi Yenan Ayaydawbon* [The Oilfield Strike of 1938], Mandalay, Kyipwayay Ponhneik Taik, 1967.

Yenan Tat Tha Athuba 1939--*Yenan Tat Tha Dukkhathe 200 Kyaw Do ie Athuba Shu Athe Khan Pwe Hpeik Kya Athana Khan Hlwa* [Request Made by 200 Oilfield Strikers who are Desperate unto Death], Rangoon, Myanma Theikpan Sar Ponhneik Taik, 1939.

www.ingramcontent.com/pod-product-compliance
Lightning Source LLC
Chambersburg PA
CBHW080635230426
43663CB00016B/2882